A JOURNEY WITH ORVIS

OTHER TRAVEL WRITING BY MOSE TUZIK MOSLEY

Love During the Time of Corona

One Man's Mountain

The One that Got Away

Travels With Buddha

Begin Within

The Elephant in the Room

If You Were With Me Now, This Is Where We Would Be

A JOURNEY WITH ORVIS

MOSE TUZIK MOSLEY

Portland, Oregon

A Journey with Orvis

Printed in the United States of America

Island Earth Press
6108 NE Mason,
Portland, Oregon, 97218

LCCN: 2024911041
ISBN: 979-8-9906526-1-3

To Martini

A veces te amo siempre

"We shouldn't forget that Herodotus is the first great travel writer as well as historian and that travel writing has a long and distinguished tradition of artifice and exaggeration. It often lets its literary ambition get the better of it, valuing a good story or an amusing quote over strict accuracy..."

—Justin Marozzi, *The Way of Herodotus*

"Nothing spoils the telling of a good story like the arrival of an eyewitness..."

—Mark Twain

CHAPTER ONE

Fossil, County Seat,
Wheeler County, Eastern Oregon, USA

Overall, my favorite traveling partner has always been Buddha (my imaginary companion now residing in a cave above Rishikesh), but a close second is my nonbinary friend Cait Z.

Cait is hale and hearty and ready to go at a moment's notice if it is someplace they really want to go. They can pack a tiny bag and slip into their traveling shoes (Ecco World Loafers, size 8) before I can slip an international SIM card into my iPhone 14. It never really matters where we are going, as long as it is someplace Cait hasn't been in twenty years or more. There is almost no place they haven't been at all. So I felt like I hit a minor jackpot when I told them I was headed to Fossil.

"Fossil?" they said. "I don't think I've ever been there."

It is one of those places, I tell them, where the elevation exceeds the population by a factor of at least five. This peaks their interest.

"Wheeler County," I say. "Just under 1,800 square miles. Population 1,421, as of the 2020 census. Though I bet some of them white supremacist survivalist types take a pretty dim view of the US Census Bureau. There's probably at least another twenty-five of them hiding out somewhere..."

"Yeah," they say, "we should visit before it gets overcrowded."

So off we go in their Highlander, a few camping supplies stashed in the back, a topographical *Oregon Road & Recreation Atlas* slotted between the front seats. They are driving and so I'm able to sit back and watch the scenery, which, going up the Old McKenzie Highway, is mostly a scene of burnt forest and in-progress housing rebuilds after the 2019 Holiday Farm Fire. Pushed by strong easterly winds, the fire started up above Blue River and then blazed west down the McKenzie valley, burning on both sides of the river and destroying the small towns along the way. Extremely devastating for the folks that lived there, though many are starting to rebuild. The burned part of the valley is a crisp landscape of charcoal stacks of seared logs that have been harvested from burned trees. Monuments of fireplace chimneys that are left over from an incinerated house. This beautiful scenic corridor of the McKenzie River, a burned-out ruin.

Past the site of the fire, the land starts getting green again and back to being thickly forested. We drive east of McKenzie Bridge and then up over the Cascades through Santiam Pass and down into the plateau of Central Oregon. We are back into the dry dusty drought of the high desert.

If you want things to change, just keep driving. At altitude in the Ochoco Mountains we find a place to camp among towering ponderosa pines, and we spread a mat and our sleeping bags out under the stars with the trust that we won't freeze to death in the night. After all, it is mid-October.

I suppose you could take heart that nowadays October in Oregon is more like September and August of years past. The temperature was in the eighties in Eugene the week before, and Cait and I went swimming in the Willamette River. Honestly, I've never swum in the river in October. I've been living out here about forty-five years. It's much warmer than it ever was. Smokier too, but that's something I don't really want to talk about.

In the Ochocos, the air was clear, clean, and crisp and the sky littered with a billion stars. I dreamed about having a cabin out here. A cabin and a girlfriend who would visit me about twice a week with fresh eggs and roast beef sandwiches. Obviously, I woke up thinking I've been way too much of a celibate vegetarian lately.

Cait likes to cook breakfast and they do sort of a poached British thing with the eggs while I burn the bacon. Everything tastes better in the mountain air, even dirt-encrusted buttered toast after you drop it off the edge of the picnic table. Yum.

It's not that long of a drive to Mitchell (pop. 124), where we check out the Oregon Hotel, which has just gone up for sale. It's modestly priced, considering it has fourteen rented rooms, two rented cottages, and an out-of-tune upright piano in the lobby. We chat with the owner, who has lived here most of her life (she migrated when she was eighteen from Prineville, about forty-seven miles to the west) and swears she'll never leave. She wants to retire now to her hobby ranch (164 acres), which is tiny by the standards of Wheeler County, where cattle roam on 26,000-acre spreads and the biggest ranch comes in at just over 100 square miles. That's a lot of cow-poking, Cait says.

We decide to not buy the hotel, though it does come under consideration. In reality, Cait wants to live an alternative lifestyle in a semi-urban housing co-op and I need only a small barn-wood shack on a running creek with no land, no responsibilities, and absolutely nothing to do but write stories or blow my brains out, whichever comes first.

Back in the car we go. Next stop: Fossil.

The road north leads through the John Day Fossil Beds National Monument (Painted Hills Unit) and the Spring Basin Wilderness (roadless, of course; a certain irony here) then up to Butte Creek Pass (elevation 3,788) then down, down, down into Fossil.

Originally the home territory of the First Nations indigenous tribes/clans Cayuse and Molalla (I doubt they were the first, but they lived here for about 5,000 years, so that's got to give them some cred...) Fossil was "discovered/founded" by Thomas Benton Hoover. Back then (1876), you could go ahead and name things whatever which way you wanted, so he called the creek Hoover Creek, and he called the town Fossil because he found some ancient fossilized seashells on his ranch (called the Hoover Ranch; now the Homer Ranch on Hoover Creek Road).

With all this renaming going on, I've decided to call the little cabin I like on the John Day River in Clarno "Mosley's Landing"...oh yeah, and I'm renaming the river. It's now the "Tuzik River," after my dear sweet mom (deceased), and the county will heretofore be referred to as Ukraine County, just in case the Russians and the Republicans win the war...)

Obviously, I could go on and on. But let's wrap this up: Cait and I landed at the Hyatt House, a beautifully restored three-story banker's homestead near downtown. Seventy-five bucks a night, with a big comfy bed, a nice bathroom down the hall, and a damn good breakfast in the morning. They liked it, stowed their backpack, and went out to make some sketches of the courthouse and the museum. They are quite a sketcher these days. Watercolors too. Did one of me that makes me look like a crotchety old man with a twenty-gallon cowboy hat and a faraway look in his eye.

"All hat, no cattle," as they like to say in Texas.

Me, I took the liberty of going shopping. First thing, the Fossil Mercantile (555 Main Street), where I purchased a rebel flag kerchief. Then on to Smitty's Antiques and Collectibles (14 Fossil Ave.), where I considered and did not buy a leather WW I ammo case ($15), a hinged tobacco tin with a nicely curved lid from British Curly Cut Bohemian Blend (also $15) , and a disabled wooden butter churn that I thought might make a nice end table for that cabin I am going to build on the Tuzik River ($35, but he was taking offers).

"What I really need," I told Mister Smitty, "is an iron fire poker to stoke the campfire."

He looked up from his Bible and eyed me curiously. "Out back," he said, with a twang that sounded somewhat Australian.

Which is why I opened the back door, stepped out into the afternoon glare, and happened to meet the imaginary dog of my dreams.

He was sprawled there in the shade of an old wagon that had a collapsed rear axle and wheels that were canted and about to fall off. The sides of the wagon were gray, desiccated wood and the painted logo of a feed store (Hoover's Hay and Seed) was just barely legible on the tailgate. His head was resting on his front paws, and he looked up at me very casually when I came out the back door.

It was hard to say at that point what sort of a dog he was. A mix for sure, some poodle in him, maybe some Scottish terrier. Nothing was for sure, and it would no doubt change as we got to know one another. But when he looked at me, we had some kind of instant recognition. I didn't really expect him to speak, but then he did.

"The name's Orvis," he said to me from under bushy eyebrows and a sagging mustache. "Where are we going next?"

And so our journey begins.

CHAPTER TWO

Lake Billy Chinook,
Jefferson County, Central Oregon

"You're going to have to talk to somebody," Orvis tells me. "It's okay if you want to talk to me. I'm a dog. Lots of people talk to their dogs..."

He's sitting in the passenger seat of the Highlander with the tip of his nose stuck out above the half-rolled window. We just dropped Cait off at Lake Billy Chinook, where they want time alone to sketch the magnificent canyon cliffs. Me and Orvis have gone off to find some lunch. Cait's hoping we bring back roast-beef sandwiches. Of late, they've got a carnivorous craving. But I'm thinking more of spinach salad and cheese puffs.

Up. up. up. When the road finally bends into a flat bench at the top of the canyon cliffs, the cell phone sparks up to its signal. A chime sounds off and I diligently pull into a viewpoint so I can read the text.

It is bad news. It is very bad news. Some of the worst.

T.F. Moon writes from Darwin, California. Her neighbor, my close friend, the Timbisha Shoshone Alan "Dry Bear" Beaman, has been found dead. This, I think, cannot be true.

Orvis, of course, has a sixth sense for these kinds of things and I'm pretty sure he knew what was going to happen before the phone even sparked. Dogs can smell these things coming in on the tide of the evening air. And who knows with imaginary dogs? They might be supernatural. They might smell things two weeks in advance. It's anyone's guess. Uncharted territory. I've never had an imaginary dog before, so I'm pretty clueless.

"It's true," Orvis says. "He died last night. In his sleep."

Dry Bear dead?

There is nothing about that sentence that I find appealing or acceptable. He was as young as me and probably healthier. Spent his whole life in the high desert of Death Valley and the sparse clean air of Mercury, Nevada. A well-known and well-respected member of the Shoshone tribe, Timbisha clan. My very best Indian friend. Well, actually, my only Native American friend. We liked each other a lot.

"Ok" Orvis tells me, "here's one way to deal with it. Don't think of him dead, not yet. Think of the best conversation you ever had with him. The best time, the funniest moments. Think of the best story you can tell…"

So we sat there, me and Orvis, in the front seats of Cait's Highlander, up there at the Crooked River overlook, with the view out the windshield of the grey and brown basalt cliffs, vertical drop 500 feet to the alluvial drift of boulders and sagebrush and a forty-five degree angle down to the shore of the lake, a thousand feet below. Autumn afternoon sun, a blue cloudless sky, a dry wind swirling, a dust devil skritching along the sandstone shelf below the parking lot. What? Dry Bear dead? No fucking way.

"Alan Dry Bear," I say to Orvis, "he didn't say much. He sort of mumbled a lot. Mumbled and smiled. Never made a big deal out of anything. Had a little dog named Joey. Drove a white Toyota Tacoma, newer than my taco truck, in pristine shape. But he wanted a new Ford F-150."

So yeah, you know, he worked hard all his life. Did a long stint as a welder at the atomic bomb testing site near Yucca Mountain. Lived with a woman up near Elko, Nevada. She died, but he never talked about it.

Dry Bear was one of my best friends in Darwin, and of late he had taken on the task of teaching me how to fish. Dry Bear had a Native look about him that is a boiled-down combination of skepticism and irony. He had a droll, laconic, carved-wood face. He was lean and thin and he kept a lot in reserve. It's an Indian thing.

I'm not exactly sure when he is joking or just trying to get through the thick skull of a classically naïve, white-man-stupid Ukrainian that there are more ways to go fishing than with a simple rod and reel. You can, he told me, use small doses of dynamite (not recommended) or, as in our current mode, a stout club of super-hard black locust with a good knob at the end and a powerful (10,000 lumens) torch (flashlight).

"That's possibly bright enough to shine right into your soul. If you open yourself to it," Dry Bear says. "You point that thing up in the sky and you can light up the Andromeda Galaxy. Though it will take a while to get there."

In our current iteration of fishing, we are planning to hunt the giant Amargosa River pupfish. This is an extremely rare variety that is said to walk the dry lake shores of Death Valley on moonless summer nights, searching for likely procreative partners and munching on whatever comes its way. Among only a handful of fish that can breathe air, it likes to dine on coyotes and jackrabbits. It is found in only one known locale: Ash Meadows.

"It's not afraid to eat a young child or two, especially if they get in its way or forget to listen to their elders," Drybear remarked. "It can be ornery due to its tough life. AND it's been extinct for over 400 years. That can be hard on any fish."

"Must make it pretty difficult to find," I say.

Dry Bear gives me a serious look and nods his head. "You bet."

The drive down to Death Valley from Darwin goes from about 5,000 feet in altitude to 200 below sea level. We transverse at least three small mountain ranges (the Cosos, the Panamints, the Chlorides, all the way to the Funerals). We pass by Father Crowley Overlook, known locally as Star Wars Canyon, where Navy jet fighters used to practice weaving and winding through the narrow canyon walls until a few years ago one pilot clipped his wings on an outcropping and exploded into a ball of flames. Local observers were shocked and saddened by the crash and had their eyebrows singed in the ensuing fireball. Dry Bear wasn't there, but he heard all about it.

It's not a long drive, but we leave late in the afternoon, hoping to avoid the worst of the heat at Furnace Creek (record recorded temperature 135 F). By 8 p.m., the temperature has dropped to a nice warm 115 degrees. As we speed through the desert, a pastel painted sunset glows behind us and the night rushes down from the eastern ridge of Zabriskie Point.

It is quite dark when we reach the turnoff to Ash Meadows National Wildlife Refuge. I am relatively sure there is no legal fishing allowed in a wildlife refuge, but I feel insecure in telling my Native companion where and when he can or cannot fish. As it turns out, shortly after we veer onto the gravel road into the refuge, Dry Bear tells me to pull over and stop. We open the doors of the van and step out into the summer desert.

What kind of heated superlatives can you use to describe 115 degrees? It's like you stepped inside a woodstove burning hardwoods. There isn't even any sun to blame. Beads of sweat pop out on your forehead and are immediately evaporated into the night air. You take a breath and feel the inside of your lungs swell with boiled oxygen. The stars, normally cold and distant, suddenly seem hot and close. The air conditioning in your car, which was once some convenient luxury, is now a lifesaving device.

Dry Bear stands next to the van and looks off to the north. The road to Ash Meadows snakes its way into the darkness. We are a few miles from the waters of Crystal Reservoir and Longstreet Spring. These are pearls of lush greenery and desert oasis where the Amargosa River (mostly underground) bubbles up to the surface and dissolves into the dryness of the desert air. Life clings to the water. Over twenty-four endemic species of plants and wildlife are found here and nowhere else on the planet.

We stand by the van for a few minutes as the night gets more dark, and then Dry Bear holds out his torch and switches on the light. A tight beam of illumination shoots off into the desert. He lets it shine for a few seconds and then turns it off.

"You see the giant pupfish out there dancing in the dark?" he says.

I take a moment to squint off into the night, but soon I have to admit that I do not see any giant pupfish.

"Yep," Dry Bear says, with a slight little wooden smile. "Me neither. Guess we came on the wrong night."

He turns to get back into the van. I begin to say something about coming all the way out here, but the heat makes conversation unlikely and gradually I think better of it. I get in the van and start the engine and we both sit for a moment in silence. The air conditioner is turned all the way to maximum cold.

After a while, Dry Bear makes a clearing-of-the-throat cough.

"Well then," he says smartly, "since we come all the way this far, we might just as well drive on to Pahrump."

"Pahrump?" I reply.

"Yep," says Dry Bear, "there's a Home Depot there and I need to pick up a few things for the house."

"How far is Pahrump?"

"Close by," he says. "Can't be more than an hour's drive from right here."

"The Home Depot in Pahrump. That's where you want to go?"

"Yep. Got to pick up a few things for the house."

"Really. The Home Depot?"

"Don't worry." Dry Bear says. "I think most of the stuff we can fit in the back of the van. The rest we can tie to the roof."

"That's why we came all this way?"

"No," he says. "But it's obvious the pupfish ain't biting."

"I'm starting to think that there are no giant pupfish."

"Well," Drybear smiles, "I told you back in Darwin they are extinct."

"Yes, you did."

"When you get to the highway, take a left," he says. "That's the road to Pahrump."

CHAPTER THREE

Garden District,
Eugene, Western Oregon, USA

At first, when we reach Eugene, Orvis gets very excited. We're turning into the driveway at Cait's house and somehow Orvis thinks this is OUR house and it makes his tail wag just to think about it.

I guess the place must smell pretty good to him. He's become a bit attached to the smell of Cait, and their farmhouse in the garden district is just an extension of their magnificence. They have done all sorts of artsy Cait-type things to it and on top of it they are a pretty good cook and keep a nice larder of things a dog might love. Like roast lamb, smoked salmon, and fresh sausages. They are no vegetarian. I've seen them polish off a heady slice of steak- and-kidney pie at a pub near King's Lynn (formerly Bishop's Lynn). You certainly don't want to get in between Cait and their steak and kidney, this I can assure you.

He tried not to show it, but I think Orvis was a bit crestfallen when we backed out of Cait's driveway and headed over to the Pine House. I've told him it was very modest. Dead-end road, gravel driveway, tiny lot, small house. I keep intending to improve on it, but, you know, life keeps getting in the way.

"Oh don't worry," Orvis says. "It will be fine."

He says this as we pull into old Lund Drive, splashing through the potholes, squeezing around a utility truck that is trimming branches from around the power lines. A massive tree chipper is grinding away. Half the street is closed down. Workers are walking around with noise-cancelling earmuffs underneath their waterproof hoodies. Nice quiet neighborhood, just like I described it.

"It's not always this exciting," I tell Orvis.

I pull up in front of the house. Orvis has half his head out the window. He's tasting the air with his nose. An involuntary shudder seems to pass from head to tail like a mild electric current. He turns to look at me with half his tongue hanging out.

"Cats?" he asks.

Two Maine Coons, I tell him. Belong to Anastasiya. Lars the Greater and Artemis the Wise. Even for cats, they're pretty aloof. Especially after Lars just won Pet of the Week.

"It's partially my fault," I say. "I wrote a letter to the nominating committee."

So then I find myself explaining: The neighborhood kids, mostly Ruby and Clementine, came to my door the other afternoon, just before Halloween, and told me they were forming a Pet of the Week Committee. They said if there were any pets I thought might be deserving, to just let them know. First thing I said was: "How about Rosy? She's a very attractive pet." That's the beautiful Husky mix that lives next door, in the same house with Clementine and her mom. Maybe I was trying to curry favor with the Committee. Setting them up with a soft lobby, so that in the coming weeks, when I do decide to nominate...well...I think that they might look at my suggestion with different eyes. I'm not saying that was my strategy...I'm just pointing out the possibility, you know, how it might look to an oversight committee, for instance.

Clementine was very firm. "No," she said. "I don't think the committee would consider Rosy. She growls sometimes..."

See? That was the clear clue right there. This was serious business. Nominate a pet that doesn't growl. Note taken. But obviously this was going to be a tough competition.

Orvis takes his head out of the window and looks over at me. Maybe I'm anthropomorphizing, but his look is a lot the same as the look Cait gives me after I ate the whole bucket of mini eclairs. He's not saying it, but what he means is: Oh no. What did you write?

Which brings us to where we insert the following paragraph (from my letter to the Committee): "As a Maine coon, Lars specializes in hunting. Though he may seem to lounge lazily in the gravel pathway that is Lund Drive, I can assure the committee that he is a wild and ferocious protector of both attic and crawl space, where he is nightly attending the eradication of unwanted pests, including, but not limited to, the invasive dusky kangaroo rat and the dauntingly plentitudenous Norway rat, known for its disease-bearing bubonic fleas..."

"I get the idea," Orvis says.

"Yeah. Lars won Pet of the Week hands down. He is pretty unapproachable right now."

So we sit there, still in the front seat of the taco truck, just looking at my house, the leaves fluttering to the ground off the Japanese maple in the front yard, the evening glow stretching a painter's light across the front porch, the skull carved into a jack-o-lantern grinning at us.

"Well, it's a pretty cute house," he says ingratiatingly. "And obviously, a great neighborhood. But I have for you just one question…"

Why is everyone so much smarter than me? This is what I think. I get an icy chill tiptoeing along the ridge of my spine. I anticipate that he will ask me something that I don't really want to answer.

Sure enough. Orvis says:

"Why would you ever want to leave?"

Instead of replying, I open my door on the driver's side of the truck and swing my legs out. Over my shoulder I glance across the front seat and look at my imaginary dog.

"Wait 'till you see the inside." I tell him.

CHAPTER FOUR

At Home at Pine Home,
Eugene, Lane County, Oregon, USA

Orvis and I settled in nicely at Pine Home.

The home is a cute little cottage close by the Willamette River in the moderate city of Eugene, which has been my hometown for about forty-seven years. I've lived at the Pine House for about ten of those years. It was a modest purchase from some friends who are now my neighbors, and it has been an excellent place to live while I sorted out my life (love, divorce, foreclosure, all of the usual life events) and gained back my personal economic security.

Of course I have modified it, added this, deleted that, expanded and contracted and re-designed. I am after all, by profession, a carpenter. But it is still a little cottage at the end of a small gravel lane and it is still quiet and snug. Plenty of room for an older single guy and his imaginary dog.

Living there gave Orvis and me a chance to get to know each other.

So let me tell you a little bit about him, and then I can describe what he knows about me. Just for the sake of a little clarity, which may come in short supply through this narrative.

Orvis got his name from a tattered old fly-fishing catalogue that was stashed next to the toilet in the outhouse behind the junk shop where I met him. Apparently, the owner at one time had the ambition to take up fly fishing. Eastern Oregon is a good place for this: plenty of small and large rivers, clear running waters, a good variety of western trout (rainbow, bull, brookies, planters), and not too many people to disturb a fellow as he stands in the middle of an ice-cold stream and tries to untangle the tip of his fly line from the brush. I don't know if the guy ever did get into the sport but at least he got as far as looking through the catalogue. Orvis is an old, well-respected outfitter based in northern New England. It is known for nice catalogues (and expensive gear).

Anyhow, it was in the outhouse that Orvis first saw his name in print, though he is unclear in telling me why he knew it was his name. Some things just remain a mystery.

Orvis is unsure about how he first arrived in Fossil, Oregon, and came to live behind the junk store. His puppy memories are dim, but he thinks he was dropped off by a family that was passing through. The family may have had too many kids and too many puppies and they might have been on their way to the migrant apple-picking country of eastern Washington (Yakima, Spokane). They may have traded him to the store owner for a used tea kettle and a cigar box filled with Crayola crayons, which was nice for the kids. This part of Orvis's story, as you can imagine, is a little vague.

It was very boring living behind Smitty's junk store. Not much was happening in Fossil. The store owner was getting older and more crotchety and he spent far too much of his time, in Orvis's opinion, sitting at the counter and reading his Bible. Orvis never read the Bible, but the old man would quote it at him sometimes and to Orvis it just never made much sense. But again, that is just his private opinion (in case any of you Bible-thumpers feel like getting offended). Religion, Orvis likes to say, is not for everyone.

So that is how things stood when I walked through the back of Smitty's and came out into the yard to see Orvis lying under the wagon. I found him just as he was ready to go. It was a lucky thing for both of us.

Myself, I didn't tell Orvis much of my own story. I didn't think it was necessary to bore him with the humdrum details. I was now an older man who was once a much younger man. In that strange way of human beings, my body had aged but it seemed like my mind had not kept up. I was getting up there, close to seventy years old, but my mind was still about twenty-five. I could feel all that aging that had taken place, feel it down in my bones and in my muscles and in my joints (especially in my joints), but in my mind I still felt about the same as it did when I was young and stupid. Only now I knew when I was being stupid. I guess you could call that wisdom.

I told Orvis that I made my living as a carpenter, only now I was getting toward the end of my run. Age and the construction business have to part ways at some point, and I was very nearly there. In the meantime, I had always been a writer and always wanted to find a good way to tell stories. I had been practicing and practicing for a very long time and felt like I was just starting to figure it out.

"But that just might be only in my imagination," I said. "It's possible that storytelling is something I will never really figure out."

Orvis was lying on the couch with his head propped up on one of the upholstered arms and I was sitting in my easy chair. He raised his head and looked over at me.

"Maybe that's what I'm here for," he said.

I considered him for a moment. He was a moderately sized dog, about forty pounds, his fur silvery gray, not too short but curly (he did not shed), and it covered his face in a way that softened him. His eyes were dark, but tended to change color with expression, brightening or dimming as he reacted to whatever you were telling him. The hair on his forehead was longer and it curled over his eyes like a single bushy eyebrow, making you wonder sometimes if he could see okay. You got the impression, with the set of his mouth and the prominence of his black nose, with the way that his eyes followed you, that he was a dog that did not miss very much. He might look like he was asleep behind that face, but it was only a clever ruse. I watched him stretch himself on my old leather couch and sort of snuggle into the cushions.

"Don't get too comfortable," I said. "We are leaving again soon."

He did not move, like it wasn't going to impress him whatever plans I had made, but he did lift his head slightly.

"Oh yeah? Where are we going?"

"South," I said.

CHAPTER FIVE

Farmhouse at River Road and Park Avenue, Eugene, Oregon USA

There is no place to park the Apache Ramada at Pine House, so I have to make arrangements to work on it in the backyard of a friend's house over on River Road. I dropped the Apache there shortly after I bought it (from a sweet young woman and I paid too much…) and it has been stuck there waiting to be remodeled and refurbished while I puttered around in the rest of my life, working and fretting and trying to imagine what I will need for the next great adventure.

Orvis, for his part, has taken to living on the living room sofa, a big weather-beaten leather couch in the front room at Pine House. He pauses only occasionally from his sleep to open his eyes and watch me as I pass by on one errand or another. I've told him that I am preparing for our journey, but he seems rather indifferent. He prefers to sleep. And who can blame him?

The weather (we must always speak of the weather) has made a quick switch from unseasonably warm Indian summer to seasonally typical mid-November ice fog. Down here near the Willamette River, the cold seems to hug itself tight to the ground along the flood plain, wrapping my neighborhood in a blanket of frosty stagnation. There is not enough heat in the winter sun to burn the fog off, and even in the afternoon we are cloaked in close-fitting gray gloom. Not quite misting, but cold and icy with penetrating dampness. If it warms up, we will get heavy rain.

I often tell the story of how, after coming out to Western Oregon in 1977, I made a call back to my mom and dad, who still lived in Connecticut. New England winters were harsh. Frozen ground, snow and sleet, plunging December temperatures. I told my dad how temperate Eugene was. No winter here, I said. Mid-January and it's forty-five degrees every day. And the rain is wonderful…

Well, now that I have lived my winters in Mexico for the past twenty-five years, I think: Forty-five degrees and rain!!!! How can anyone live like that?

Which makes no never-mind if you are a dog on a warm leather couch and have someone to feed you twice a day. I don't think Orvis has even BEEN outside in two or three days.

So he hardly plucks his ears up to hear me speak of our coming journey to Los Cabos.

"Yes sirree Bob!" I say. "We are packing up the old mule train and heading south on the interstate."

He comes out of his dream world for a moment and looks up at me from the couch.

"Who is Bob?" he says. "And what is south?"

"South is ninety degrees left of west. West is where they used to tell men to head when they were young and seeking their fortunes. As we have already made our fortune, such that it is, we are heading south to seek the beach, which is far more fun than any fortune."

"Sure," Orvis says. "But is it any more fun than the couch?"

He pretends to go back to sleep as I explain to him that in order to reach the beach and the somewhat mythical destination of "Surf Camp 22," we are going to have to do something called "work," which I assume from his posture is not something he is even remotely acquainted with.

"I've purchased a collapsible dwelling," I say, speaking into his dreamworld. "It is called an Apache Ramada. Very nice, if somewhat older (I do not say that it is actually a 1977 model). It's going to need a few things. A bit of tweaking, is all."

Orvis moves in his sleep. His legs twitch, as though he were running away somewhere.

"Not much really for YOU to do," I assure him, "other than watch and learn."

Now his legs are moving into a gallop. Or maybe he is swimming. It's hard to tell.

I think he may be running away from work. I begin to wonder if I have chosen the WRONG imaginary dog.

The weather does not improve for several days, and now, by the middle of November, I am working with numb fingers and an icy space of exposed skin on my lower back where my Carhart winter trousers separate from my thermal long-sleeve Whitley Carpenter's shirt. A pair of all-encompassing blue-green coveralls, zipped up to my throat, cuts the chill, but only in half, and I find myself boiling the kettle in my benefactor's kitchen and brewing cups of industrial Earl Grey tea in an endless chain that is interrupted only by a total unzipping of everything as I pass my personal fluids onto the surrounding shrubbery.

Cold. Gray. Wet. This is exactly the sort of lifestyle I have been trying to avoid.

The Apache Ramada is of clever design. Solid walls that fold into each other, lots of windows. Two beds, a kitchen with stove and sink, refrigerator, storage cabinets. A tiny port-a-potty.

I immediately decide to rip it all out. Clear the decks. Start again. Basic structure okay as it stands, everything else goes.

I start with a new floor, walls paneled in western red cedar, cushions reupholstered, electricity rewired (solar electric system), beds re-bedded. Fresh and tidy and every possible crevice and hole filled with caulk and spray foam to prevent, at least initially, the intrusion of mosquitos, flies, wasps, Africanized honeybees, scorpions, centipedes, tarantulas, field mice and the rattlesnakes that eat them.

This all takes several days of shivering and working on my knees while Orvis sits on the front seat of the taco truck and naps.

But by Monday morning, I tell him that we are almost ready to go.

"South?" he asks.

"To the desert, the sun, the beach, the home of fish tacos, fresh camarones, ripe avocados, mangos in season, surfer girls, and an occasional Frenchman. It's all only 2,300 miles and just over $800 worth of petrol away. Five days driving, max."

"Great," he says with a yawn. "Wake me when we get there."

CHAPTER SIX

Peace Symbol Barn, Near Gospel Flat,
Bolinas Lagoon, Northern California

Hope is coming in very small quantities these days. So we have to cherish it whenever we get a whiff.

This is what I tell Orvis as he tries to sleep in the front seat on the very long drive down the interstate from Western Oregon.

We left the Willamette Valley in early morning darkness, the road wrapped in fog, and it soon became apparent that the Apache Ramada is comfortable at a modest fifty-two miles per hour and no more. Faster speeds make her very nervous, and she begins to sway across the slow lane of I-5, causing the speeding tractor-trailers to sound their massive warning horns as they steam past (doing seventy-five) in a passing lane choked with mist. It makes for a bit of white-knuckle adjustments in the taco truck, steering-wheel moves that are too exciting to be much fun. I'm glad Orvis is happily snoring in the passenger seat. He doesn't need to see this.

So it is going to be a long, slow slog on our drive to Thanksgiving dinner in West Marin County, Northern California. We are only to Grant's Pass when a weak sun rises, which slowly wakes the sleeping dog. He comes to consciousness nose-first and seems fresh for conversation.

"What's going on with the anxiety?" he asks. "I smell stress."

"Nothing to worry your poor little dog dreams about. A pinch of traffic is all."

"Did you take your blood pressure medicine?"

"And the anti-inflammatory. At the next truck-stop. With the gasoline."

"Good. I could use a stretch," Orvis says.

Mostly I buy my gas at the Indian casinos, where it is cheaper because of less tax. Somehow, I think I am contributing to the Native American Movement by shopping there, which is a very tiny way of saying I support Indian rights. I am a Native American myself, being born in Oxford, Connecticut, but my Eastern European ancestry (full-blood Ukrainian) separates me entirely from being a member of any First Nation tribe. It's not my fault, but I still like to support them.

Orvis takes an imaginary whizz on a Christmas tree planted in the parking lot while I seek relief in the men's room. I'm tempted to put a few coins in the slot machines that line the hallway to the truckers' shower. Maybe win enough to pay for a tank of gas. Maybe lose enough to make myself feel good about charitable giving during the holidays. But because I know Orvis is waiting in the cold, I pass the opportunity by. I need to save my luck for the challenging drive ahead. Don't want to run out of luck out on the Interstate.

When we are back out on the I-5, going fifty, we have plenty of time to chat. But there is only so much you can say to an imaginary dog. It's like talking to a child, really.

You try to be entertaining to keep their attention. You have to tell stories. Even if they are disappointing ones. Even if they are sad. And, of course, Orvis has lots of questions.

"What is this thing called "Thanksgiving?" he asks.

A made-up holiday roughly corresponding with traditional celebrations of the fall harvest and times of plenty. Clouded in the modern American psyche by false stories of peace and harmony between European invaders (Separatist Pilgrims) and the Noble Savages (mostly the Wampanoag) who shared a feast in early November (circa 1621) before the onset of the harsh Massachusetts winter. They all gave thanks, for peace, friendship, goodwill, and the fact that they were alive at all. The Pilgrims had just survived a rough journey across the North Atlantic in a cramped sailboat. The remaining Wampanoag had recently survived (barely and in a much-reduced state) the ravages of smallpox, yellow fever, and leptospirosis (most deadly of all). The Puritans thanked God. The Indians thanked Mother Nature. Then they ate a big meal as though it were their last. Later, the white guys wrote the history books and the Indians became extinct (mostly).

"It's about the same now," I tell Orvis, "We are still in denial around how we treat minorities and on Thanksgiving we eat like we're going to starve."

But we are still thankful.

"Thankful..." Orvis says thoughtfully. "I'm thankful to be pure poodle."

This makes me cringe. It makes me feel guilt. It makes for a very awkward silence.

Orvis believes he is the smartest and most elegant of all dogs: A French Poodle. I haven't had the heart (or the nerve) to tell him the truth.

But, like I said, it's a very long drive and now, what with the short winter day, it is dark in the cab of the taco truck. Dogs can smell even better in the dark. It's pretty easy for Orvis to sniff out the facts, or at least the lack of truthfulness.

So it's time to seize the moment, clear the air, scrub the decks, and admit there is an iceberg on the horizon.

"Poodle?" I finally say. "You are more than a mere poodle. Even a French one. You, my good dog, are a MEXIDOODLE."

It gets his attention. But also arouses his skepticism. He comes from a place of only half-believing anything I tell him. Like a typical teenager.

"What," Orvis says quietly, "is a Mexidoodle?"

It's best, I think, if I just tell him the whole story. I begin: "Back in the time of the ancients, when the world was a much smaller place and the forests were still filled with wild dreams..."

I can hear him snorting in the dark. He turns his head toward me and I see the night glow of his yellow eyes. He gives a little growl. This stops me in my literary tracks.

"Just give it to me straight," he says. "I'm not a child."

I let out a long breath and begin to inhale an even larger one. The cab smells like my decaying imagination.

"Your grandfather was a full standard poodle. He was named Ace. He had a cigar-smoking friend named Charley who used to take him to the movies. Down in Los Cabos. This was when there was a thing called Cinema in the Sand. They showed films on a big screen at Shipwrecks Beach. One night, before he got snipped, Ace got bored with the film (an Academy Award winner entitled *Birdman*), wandered off down the beach during intermission, and ended up meeting a rancho dog named Perocita Marie. It was a very dark and romantic night. Marie was in her moons, Ace was feeling randy. They became your grandparents."

The darkness in the cab seems to get a little darker. Orvis is very quiet. The interstate rumbles by, tires on concrete, a vibration from the travel trailer as it sways behind us, headlights in the northbound lanes that burst into little star clusters in my night vision.

"What kind of dog was Perocita?" Orvis asks.

"Full-bred Mexican rancho. Shorter legs, longer body. Front curl ears, busy eyes. Smart as they come. She had several litters, all of them geniuses."

"And my parents?"

"There it gets a little murky. I'm not exactly sure."

"Beautiful and super smart, I'm assuming."

"Obviously."

There is a palatable lessening of tension in the truck. Orvis is motionless for a few minutes while he thinks about it. I can tell he doesn't believe me. Finally he yawns and lays down on the seat. He mutters the word "thanksgiving" and then in a few more minutes I can hear him sleeping.

Of course I wake him up on Thursday and share my dinner with him. We made it to Bolinas Lagoon, got to spend a couple of nights with my friends. Perfect weather. Perfect food. Everything perfect and a truckload of things to be thankful for. A couple of days later, we hit the road again for Southern California and the Mexican border.

We are both wide awake and singing songs to one another on Saturday night at 9:17 p.m. A very long day of driving, and we should have pulled over before dark, but it was going so smoothly…

In the middle of Interstate 10 East, there must be a crease in the road, a short ledge of concrete, a pothole, a piece of truck tire, something there that I don't see in the moonless night. We are not going fast, but fifty mph is still fast enough, and we are virtually surrounded by speeding traffic going much faster.

In the flash of a second (by flash I mean like a fireball explosion), the Apache Ramada breaks its axle. Our tow hitch twists, the frame of the trailer hits the concrete of the interstate, and we are engulfed in a shower of sparks as we begin to fishtail. In both my side mirrors and the rear-view mirror, I see what looks like a fallen meteor chasing us down the highway. So many sparks it looks like the Apache is on fire. Truck horns are blasting on either side of us and I'm struggling with the wheel to try to stop the skidding, struggling to keep the taco truck from flipping over, as we skid sideways toward the right embankment.

I can't say how long this lasts. It feels like several minutes, but it was probably about five long seconds. Eventually we are sitting upright on the shoulder of Interstate 10, my hands frozen to the steering wheel, the beautiful Apache Ramada a heap of twisted leaf springs and broken wheels in the gutter behind us.

Silence in the cab and we can hear ourselves breathing. My heart is racing, but Orvis seems as calm as ever. There is a long pause in time and space. He takes a deep breath, almost a yawn.

"Well" he says. "There it is then. Just like the Pilgrims."

I look at him, but I don't say anything.

"Thankful to be alive." he says.

I sigh heavily and then I dial 911.

CHAPTER SEVEN

Los Pinos Fresh Aire Motel, Palm Avenue, Beaumont, California. Room 102

There was never any indication, not the slightest hint really, that Orvis would so quickly become an ardent football fan. A TELEVISION football fan. Four games a day. From 2 a.m. till noon. No sleeping in between.

No, I'm not talking about American football, which is played mostly with the hands and body. I'm referring to football played with the feet. A sport of the world. A poor people's sport. FOOTBALL. That which Americans call soccer, though no one seems to know why.

An early Christmas miracle is happening nearby. About five blocks from our funky hotel room, the Apache Ramada is being resurrected. We towed the remains of it to Carson Trailer and Steel Fabricators on 6th Avenue East. They have told us in very optimistic terms that for a few thousand dollars, they could Frankenstein it back into a certain road-readiness. New axle, new wheels, new brakes, some frame straightening…at least enough to get it another 1,254 miles south to be parked forever at Surf Camp 22. They spoke mostly Spanish at Carson Trailer. For some reason that felt very reassuring.

In the meantime, the tow truck driver guided us to a cheap motel. I love cheap American motels. They are usually run by a tight family of East Indians. When you open the door of the check-in office, there is almost always the smell of curry being cooked somewhere. The woman who does your paperwork has a motherly smile and a thick Indian accent. "You must remember sir, there is no smoking in this room. You must be advised, sir, never any smoking…"

Anyway, Orvis and I settle into room #102. Of course, the first thing he does is switch on the television.

It is tuned, naturally, to the local FOX station.

Okay, don't get me started about the FOX News network of liars and thieves. As I am a former news journalist, I abhor what FOX News has done to the truth. So I won't even start. But when Orvis turns on the television, FOX has turned itself suddenly into a sports network. And the sport they have purchased?

The FIFA World Cup of football.

Okay, we can call it soccer. In America that is what we call it. I've been a fan all my life. I spent over twenty years as a professional soccer referee. In the USA, that means I officiated high school, college, and city league games. I made about $2,000 in a good year. But it taught me to love the game.

The best soccer competition (other than the European Champions League) is the quadrennial celebration of the Federation of International Football Association (FIFA) World Cup Finals. Currently, thirty-two nations make it to the finals (out of about 193 countries who compete). Like the Olympics, you have to qualify to play for your country (ancestry, citizenship, marriage, native birth) and you can only choose one country to play for. It is an honor to be selected and it is a huge honor if your country wins the tournament. Only eight countries have ever won the World

Cup. Brazil has won it five times. The USA has never come close (but maybe this year?).

I love watching the World Cup. Last time it was played (in Russia, 2018), I watched every game. That's sixty-four two-hour games in two weeks. Exhausting. It's usually played in the summer (June/July). This year, because of the climate of the host country (Qatar is very, very hot in the summer), it is being played in the late fall. This is the first time it has been played in an Arab nation. This has caused a lot of controversy (women's rights, slave labor, bribes, petrodollars, alcohol sales, accommodations, you name it, there have been many problems). But as it so happens, it coincided nicely with my travels. Or should I say, my forced stay in Southern California, which is not one of my happy places in the world.

Orvis and I are confined to a motel room while the fabricators rebuild the Apache Ramada. There is little to do other than write little stories, read little books, and watch a little flat-screen TV.

As you can imagine, the TV is constantly tuned to the channels broadcasting the FIFA World Cup. I have a chair pulled up in front of the screen. Orvis is lying on the extra bed. I thought he would sleep through most of it. But no.

All of a sudden, Orvis is a huge soccer fan. And his team? France.

"France?" I say. "Why France? They won the last time. Two of their best players are injured and not even on the roster. Sure, they have Mbappe and Dembele, two great strikers. But that is not a very imaginative choice."

"Why France?" he replies. "Because they are French."

Now I am thinking: Why did I imagine him as a poodle?

"What about Mexico?" I say. "What about the USA?"

"Not a chance. I am not one to choose the underdog. I rather pick the top dog. The thing I like about France is that they win ALL their games. It is so much more relaxing that way..."

Suddenly I notice he is speaking with a French accent. I say to myself: What have I created?

But he has a point. I am a total fan of the USA. And every game is tense and intense. The last ten minutes of the game against Iran almost gave me two heart attacks. It was their first win and it was not in any way easy. Our star player gave up his private parts to score the winning goal. I felt like I was the one who got a knee in the balls.

Anyway, we are forced to watch every French game and of course, France always wins. Eventually the Apache Ramada will be fixed and we can continue driving south into Mexico. There will be no easy access to television coverage of the World Cup. I tell Orvis he better enjoy the games while he can.

But he is not listening. It is between games and he has locked himself in the bathroom with my smartphone. I'm not sure, but through the door I think I hear him singing. Over and over again he seems to be practicing one song.

In a minute I realize it is the French National Anthem.

A few hours later, when France actually drops a game 0 to 1 to lowly Tunisia, he is so deflated I have to pick him up off the floor.

It doesn't help when I say to him: "Hey, that's the beauty of the game."

I have to turn away so he won't see me smiling.

CHAPTER EIGHT

Transpeninsular Highway,
BCS, Mexico

I have to explain to the young man at the border that the Apache Ramada can no longer open up to reveal its contents. There has been an accident, I tell him. The opening mechanism is broken. Besides there is nothing interesting inside. Just stuff for "mi campo."

"No armas?" he says. "No drogas?"

Nary a one, I tell him. Just the usual stuff. You know: A fridge, a stereo, a bunch of old plywood, a septic system, lots of books…

It is a little after 6 a.m. in Mexicali and the eastern sky is rosy with the…well, I would like to say the coming dawn…but actually it is rosy with pollution. That industrial haze that hangs over Mexican border towns, a mix of truck exhaust, factory exhaust, desert dust, chemical off-gassing… really, who knows what is in the air over Mexicali, but it sure looks like if you live there, you won't live there for long before your lungs give out.

The young man is tall and thin and looks quite guapo in his khaki uniform. He is a fine example of a border guard. He looks like he could be a real stickler for details. Intelligent, attentive. Certainly the sort of tall young man that I would want guarding MY border. Does this mean I could be in trouble?

Well, this is what I can tell you: In years past, coming into Mexico was a crapshoot. There was never any telling if you would sail through or be hassled by an underpaid official who could come up with a myriad of reasons why you or your rig did not conform to regulations. This underpaid official would then offer to clear your paperwork for...let's say...1,000 pesos. Cash. Paid to his pocket. That was the reality of Mexico.

But then we had this thing happen: a worldwide pandemic. Suddenly, people stopped traveling. Suddenly there were many fewer tourists coming across the border. The tourist industry, which is a particularly large part of the economy in Baja California, tanked. It was painful to everyone. But most Mexican officials got the message: Do not hassle the paying tourists.

So this is what happens. The fine young man asks me politely for my paperwork. License, registration, title and registration for the Apache. I even show him my passport. I help him match the registration number to the license plate. He looks at me rather dubiously and then he moves the plastic barrier blocking the lane and waves me through.

Orvis, who has been curled up on the front seat pretending to sleep, opens his eyes and looks furtively through his bushy eyebrows.

"You can relax," I tell him. "We are safely in Mexico."

We both feel that surge of happy adrenaline that one experiences after successfully crossing an international border. That feeling of "well, they didn't catch me this time." Though it is an open question as to who "they" are and what they would catch you for.

When we are only ten or fifteen miles south of the border, I can already tell that Orvis is waking up to the new countryside.

A drive down the Baja California peninsula is an unforgettable experience. There is one road, mostly two lanes with no shoulders. It is called the Transpeninsular and it was completed in the early nineteen-seventies. It winds its way back and forth in three long switchbacks from the Pacific Ocean to the west and the Sea of Cortez to the east. Eleven hundred miles from the US border to Los Cabos.

The scenery is a desert panorama of geologic anomalies. Mesas, canyons, and volcanos. Blanketed with the typical flora of the Sonoran Desert: Cactus (saguaro, cardon, candelaria, ocotillo, biznaga), trees (palo blanco, pinos, boojum, ciguela, lomboy) underbrush (fireweed, tumbleweed, sage) and seasonal flowers (poppies, lupines, owl clover). It is almost always sunny and sometimes windy and there are dust devils that swirl along the road as you drive south. Dust devils and road runners dart across your path, and maybe it's a warning or maybe just a welcome to the Outback.

I roll the windows down when we get south of San Felipe. Orvis leans his head out and takes full advantage of the fifty-mile-an-hour wind that races through his face. There is that digitalis smell of the desert. Fresh clean air scrubbed by mountain boulders and the saltwater filter of the ocean. He pulls his head back in the truck and looks over at me.

"Luxurious," he says. "When do we get there?"

I wish at that point I could have told him what we still had to go through, but then again, I'm glad I didn't know myself.

CHAPTER NINE

La Paz,
Baja California Sur, Mexico

Life can be hard. I know this. I know that there are things that happen that you cannot control. Difficult and sad things, even tragic ones. Bad stuff happens to good people. Any manner of bad stuff. Random incidents of suck-worthy stuff that the Universe throws your way to remind you of your total insignificance. It can be a dangerous world and an unfeeling one. One minute you're driving down the highway, singing road songs, and the next…

What I find really fascinating, however, are the things, both dangerous and stupid, that you do to yourself when you know better; when you know from experience, long vast experience, that you should not be doing them. These are significant things like: Never Drive at Night in Baja. Things like: Pay Attention to Your Gas Gauge. Simple, easy things to remember. It's not rocket science or brain surgery. Life is hard and the world is uncaring enough that you don't have to help promote the dark negativity by being so supremely stupid.

Orvis, that good dog, that supremely good dog who thinks, or wants to think, that he is a French poodle, is counting on me to get him all those long sinuoso miles down the peninsula to the mythical place called Surf Camp

22. He is trusting me to get him there safely. You would think that I, as a responsible pet owner, would be more careful.

I can't remember how many times I have driven the Baja Transpeninsular from the US border to the southern tip at Land's End in Cabo San Lucas. It is certainly more than thirty, probably more like fifty times. I was traveling to Surf Camp long before it was even called Surf Camp. I started in 1988 and did it almost every year since 1996. Back and forth. That adds up to a lot of driving, something like sixty-thousand miles of driving on that one road. I guess I know it pretty well.

Many times I did this drive by myself. Often I would listen to audio books. First tapes, then CDs, then an iPod, now audio from my smartphone. There were many compelling stories that I listened to, and they would help me pass the time as I travelled on the endless, twelve-hour-per-day drive. This year, there was a particularly good one. A favorite writer (Amor Towles), a great story (*The Lincoln Highway*), and a fine production. I was completely enraptured. Even Orvis liked it. Well, at least the beginning, then he kept falling asleep.

Close to the end of the story, we were on the road from the Pacific Coast town of Ciudad Constitucion to the capital city of La Paz, which sits on a large shallow inlet of the Sea of Cortez. One of the long switchbacks from coast to coast. It was late afternoon. The part of the story when they drive up into the Adirondacks to get Woolly's inheritance money. What was going to happen? Were they actually going to get away? I was enthralled.

The highway from Constitucion to La Paz is one of the less dramatic stretches of the Transpeninsular, but that said, it is still an interesting challenge. From west to east it starts out surrounded by the agricultural fields of the vegetable industry. From that level fruitful plain it stretches across the Llano de la Magdalena, a flat plain sloping toward the Pacific and Magdalena Bay. Then the road climbs up through the hills and then mountains of the peninsular spine, referred to variously as the Sierra los Filos del Treinta Y Cinco, or sometimes Tres Mesas, those being Mesa Aqua Blanca, Mesa Quelela and Mesa Cerro Colorado. There is a bit of a narrow pass at the turnoff for Rancho Matape. After that it is a steady descent toward the southwestern side of Bahia de La Paz.

I was concentrating on the story. What was Woolly going to do? Was Duchess going to be able to break into the safe? Was Emmet going to get there in time to stop him? These were all burning questions, so I cannot tell you when my "Low On Gas" warning actually started flashing on the dashboard of my truck.

Orvis woke up just as Emmet pulled the 1951 Chrysler, now painted a bright yellow, into the driveway of the Adirondack Hunting Lodge. He was walking up to the front porch and he could hear the clang of metal on metal as Duchess hit the door of the safe with an axe. Orvis stretched his neck and sat up on the front seat of the taco truck. He looked over at me.

"What's that light flashing on the dash?" he asked.

Emmet came to the front door. It was locked. He wrapped his hand in his coat sleeve, took a short, sharp swing to break the glass…

"The light?" I said. Now I was also looking at the dashboard. There was the speedometer (going about 45 mph or 70 kilometers per hour) Next to it was the tachometer (registering about 2,000 RPM), and then over to the left the gas gauge and the warning light. The indicator needle was sitting right over the letter "E."

Could I really be this stupid? Could I have actually accomplished this amount of brainlessness? Was it possible to even exist as a human with my current level of incompetence?

"Oh, that's just a light that says we're a little low on gas," I told Orvis. "We'll probably have to stop at the next petrol station."

"Great. I could use a little break. How far is the next station?"

"In La Paz." I swallowed and did a little cough. "It's the next town. Coming right up."

Which is just about when we passed the sign that said: "La Paz 96 kilometers."

Which is also about the time I completely lost track of the story being told on my truck radio. Did Emmett kill Duchess? Did Billy find a way to open the safe? I may never know.

Because in my mind I was doing a calculation. It went something like this: Divide by eight, multiply by five? Or is it: Divide by five, multiply by eight...oh Jesus, however I tried to translate kilometers into miles, it seemed for sure that we were going to run out of gas. Ninety-six kilometers is about seventy miles. My reserve in the gas tank when the light comes on? Maybe about two gallons? I should know that, right? Let's say it is two gallons. Let's say the taco truck, while towing the Apache Ramada, even with the new axle and the bigger wheels...oh jeez...let's say it's even getting twenty miles to the gallon (which is vastly optimistic...it MIGHT get fifteen mpg going downhill)...oh my gosh, two gallons at that rate of consumption gets us forty miles… forty miles is not ninety-six kilometers, at least not in this quadrangle of the universe.

"You should just relax," I tell Orvis. "Maybe take another nap."

"What's wrong?" he sniffs at me.

"Well…we have a little situation that could become a little problem."

This is what I don't mention to him: If we run out of gas, the engine stops. When the engine stops, so do all the other power systems in the truck. Systems like the power steering and the power-assisted brakes. There is absolutely no shoulder on the side of the road in this section of the Transpeninsular. Only two narrow lanes. So if we don't happen to be at a turnout when the engine gasps its last breath of gasoline, we are stuck in the middle of the road. Going downhill, it will be kind of hard to stop. Going uphill, it will be hard to steer. In traffic, with Mexican tractor-trailer drivers bearing down on us……yikes, I don't even want to think about that.

So what do I do? Should I just find a place to pull off and then try to flag someone down to help?

Should I just keep going and see if somehow we have more gas than I think?

The worst thing about panic is that it feels like panic. It feels like one huge, deadly, unanswerable question. A minefield of what-ifs. (Actually, that should be a mind-field of what ifs.)

But I am a seasoned traveler, and problems are nothing new to me. So I go beyond the what-ifs of the situation straight to the part of self-castigation.

"HOW THE FUCK COULD YOU BE SO STUPID!" I say to myself.

And then, as though he can read my mind, Orvis says:

"We're going to run out of gas. Isn't that what the little light means? That's kind of a stupid thing to do. Should we get some more gas before that happens?"

"For sure, Orvis. We will stop at the next filling station."

"Really? Can we make it that far?"

"Of course." I tell him. "No problem."

CHAPTER TEN

La Paz (part 2)
Baja California Sur, Mexico

I developed this theory of human knowledge many years ago. Thinking of the total sum of everything we know about everything there is, I envisioned a sphere. Something like a weather balloon. This sphere contained all knowledge. As the human race learned more about the universe, the sphere expanded. As the sphere expands, the surface area increases. This surface area is the boundary between what we know and what there is to know. The universe is basically infinite. As we gain more knowledge, the sphere gets bigger and the amount of stuff we learn increases and the boundary keeps expanding. So therefore, the amount of knowledge we don't know also keeps getting bigger.

This means we can never know everything. There will always be things that are unexplained. There will always be magic.

Even though I told Orvis that he should relax, maybe take a snooze as we drove those last ninety kilometers into La Paz, he did not take my advice. Dogs are like that. Sometimes they take their cues from human body language. Or from the smell of human sweat. Or the sound of grinding teeth…

I have to say that I was a little stressed out. The gas gauge was on empty. I was towing a pop-up trailer that was overloaded with my stuff. My truck was getting lousy gas mileage. I had about fifty miles to go to the nearest gas station. What was the smart thing to do here?

Should I just find a place to pull off the road and then flag someone down to take me to a Pemex? Leave all of my stuff and my dog and my truck by the side of the road for who knows how long? It was December, a time of short days and long nights. It was late afternoon. Leaving my truck seemed foolhardy. My dog was imaginary and I couldn't really expect him to guard everything.

So I clenched the steering wheel, gritted my teeth, and kept driving.

Orvis sat bolt upright in the passenger seat. He kept tilting his head from side to side, as though he were trying to understand the situation. His ears were flexed as though he could possibly hear something that would explain the level of stress that had invaded the cab of the truck. Every couple of minutes, he would lean forward toward the windshield and squint into the distance to see if he could spot an omen of our immediate future. Dogs can see over the horizon; did you know that? Sometimes they can see things happening on the other side of the planet. It's why they bark sometimes when it seems like there is nothing to bark at.

I slowed the taco truck down to about thirty-five mph. I coasted sometimes when we came off the top of a hill. I tried to draft behind a passing semi-truck. But mostly I just said a lot of prayers.

"Oh sweet Jesus, don't let me run out of gas."

There is a Saint Christopher medal hanging from the bracket of my rearview mirror. It was given to me long ago by

Ms. Leeann Parker in San Francisco when she wanted to try to protect me on my travels. It has always hung from the mirror of whatever vehicle I have owned, and I have to say that it has been mostly effective. Saint Chris is the patron saint of travelers. I didn't know that he was also the patron saint of gasoline.

From the top of Chapala Pass there is a long steady descent down into the Bahia de La Paz. About halfway down the steady descent, there is a dip in the road and a military checkpoint. This is where bored young soldiers ask you where you are going, where you have been, and if you are on vacation. Sometimes they ask for batteries for their flashlights. Or maybe a pack of cigarettes. Some people even give them cookies. And sometimes they search your vehicle, if they are especially bored or if they suspect you might have armas or drogas.

This time, when I stopped at the checkpoint, the soldiers were very nice. They did not want to search my camper. They had me roll down the back windows so they could look at my luggage. When they were done, I asked how far the nearest Pemex gas station was. They pointed from where I had just come and said about 100 kilometers.

I think they were just messing with me. Maybe they get this question a lot, because they were certainly well-prepared for my next question. Which was: Do you have any gasoline you can sell me?

"*No, no, senor*," they smiled at me. "*No gasolina aqui*."

When we cleared the checkpoint, Orvis said: "They weren't very helpful, were they?"

"I think they probably enjoy talking to tourists like that. We should have given them cookies."

The taco truck was definitely running on fumes at this point. I put her in low gear and kept driving. We were climbing up out of the dip to another hilltop and I could just feel the engine sucking at the fuel tank as we slowly pulled our load up to the next pass. I let out a long breath when we reached this summit—off in the distance we could see the Sea of Cortez.

"I can smell the ocean," Orvis said with a sniff. "It can't be far now."

Oh Saint Christopher, lord of travelers and petrol, please make us some more gasoline molecules to help our empty tank. Oh universe, please create the energy to deliver us to Pemex. Oh Lord, won't you buy me a Mercedes-Benz…

I kept the engine running but shifted out of gear, and we glided down the long straight hill that slopes toward La Paz.

Like I said, some things you cannot explain. There are forces in this multiverse that act in unknown and unpredictable ways. The quantum mechanics of hope and delivery and good luck. The answers to prayers. The miracle of Baby Jesus, and Christmas, and Santa Claus and Rudolph the Red-nose Reindeer. You name it. I have one to add to the list.

At the bottom of the long sloping road, where the Transpenisular intersects the road to the north bay, tucked behind a OXOXO convenience store, there was our Christmas present. A Pemex station!

I glided the truck and the camper into the left lane and coasted into the parking lot. When I put it back in gear, we drove a few yards to the side of the gas pump and the engine died.

Orvis looked over at me and heard me let out a deep breath. I leaned my forehead on the top of the steering wheel.

"Merry Christmas," he said.

CHAPTER ELEVEN

La Paz, BCS,
MX Part Three

I know, I know, I know what you are thinking: When is he going to wind this thing up? I mean how many more misadventures is he going to put us through? When is he going to get to this place, this mythical Surf Camp 22?

Well dear traveler, let me tell you, a journey is not always so cut and dry. It's not just: get on a plane, get picked up at the airport, get whisked away to your all-inclusive resort and spend the next fortnight drinking pineapple margaritas. Surf Camp is not all-inclusive. In fact, Surf Camp is totally non-inclusive, as you will see if you can just be a little more patient.

It had taken us an inordinately long time to get from Constitution to La Paz. The sun was at our backs for most of the drive and it kept getting lower and lower in the sky as is its wont. While we were in the Pemex station getting gasoline, it dipped below the western horizon.

So it was in the light of the evening gloaming that we watched the dial on the gas pump reach 69.87 liters. As far as I know, dear reader, my gas tank only holds about sixty-five liters. Again, like I said clearly in the last posting, some things just cannot be explained. But I did not question the young man pumping the gas. I just paid him and gave him a good tip and felt quite content with my full tank and the knowledge that I had probably also drained my account in the good karma bank. Heck, what is good karma for if you are not going to spend it?

I have some very old and very dear friends (Betsy and Cactus) who live in La Paz. In fact, they live in the northern suburb of Centenario, which is probably less than two miles from the Pemex station that just saved us. The problem was that I had been texting them and calling them for the last couple of days and I had not heard back. Probably their number changed or my cell phone service is screwed up (shout-out here to Verizon). Anyhow, I didn't quite feel comfortable just dropping in on them. And it was no longer an emergency. And if I kept driving, we would get ever closer to Surf Camp.

Yes, Surf Camp 22, which had now become a mythical Shangri-la. Would we ever get there? Did it really exist at all? Or was it just another weird swirl in the time-space continuum that had become the genesis of my imaginary world? If I could have an imaginary dog, it seems quite plausible that Surf Camp was also imaginary. Maybe I was, in reality, lying in a hospital bed somewhere, deep in a coma, dreaming my very existence, and Surf Camp was just a side effect of the anesthesia. Well, dear reader, we might never know…

Ok, ok, stop that kind of debilitating thought.

Well, yes, it was getting into the evening, and I do not like to drive after dark, but the road was beckoning and now we had a full tank of gas and so…yes, this is how I make bad decisions.

The city of La Paz is the only place in the entire Baja Peninsula that is actually like being in mainland Mexico. Like in real Mexico. Not the Mexico of the border cities, which is a weird blend of wealth and poverty and the strange mix of destitute refugees trying to cross the border. And not the even weirder weirdness of the tourist cities, picturesquely on the ocean, dominated by luxury resort hotels, Gucci stores, and Mercedes dealerships, with a population of transient wealth, second or third homes, and an impoverished barrio stretching off into the inland desert. (See San Lucas, or San Jose.) La Paz is an actual city, with a long history, a central zocalo, a three-hundred-year-old cathedral, a bustling waterfront, and a population of middle-class Mexicans. La Paz is Latin American. La Paz is Mexico. A close (smaller) cousin of Guadalajara, or Puebla, or Veracruz, or any number of other Mexican cities.

Which is to say that you really don't want to be driving there after dark.

Not only because it is confusing, or possibly dangerous, or impossible to find your way out of until morning, but because there is take-no-prisoners traffic. Rush hour traffic. Hardworking Mexicans trying to get home to a couple of cervezas and some warm tortillas. Please get out of their way.

My normal route south takes me around central La Paz. There is a cutoff road to the west, out near the airport, a shortcut that takes you south toward Todos Santos. I know the route well. But now it was five-thirty in the evening and getting dark, and the traffic was slow and stalled and I had been driving all day and things had been a little stressful, and...

Before I knew it, things got a little quirky. Soon it was really dark, and I had my headlights on and I was a bit south of La Paz and traffic was finally thinning out and I thought I would soon be released from the hell of the nighttime city. Really, I almost made it out. I was minutes away from freedom.

Then there were flashing blue lights behind me. And then a loud siren. And then in my mirrors I could see it was a police wagon. And then I realized that I was being pulled over.

Oh, fuck.

I pulled the taco truck and the Apache Ramada off onto the side of the highway, into a dirt parking lot. There were two police cruisers, one on either side of me.

I turned to speak to Orvis, to tell him to lay low, just hunker down and be patient and I would take care of this, and that there was nothing to worry about, I mean I hadn't really done anything wrong. I turned to explain all this to him and that is when I noticed.

He had already crawled into the back, into the space down on the floor between the seats, and he had made himself small and dark and well-hidden. I could just see his eyes glowing in the dark, and they spoke to me in a deep voice that said:

"You're on your own, buddy."

CHAPTER TWELVE

Slightly south of La Paz City,
BCS, MX

I am not writing from prison, so you who are authority-adverse can relax. I have a long history of being stopped by the Policia in Mexico. Though I must say, I handled this time a little bit differently.

Perhaps we can back up a little bit here. All the way back to the 1950s and 60s when I was growing up in America. My family was strictly working-class. My dad worked in a factory; my mom was, what they called then, a "housewife." I went to public schools (Seymour High School), public university (UConn). I had all the advantages of the middle class. I spoke only English. I was male. I was white. (Still am, as a matter of fact). When I was ten years old, I wanted to be a G-Man (that meant, at the time, an FBI agent). I wrote letters to J. Edgar Hoover. He wrote back. I swear, this is all true.

Which is to say that I had a strong and admiring view of the police. I was in love with democracy and the rule-of-law (still am). I became a journalist instead of a lawyer, which was probably, in hindsight, a bad move. At least financially. But through it all, many, many years of travel all over the United States and much of the rest of the world, I had a good relationship with the police. Hey, I'm a white guy.

They don't shoot me when I get out of the car. Mostly they leave me alone. Mostly I don't commit any crimes. I drive like your grandmother (slow and in one lane only). I smile when I see a police person and (mostly) they smile back.

So I actually had a bad attitude when I first came to Mexico and got stopped by the police. In Mexico, the system was different. A policeman bought his own equipment and his own territory and was paid very little by the government. This meant they basically survived on bribes. If you were a tourist driving in Baja, they stopped you for whatever petty offense they could find. Then they took your driver's license and they didn't give it back until you paid them. In cash. No writing you a ticket. No judge. No jury. Just you and the cop, one on one, how much can he scare you and take your money.

This always rubbed me the wrong way. This was not right. It was not the rule of law. Several times, I almost got myself in deep trouble by refusing to pay the bribe. It was especially bad on the way BACK into the U.S. Just before the border going north, you would get pulled over. They knew you were heading home. They could easily get 500 pesos, because they had you. They threatened to take you in, not let you leave. It was a pain in the ass.

The police in certain areas were notorious. One of those places was La Paz.

So when I got pulled over on that night in early December...after I had driven that long highway 2,100 miles from Eugene, Oregon, USA, after I had gone through everything, a broken axle, a $3,000 repair, running out of gas, a smart-ass dog as my only companion...

Well, how can I explain it? I had had my fill. The universe was messing with me too much. I snapped. I decided to mess with the universe...

Probably a bad idea, but like I said, I was at the end my rope.

So if we set the scene, it would look something like this: A dirt parking lot on the southern edge of La Paz City. The taco truck accompanied by the Apache Ramada parked in the middle. On either side a Policia cruiser marked Policia Municipal. In the backseat of the truck an imaginary dog, hunkered down, inwardly grinning, just waiting to say, "I told you so."

I got out of the truck. The police captain got out of one of the cruisers. I said (in bad Spanish):

"What is the problem?"

He said (in perfect Spanish): "Your lights are out on the trailer."

I walked to the back of the truck and noticed the electrical connection for the Ramada had come loose. I reached down and jiggled it. The trailer lights came on.

"I am very sorry," I said. "It was a bad connection."

"Very dangerous," he said. "Let me see your driver's license."

I took out my driver's license and handed it to him. He put it in the left-hand pocket of his shirt.

"Very, very dangerous," he said.

"I'm not giving you money," I said.

He started to walk away with my driver's license in his pocket.

"One moment please," I said. I opened the door of the truck, reached in, and got my smartphone. I turned to him while holding the phone and I said: "I'm going to use this to translate."

He looked at me. I said loudly (this time into the phone), "Siri create a live link to Facebook."

If you think that Mexican police captains don't understand English, you would be wrong. This one certainly understood.

And like I said, I was at the end of a long day and I didn't feel like eating more shit.

I held the smartphone in front of me and took a photo of him. "Please explain why you are stopping me," I said.

There was a complete sea change in his attitude. He stood up straighter. He spoke more politely. He went into a long speech about how he was a captain in the municipal police and how it was his duty to protect tourists, and how it was necessary to make sure everyone was safe. It went on a bit. Then he took my driver's license out of his pocket and handed it to me. "Please drive safely. And enjoy your vacation," he said.

He got back into the police cruiser. And they left me there in the parking lot.

When I got back in the truck, Orvis was in the front seat. He had an amazed look on his face. He smiled and showed all his teeth.

"Wow," he said, "that was cool."

CHAPTER THIRTEEN

Surf Camp 22, Shipwrecks Beach, BCS, MX

I will freely admit that it was not the most auspicious of beginnings.

Surf Camp was a wreck. My imaginary dog refused to leave the beach, where he was sure that at any moment he would meet a French poodle who liked to surf. Though the ocean was warm (about seventy-seven degrees), a cool wind was beginning to blow from the north. The waves were moderate, the water clear, the fishing boats were bringing in good-sized dorado. There was nothing to really worry about, but there was a lot to do.

For reasons that are beyond the scope of this narrative, a visitor (Our British Friend) who was tentatively scheduled to arrive in about ten days was instead coming on Tuesday morning. Today it was Sunday. There would have to be a mad scramble to accommodate her.

Let me explain about Our British Friend: She is a mature and sophisticated woman of refined tastes, frugal sensibilities, and worldly experience. She has traveled the planet, raised brilliant children, written and performed amazing songs, and is an accomplished designer/artist. I have learned to not question the universe about this, but for some reason she finds me slightly entertaining. It is always an honor to have her as a guest at Surf Camp.

Ah yes, Surf Camp. Which, at this present moment of our story, is basically a heap of debris mixed with a load of miscellaneous things that have been disgorged from the Apache Ramada.

The Apache Ramada is a bit worse for wear, having been, as you will recall, dragged down the interstate skidding on its underbelly after the wheels fell off.

Surf Camp is based around a 1952 Boles Aero travel trailer. This is a close cousin to an Airstream, basically an aluminum shell stretched around metal struts with windows cut in at strategic places. It has sat in the Baja desert for at least thirty years. The wheels are long gone and the interior has been completely gutted and the glass broken out of most of the windows. The roof is a sieve that filters the sunlight nicely but would be completely ineffectual in a rainstorm. I use it mostly for storage, but I have a little writing table at one end that I use to remind myself that I can write stories almost anywhere. Even surrounded by peeling plywood and broken glass. You would get a good laugh if you could see me writing this.

Next to the Aero, the Apache Ramada (1977) looks modern. With much effort and maneuvering (you can move almost anything with a big enough lever) I am able to get the Apache situated in a space that is perpendicular to the Aero. I take the wheels and the new axle off and lower it onto concrete blocks. Now the two old ladies can leisurely spend the rest of their years, side by side, moldering into the desert landscape. I'm sure they will be here longer than I will. Probably longer than I will even be on this planet.

The trick now is to build a shade structure between the two travel trailers. I have a stack of salvaged timbers (some of which once supported the movie screen I built for something called "Cinema in the Sand") and some black palm poles which are like iron and never rot. My job is to configure them into a stable-enough structure, cover them with a big shade tarp, and then tie it all down so that the north wind, when it comes a-calling, does not sweep us all away.

I'm somewhere in the process of doing all this when Tuesday shimmies up the calendar and Our British Friend arrives.

"Fabulous," is her first word when we reach Surf Camp. "Grandly optimistic, wouldn't you say? Tip-top and filled with potential. When will we be hiring the construction crew?"

Of course she is joking, as she knows there is no construction crew and no money to hire one if it even existed. But really, Our British Friend is game for just about anything. Soon her sleeves are rolled up and we are working to get the place together. At one point she is out in the yard folding up some extra tarps.

This is when I hear the words that a host never really wants to hear from someone who is visiting:

"What sort of snake do you think this might be?"

Our British Friend is standing with the corner of a brown tarp in one hand and she is pointing to a snake she has just uncovered. The snake is about five feet away. I can see it tasting the air with its tongue.

"You might want to step back a bit," I tell her. "Move slowly."

"It's very beautiful," Our British Friend says.

"Yes," I say. "It is a very beautiful rattlesnake."

I am begged by my subconscious to pause for a moment to add a bit of exposition to our story, as I have been reminded by myself that perhaps I have not been painting a clear and true picture of this country and its environs.

Despite what I have told you about the vagaries of travel in Mexico, I would not want you to have the impression that it is an unwelcoming country. I think that we, in the America of the United States, tend to have a condescending view of our neighbors in the other Americas. This is especially true of Mexico. We tend to see Mexico and Mexicans as a rough-and-ready blend of emotion and physical intensity. We see them as hardworking and unsophisticated. We see this, I think, because most of the Mexican folks we know in the United States have come there to make money. Most of them have been disenfranchised in one way or another in their home country. They have come to our country (USA) to try to remedy that. This is how we know Mexicans. But this is not how Mexicans are.

The vast majority of Mexicans are modern and sophisticated, culturally diverse, family-oriented, proud, strong, and relatively wealthy. They are a very warm and welcoming people. They speak very good Spanish and many of them speak two or three other languages. They have the same problems that all countries have. Problems of violence, drug addiction, economic stagnation. But in general they are not out to harm anyone.

I cannot, however, say this of the other creatures who inhabit the landscape of Mexico, especially in Baja California.

The landscape here is not for ninnies. It is not for the faint-of-heart. Not for the bug-fearing. Not for those with (word for fear of snakes).

I am an old Baja hand. I've slept with centipedes. Had scorpions scoot across my feet in the shower. Swarmed by African honeybees, attacked by red fire ant armies, beset by crowds of field mice, stickered by all manner of cactus.

But I never got bit by a rattlesnake.

And Our British Friend, who is very far from a ninnie, also has not been bitten.

We backed slowly away and let the snake continue to taste the desert, hopefully finding a path to its home under some safe and secure rock, a fine nest of warm sand and mouse bones.

"I think we should take a little break," I said. "Maybe relax with a good cup of tea."

"Fabulous," she said. "I'll put the kettle on."

CHAPTER FOURTEEN

Christmas Eve, San Jose del Cabo, BCS, MX

Orvis has picked himself out a nice comfy spot at the peak of a very tall sand dune that overlooks the left-handed break at Shipwrecks. He lays there in the sand most days and keeps a constant watch over the beach and the ocean horizon that stretches about twenty-five miles to the east. At first he wasn't sure what he was looking for, but then…well…I'm sorry to say I'm partially responsible.

For several years I have spent the holidays living alone. Not really isolated, because I have lots of nearby friends, a large extended family of people I am close to, plenty of company if I want it. But in my household, where I live, my little unit of life, I have been alone. This has been entirely of my own choosing. This season is different. Our British Friend is here. I have an imaginary dog to watch over. We are something of a little family.

And I am (only somewhat) embarrassed to say it brought out the worst of the Christmas Spirit within me. The spirit of a Christmas tree. The spirit of gift wrapping. The spirit of ginger cookies and toy soldiers, sugar-plum faeries, reindeer on the rooftop, Old St. Nick, and, of course, lots and lots of shopping. For all those gifts under the tree. What fun, eh?

Our British Friend takes a completely polar opposite approach to Christmas. No gifts, no tree, no Christmas carols or Old St. Nick. Just a nice quiet time with a good book in front of the fireplace. (We have, by the way, the BEST fireplace at Surf Camp.) Maybe a slice of turkey or some BBQ shrimp on Christmas Day.

She is, however, an artist, and when I challenge her to come up with a Christmas tree that is a work of art...well, she delivers in spades.

My mistake is that I leave the two of them alone. Orvis is up from the beach for a visit. Our British Friend is in the comfy chair reading Ann Patchett. I decide it is a good time to drive into town for supplies (and a little Christmas shopping, yum yum). I'm gone for several hours.

Which is about all the time it takes for the two of them to come up with the following Christmas narrative which, I forewarn you, I had no part in.

From what I can tell, Orvis asks Our British Friend about Santa Claus and the meaning of Christmas. She is probably not the best person to ask about this. Our British Friend was raised as an Anglican. Her parents bought an old rectory in a village that was part of the Sandringham Estate. This is one of the properties owned by the Windsor family in England. They are best known for a person named Queen Elizabeth II (deceased) and the present King of England (Charles III). Sandringham was where the Windsors came home each winter for Christmas. Our British Friend had to suffer through six weeks each holiday season of having the royals and all their retinue in her backyard. Literally her backyard. The rectory backs up onto the King's Deer Park. Sandringham House is on a hill not far distant. At her elementary school (two blocks away), Our British Friend had to learn the correct way to curtsey when the Queen came by to hand out little Christmas gifts to the village children.

Well then. Does Our British Friend now believe in the miracle of the birth of Jesus and the magic of Old Saint Nick? I haven't specifically asked her, but I would say no. I would say that on the spectrum of Santa's Elves on one end and the Humbug of Scrooge on the other, Our British Friend is rather well toward the Scrooge end.

And, you know, Orvis is kind of naive. He is a young dog filled with hope and desire. You tell him about other imaginary beings (like Jesus, Santa Claus, Bigfoot, whatever), he BELIEVES you. Because what imaginary being DOESN'T want to believe in other imaginary beings?

So Our British Friend makes this mistake (which is very easy to make): She over-compensates.

Rather than telling Orvis the awful truth about Christmas (plastic toys, diabetic sugar rushes, over-consumerism, Walmart stampede shopping, stale Christmas carols), Our British Friend decided to make up a cute little story.

"Santa Claus," she tells Orvis, "comes to Baja riding on the back of a whale. He has a sleigh filled with Christmas presents that is pulled by magic flying dolphins. He stops at every camp to give the good children and little nice dogs their presents and have a cup of tea with a crumpet. Or it might be a shot of tequila with a wedge of lime, I'm not exactly sure about that."

Orvis looks at her with suspicion. "What kind of whale?" he asks.

Our British Friend does not miss a beat. "A humpback," she says.

"Do the dolphins actually fly, or are they just jumping?"

"Right-oh. Maybe just jumping."

"And what kind of presents does he bring?"

"Oh my, all sorts of magical stuff. Little stuff, big stuff. Lots of stuff. And sometimes, if you are really good, he brings you your heart's desire."

"Which in my case," Orvis smiles, "would be a French poodle who surfs."

"Well," Our British Friend replies, "there are limits..."

Of course I am making up this conversation, because I wasn't actually there and only heard about it later from Our British Friend. When I return from my excursion into town, I have my own little fantasy world to spring on everyone. I have made plans for Christmas Eve.

"It's only two days away," I tell them both. "I've reserved a nice hotel room, right downtown. I found a secret walk in the estuary where we can go birdwatching on Christmas Eve and then over to the turtle sanctuary, where at 6 p.m. there is a release of baby turtles into the ocean. Then we can go back to the town square and attend the Misa de Gallo. That's the Catholic mass on Christmas Eve when they bless the Baby Jesus, and there is a procession from the church to the zocalo. Sixteen men carry Baby Jesus on a litter and place him in the manger. The Wise Men are there and a cow and a lamb, and Mary and Joseph and then later I think Adam and Eve show up and of course God comes down about midnight."

They both looked at me like I was crazy.

Our British Friend is skeptical and unimpressed. Sixteen men carrying Baby Jesus is just not her kind of thing. Orvis, on the other hand...

Orvis is having none of it. He is adamant that he will spend Christmas Eve perched on his sand dune waiting for Santa Claus on the humpback whale, with the magic flying dolphins that are probably just jumping really high. He wants to be sure that Santa knows what he wants for Christmas.

"A French poodle who surfs?" I ask him.

"Exactly." he says.

See, that's the thing about Christmas. At least the modern Christmas. It is set up to disappoint you. Like when you really wanted the Dick Tracy television/telephone watch but instead your parents got you a bicycle. Or the time they gave you socks and new underwear. And said it was from Santa.

I mean what was Santa thinking? Socks and underwear?

But I am not going to try to explain to Orvis that he will probably NOT see Santa Claus riding a humpback whale with flying dolphins. I will not explain to him that Santa is the anti-quantum sort of a thing. He is only there when you can't see him. When you fall asleep for five minutes and then open your eyes and the milk and cookies are gone. I will not try to explain the way of the world to my imaginary dog.

He's just going to have to learn for himself.

CHAPTER FIFTEEN

Boxing Day, Surf Camp 22, Shipwrecks Beach

I think that the days between Christmas and New Years are the perfect days to speak of our addictions. This gives us four or five days and long nights to: One—examine our habits, especially the bad habits, the ones we need to eliminate, and two—indulge them to the max. Then on New Year's Day we can make a resolution to break these habits. Of course, we all know how New Year's Resolutions go...but still it's a good time of year for this sort of thing.

My personal addiction, the one that will probably end my life prematurely (such a loss to literature!) is to SUGAR. Yikes! This is a bad one. Probably worse than cigarettes. Worse than alcohol. Up there with heroin and meth. Though I've never done any of those, especially the cigarettes.

Christmas Day dinner is a fiasco for my insulin lymphatic system. My sugar addiction is out of control. I'm lucky I don't pass right into a diabetic coma.

We are extremely fortunate this year to have a geographically and culturally diverse group of people at the dinner table. Surf Camp is perfect for hosting dinners, up to twelve people before the chairs run out. On this Christmas, we have a range that goes as far north as southeast Alaska, as far south as Mexico City, as far east as Biarritz, France, and west to who knows where, probably Hawaii, I guess.

There are three solid languages spoken at the table, four if you count my fake Ukrainian, five if you count the Italian names of some of the dishes. Of course, what it all boils down to, finally, is dessert.

Alaska bakes an extremely luscious citrus meringue pie, akin to key lime, but far more sophisticated. Biarritz brings the cheese (in France they eat cheese before AND after dinner), an amazing Conte, a perfectly aged Roquefort, a fine Burgeon-desonne. And Mexico City? Well, what can I say, Mexico City brings dulce de leche, tamarindo in little clay pots, an entire Rosca de Reyes Tradicional. Alongside all this, we have dark chocolate-covered almonds from California Norte. We have Trufas Espolvoreadas con cocoa. We have English creme-filled biscuits. We have the beginning of a sugar-addict's nightmare.

I would like to tell you that I resisted all of this temptation. But that would be false. I'm indulging until New Years. But then…

Orvis is taking in all of this scene from a relaxed pose (which is a lot like sleeping) as he cuddles himself in the big blue chair next to the bookcase. I bought the big blue chair last year from the Gringo Second Hand Store. I was thinking it would last about one year before the mice and snakes took over the insides, but to my delight it was entirely intact after I stored it in the aluminum travel trailer. I think it was so hot in the trailer in the summer that not even the snakes and mice could handle it and they did not nest in the big blue chair. Now Orvis has taken it over as his favorite place to lounge while he watches camp life transpire.

Orvis spent much of Christmas Day in contemplation. I returned with Our British Friend from our Christmas Eve excursion about mid-morning. I expected to find him all excited and ready to give us a vivid description of Santa Claus and the Humpback Whale and the Flying Magical Dolphins. But he was rather subdued. I left to gather some firewood for the evening campfire, and he told Our British Friend what had happened.

"I was right there. It was perfect," Orvis said. "A completely commanding view of the beach and the ocean. I watched as Orion climbed up into the sky. I saw the Big Dipper rise in the east and I followed the North Star perfectly, knowing that's how you navigate the night. I swear I only dozed off for five minutes…maybe ten at the most."

"Yes." Our British Friend said. "You probably just missed him."

To his credit, I think that Orvis is more disappointed with himself than he is with Santa Claus. Santa did not bring him his heart's desire (a French poodle who surfs). Santa brought him instead a Spanish/English dictionary. You would think: not a very sexy gift. But it turns out Santa was looking out for him. Santa was looking into his future.

So this is where we have to introduce a new character. She is sitting in the third chair on the left side of the table and her name is…well, let's say her name is Maria Louisa. (because of the vagaries of social media I rarely use anyone's true name). She is originally from Mexico City but has lived at Shipwrecks for a few years. She lives alone up on the bluff above the Tribe Arroyo in a house (well, that's a stretch, for sure, it's not really a house, it's a jumble of falling down timbers with a cement floor) that was built by old Leon who has since passed, but before his last breath gave her permission to live there. It gets complicated, but last year I met her on the beach, befriended her in broken Spanish, introduced her to my other friends, and now she is a solid member of the Surf Camp 22 Dinner Club. Her Spanish is perfect. She's working on French and English. Oh, yes, and did I mention? She surfs like a maniac.

Maria Louisa is a classically beautiful human. Small, thin, and athletic. Brown skin that shines like gold in the winter sun. Dark eyes and hair and a face that transports the observer to an ancient world of Aztec royalty. Seriously, you could easily imagine the Jaguar Warriors fighting a deadly round of futbol over the opportunity of her favors.

Along with physical beauty, she is additionally wrapped in a psychological enigma that we all seem unable to explain. Our English Friend, whose Spanish is much better than mine, says Maria Louisa is on a spiritual quest. Being alone and with the ocean are her devices to find her inner truth. Everyone else wonders why she is alone, as she is young and beautiful and certainly not without male suitors.

I've been watching as Orvis begins to notice her. Tonight at Christmas dinner, from his view at the big blue chair, he can only see her profile. But that is the most magnificent view of her face. The high forehead, tall cheekbones, and royal crook in her nose. The profile of a princess. Or queen of the playa.

There has been very little swell and no good surfing waves in the ocean this holiday season. So Orvis hasn't even seen her surf yet.

So I end Christmas Day thinking: Can an imaginary dog, who thinks he only wants a French poodle, fall for an Aztec Princess from CDMX? A princess searching for her inner dreams?

It's beginning to sound a lot like fiction to me.

But what do I know. I'm just a writer.

CHAPTER SIXTEEN

Las Arbolitas, Cabo del Este, BCS, MX

Orvis tells me that I have to stop writing about him. He says that things are getting too weird and unbelievable and that I will lose my credibility as a writer.

"I'm not sure I have much credibility to lose," I tell him. "But I see your point."

Why do I know that things are getting too weird and unbelievable? Because this is what happened yesterday.

I was on my way into town, and let me explain this, there are two parts of the road into San Jose del Cabo. The first part, out near Shipwrecks, is all dirt and rarely graded or repaired, and somewhat gnarly depending on the season. The second part is paved. Basically a two-lane highway where everyone can drive like a maniac and the livestock are constantly in peril. Buzzard's Highway, I like to call it, because of all the roadkill. This weird thing happened on the unpaved dirt part of the coast road, not far from the turn-off to Surf Camp.

Listen: I can't make this stuff up, really, I can't.

I was driving very slow, because I always drive slow on the rough road as I do not want to screw up the taco truck, which has been a solid and faithful companion these last years and deserves a long and well-maintained life. Even though I was going slow, I hardly noticed this thing in the middle of the road. Yes, right in the very middle of the road. I actually drove right past it. It looked like a wriggling mass of…what? Then I thought: What the heck was that? I thought: A rattlesnake that got run over by a truck? Something dying a terrible death?

I stopped. I put the truck in reverse. I backed up carefully until I was right beside the unidentified wriggling mass. I looked out the driver's-side window.

Okay, wildlife enthusiasts, please take note: This is nothing you are going to see on the National Geographic Society Nature channel.

The whirling mass was not a dying rattlesnake. It was two chipmunks in a fight to the death.

Yes, chipmunks. We have them here. Those lovely furry ground squirrels, so cute and cuddly, the ones that dart around looking for food and avoiding being eaten by…well… any manner of things, from hungry snakes to hawkish eagles to night owls. It was mid-morning, and here were two chipmunks fighting each other in the middle of the road.

I don't mean like they were just just sparring and chuckling at each other. I mean like locked in a death grip. Snarling, bleeding, with their teeth bared. As I watched, they separated for a second and then hurled themselves at each other, became a whirling ball of fur and fangs, and tumbled off to the side of the road.

"Hey!" I yelled at them. "Cut that out!"

They stopped for half a second, looked at me, and then looked at each other as if to say, "Who the fuck is that?" and then whammm, went right back to fighting.

I have to say there was something about this that I found deeply unsettling. I mean it was two days after Christmas…

And the CHIPMUNKS were fighting? What was this world coming to?

It harkens to memories of youth (as does everything these days). You might know, if you are of this era, about the Three Chipmunks. You might remember their famous Christmas Song ("Christmas Don't Be Late"). It made the words "hula hoop" famous. There was always a bit of conflict among the Three Chipmunks because the one named Alvin had trouble with group cooperation. But really, they were a comedy team. We never saw them fighting to the death. And certainly not at Christmastime.

I believe the inner child in me found this profoundly disturbing. I was always in love with the fairy tale that Christmas is about peace on earth, goodwill toward humans. Not Chipmunk gladiators killing each other in the middle of the road.

Well anyhow, I left the Chipmunks there on the road to their own tragic fate and proceeded on my errands. I had plenty of time for contemplation on the drive into town and then the return trip to Surf Camp.

And I came to the conclusion that Orvis was correct. Things were becoming too real, or too surreal, or too something. Friends were writing me to say they really wanted to meet Orvis. I felt as though I had stretched the narrative to its limit. It was like some metaphoric bungee cord that was pulled to its ultimate length, couched in the desire to reach that final hook, but not quite long enough. At any moment it could reach the end of its tensile strength and snap back to poke your eye out. Or at least give you a good bruise on the forehead. One snap and you wished you had stopped stretching it two seconds ago.

Our British Friend and I are going to head out on a little excursion up the coast road. A few days away from Surf Camp. Orvis is going to stay with his new friend (Maria Louisa).

I'm going to take some time off. And hope I don't dream of murderous chipmunks.

CHAPTER SEVENTEEN

La Ventana, Cabo del Este (Norte), La Paz, BCS, MX

Our journey northeast along the cape is magical. We leave Surf Camp in the late afternoon, and by sunset we are having dinner with friends near Vinorama. Their house is perched on a sand dune above a private surf break. The view is empty beach and ocean for several miles in each direction. It is a bit lonely out there, but we sing Beatles songs after dinner with three voices and one guitar and then we sleep in the back of the taco truck and watch for *estrellas fugaces*. I see four strong ones and then show Our British Friend how the belt of Orion points to Sirius the Dog Star.

"It's a very average star," I tell her. "A class A-1 white hydrogen star on the main sequence. Only about 1.8 times the radius of the Sun. With medium-range luminosity."

She does not respond. Maybe she is asleep. Maybe she is just tired of my voice. But this doesn't stop me.

"But it's only 8.7 light years away. So to our eyes, it is the brightest star in the sky. After the sun, of course. All the other objects are only reflecting the sun's light. But Sirius burns on its own. There may be a lesson here."

"Shh," she says. "Your voice is scaring away the falling stars. I want to see one more before I fall asleep."

Yes, it is a magical journey up the coast, but the magic is not in the scenery.

The road at Shipwrecks is a rough dirt track that hugs the coast and gives access to the numerous beaches and surf breaks that line the lower East Cape. Fourteen miles of this road have disappeared. That would be the section from Playa Tortuga south to La Laguna and Playita. This section has been bought up by large corporations and resorts. They have built a paved road further inland at great expense just so they could own the beachfront. This tendency will no doubt migrate further along the East Cape. But for now, from Shipwrecks north there is still only one traditional road along the coast.

Dirt roads in this part of Mexico are both annoying and authentic. Mostly they keep the less hardy tourists at bay. They keep the beaches empty and the ranchos rustico. Cattle in the road, goats herding like ghosts through barbed-wire fences, roosters strutting, roughly painted wooden signs selling farm cheese. There is the occasional well of brackish water, the smell of manure, a cabrón sitting on his horse in the shade of a spreading ficus tree.

Think of clouds of dust. Berserk surfers driving double doubles (Mexican for four-wheel drive), bouncing and swerving at high speed off the washboard as they chase a reported swell up and down the coast. Gearheads wearing helmets and headphone radios tearing up the road and the beach in high-tech side-by-sides just because they can. In between the calm isolation and enduring rustification, it is a countryside of infernal combustion engines and ugly human nature.

But I thought you said it was magical?

Ah yes, that's the trick, isn't it? The magic flows from the observer to the observed. Our British Friend spreads the magic with her fine ink fountain pen and watercolor brushes. Myself, I use words.

Our Vinorama friends suggest Los Arbolitos. It is a short drive to the north, just around the point of Los Frailes and before the cape of Cabo Pulmo. It turns out to be a series of picturesque bays. Scalloped shells carved into the short cliffs. Fingers of barnacled stone reaching out into the Sea of Cortez. This is the south end of the Cabo Pulmo National Marine Park. It is known worldwide for the ecological program that actually saved the coral reefs and restored the marine habitat. No fishing or harvesting shellfish is allowed. It is not pristine, but the snorkeling and scuba diving are excellent.

The camping is quite a bit less so. Mostly an undeveloped parking lot in a sand arroyo. Cattle tramp through at will. Roosters begin crowing at three a.m. By six, they start the generator. It gives us a good laugh. Neither Our British Friend nor I sleep much.

The magic here resides in the fact that there is no wind. I've never understood the complexities of weather and climate, but for some reason the north wind that has been blowing steadily all season has stopped. Well, not exactly. It actually swung south. A bluster of southern wind is battering Surf Camp while we are not there. But here at Cabo Pulmo, the cape turns east. At Los Arbolitos and further northeast to Los Barriles and La Ventana, it is calm. The ocean is smooth. The water is warm. The strong south wind is blocked by the headlands.

We linger to create a few sketches and some word phrases and so it is very late when we finally reach La Ventana. I've made arrangements to meet some folks from Oregon who have a winter house there, another English friend and her fly-fishing husband. The town is built along the spectacular Bahia Los Muertos, which is protected by Isla Cerralvo. This island appears as a mountain range rising up out of the water in the north. A channel between the island and the mainland provides a chute for the north winds, and La Ventana has become a mecca for kite surfers and wing enthusiasts.

Again, it is late, and rather than find a place to camp I pull into the parking lot of the first hotel we come to. It is the Villa Paraiso. Built into a cliffside. The patrona sizes us up. Our British Friend is always lovely, but I am a bit scruffy with a scratch of beard, sunburned cheeks, a hairless head tattooed with scrapes and scars where I have butted into too many head-height and unyielding objects. She offers us the most expensive room she thinks we can afford. It is down five sets of stairs (eighty steps, we counted) and out on a point. Very nice, even if we have to share the veranda with a group of Swiss-Germans who are loud and over-excited with the prospect of cheap tequila.

There is nothing better than the blessing of good friends, and though we are very late finding our way in the dark to their house, our fellow Oregonians welcome us with tea and mincemeat pies (Our British Friend notes that we are served Marks & Spencer's pies, which do not grow in Mexico but had to be imported especially for the holidays from somewhere at least 7,000 miles away). The conversation is excellent, we are introduced to their brilliant daughter from Portland, their new dog (Fiona), and all is well and fine and good…until they ask about Orvis.

"It's funny," I tell them, "I haven't thought of him in a few days. I'm sure he is alright."

They look at me with both suspicion and skepticism. It turns out it was Orvis they really wanted to meet.

After an awkward pause, Our British Friend turns to me with her pretty hazel eyes and her rising eyebrows.

"It's been a delight," she says. "But really, it is late and time for us to go."

Gracious goodbyes and we climb into the taco truck.

"What?" I say. Our British Friend is shaking her head when we drive away. "I didn't know they only wanted to meet Orvis…"

But there is no answer. Am I projecting or is there disappointment and criticism in her silence?

After a few miles, I decide it is all in my imagination.

CHAPTER EIGHTEEN

Cabo San Lucas, BCS, MX

It turns out that Maria Luisa is much more of a cat person than a dog person.

I try to explain this to Orvis when we return to Surf Camp and he is sitting outside the gate with a bit of a forlorn look in his eye.

"There are dog people and there are cat people," I say. "Dog people like dogs. Cat people like cats. That's just the way it is."

"Cats are constantly killing things," Orvis says. "They lay around all day purring and then in the night they go hunting. Just for fun. They like to torture whatever they catch. It's kind of disgusting."

"Great for controlling the vermin," I tell him. "Some people like that."

"Constantly killing things," Orvis replies. "I had to call in the coyotes to get them to stop."

"You did WHAT?"

Something of an explanation is due, I think. Maria Luisa now lives back in the desert. She got a position caretaking a small rancho owned by Big Wave Dave and Paulie the Screw. The rancho is a bit of a wreck. The solar electric system is defunct and she has only a feeble gravity feed from the pila for water. It's somewhat rugged, but that is how she likes it.

However…that far back in the desert you are much closer to wildlife. It's fox and coyote town back there. Rattlesnake heaven. Centipedes the size of small vacuum cleaners.

On his second day out at Maria Louisa's, Orvis began a little howling at night. Just loud enough to be heard for several miles in the stillness of the desert. Not too much past midnight, but folks go to bed early out on the East Cape. In Coyote language he was saying, "Come eat these cats, they are killing every bird and gecko they can find."

"The coyotes didn't actually catch the three cats," Orvis told me. "But they put a good scare into them. The cats spent four days hiding under the bed. And no purring…"

So much for farming out Orvis.

Honestly, I was just as happy to have him back even if he did get kicked out of Maria Luisa's for cause.

"Well, never mind, pal," I said. "We are glad to have you home, and just in time to come with us on a Bikini Expedition to San Lucas."

This pricked up his ears. Soon I was explaining about bikinis.

I cannot testify to the veracity of this explanation, but the story is told that shortly after the United States of America tested an early hydrogen bomb on a speck of land in the South Pacific that was named Bikini Atoll (Perhaps you've seen the famous footage of the explosion. The mushroom cloud, the tidal wave, the capsized warships, the giant ants and tarantulas, the mutated sharks as big as aircraft carriers that were left over after the nuclear test), a new style of bathing suit began to appear on American beaches. It replaced the common one-piece woman's bathing suit with a much more immodest two piece. Perhaps the mushroom cloud was so phallically erotic that a marketing genius could not help himself (it was no doubt a man) and coined the label "bikini" for the new fashion. The word "bikini" became synonymous with a two-piece suit that ranged anywhere from boxer shorts and a jog bra to a string thong barely separating the buttock cheeks and two postage stamps over the breast nipples. Currently (not that I am a trained observer), the bikini seems to have shrunk in size and grown in price. As you know, there is little logic to be found in the science of women's fashion.

"Our British Friend," I tell Orvis, "has decided she wants a tanned tummy."

This imaginary dog looks at me like he can't for the life of him imagine why she would want that.

"It's a woman's thing," I explain. "Always best to go along. Besides, she will look great in a two-piece."

Thus begins the Bikini Expedition.

I should say here that it takes a lot to get me to go the twenty miles or so southwest to Cabo San Lucas. "Cabo," as we call it locally, is something of a pit. If you could make a list of all the worst things that could be done to a unique and beautiful bay and the pristine beaches that surround it…I mean, seriously, think of the worst things short of detonating a nuclear bomb, well…there in your imagination would be a good description of Cabo San Lucas.

I'm not even going to go into an explanation of what it once was. A wide sand arroyo that emptied into a half-moon bay. A finger of stone stretching out to a tidal arch with a perfect north-facing beach nestled into the cliffside. A sleepy fishing village with a dirt air strip and some of the best marlin fishing in the world. It deserved to remain undiscovered, but of course it didn't.

Still, it definitely did not deserve to become what it is now. A cruise ship destination. An expensive marina with so much pollution you can smell diesel fumes wafting off the surface of the water in the morning. At one point I had friends who owned a tall ship (the *Talofa*) based in the San Lucas marina. Waking up on board in the marina was like being in a Big-Rig parking lot. Gasoline and diesel fumes to fill your lungs. Garbage floating by. The ship was a beautiful work of art. The setting was not romantic. They moved to the Caribbean.

Surrounding the marina is a *malecón* walkway. Fine in concept but now too narrow to accommodate the tourist traffic. The *malecón* is lined on the shore side with restaurants and bars. Also rather European with corresponding prices that also seem pretty European. Everyone here is under assault from constant hectoring by salesmen trying to push one thing or another. Fishing excursions and whale-watching, a romantic water taxi ride to Lover's Beach, snorkeling with a group of thirty to see the one angelfish still living in the bay.

Above and behind the restaurants are high-rise hotels. This would be okay, also rather European in some ways, if the hotels were ever finished. It has been at least twenty years since many of the structures were started. Many of them are still multistory hulks of concrete shell with rebar sticking out, existing in some kind of cement stasis like they were designed to be on the set of a horror movie, or the background for some punk-rock music video.

I think you get the picture. The rest of San Lucas is about twenty blocks deep and most of the real estate is occupied by tourist shops selling tourist junk and nightclubs selling human flesh in one form or another. This is your kind of place if you find porn movies interesting for their plotlines. I won't say more.

Ok, so why go there? Because Our British Friend wants a new bikini and I know that at one end of the San Lucas *malecón* there is a marble and travertine shopping mall that will have all manner of beachwear. High-end beachwear. Bikinis of quality design and manufacture that are worthy of her taste and dignity. Something sexy and modest at the same time. Clinging in the proper places, accentuating at the improper ones. And I'm buying, so she can't object to the price. Within reason.

Seriously, this becomes a freaking expedition. I have to cut my way through the traffic as though we are slicing our machete-way through the jungle. At every turn there is some yahoo taxi driver ready to cut me off and crush the toes of the taco truck. We reach the parking garage below the mall and I have to fight for the last remaining spot. Whom will I have to kill when we are trying to get out of here? I try not to think about it.

I tell Orvis to stay very close and not say a word. If he gets lost here, there is no telling. He will be "rescued" by some tourist from Minnesota and spend the rest of his life living in snowdrifts outside Minneapolis.

"You ever seen a snowdrift?" I ask him. "Frozen water everywhere. So cold your eyeballs freeze."

Our British Friend is aghast. Why did we come here?

The bikinis. They are of modern design, but about ten years behind the "Me Too" movement. Which is to say they are designed for thin nineteen-year-olds bred by fashion magazines for their unusually large chest structures. Or forty-five-year-olds who have been surgically augmented. The brands? Billabong, Surfer Girl, Point Break, French

Kiss, Ocean Pacific. Where are Title Nine and Patagonia? Maybe even Nike or Adidas? Something reasonably modest. Athletically sexy. Empowering.

It is no-go with the bikinis (anyway, Our British Friend would break my arm before she let me pay $275 US for two, possibly three, little triangles of Lycra). We take a quick walk through the downtown. I point out the Giggling Marlin. Squid Roe, Cabo Wabo, The Hard Rock Cafe. She is not impressed. And Orvis remains just as silent as I suggested. I think the large friendly couple we ran into coming up from the parking lot (they were Americans from Green Bay wearing t-shirts that said, "We Care," and underneath, "Wisconsin Pet Rescue Society) scared the bejesus out of him.

Many, many expeditions have failed throughout history, and why should ours be any different? I fought my way out of central San Lucas like a bloodied Conquistador on the outskirts of Tenochtitlan. Taco came through without a scratch. On the outskirts heading back toward San Jose, I took a wrong turn and we found ourselves in the parking lot of Walmart.

Listen, before you judge, I know that no self-respecting, progressive hippy would ever deign to pass through the doors of a Walmart, even on foreign soil. But they have no Walmarts in England. Our British Friend (non-prejudiced) suggests we stop for groceries. I mean we were already there, right?

It's a superstore. Why didn't I think of this? There is an entire section devoted to bikinis. Our British Friend soon finds one that she likes. The price is 359 pesos. (Look at the exchange rate, do the math, about $16 US.)

When I am purchasing it at the checkout stand, the lovely young Mexican clerk smiles sweetly and says, "*uno momentito*." She removes the anti-theft ring from the garment and that is when we notice that the bikini is on sale. Half off.

Clean living, my friends. That's the only way I can explain it. Clean living.

And let's raise a non-alcoholic cocktail to the ultimate success of the Bikini Expedition.

Even Orvis is smiling.

CHAPTER NINETEEN

Surf Camp 22, Shipwrecks Beach,
Cabo del Este, BCS, MX

Our French Friends arrive shortly after Groundhog Day. They have come from Saint-Jean-de-Luz, a satellite town of Biarritz. I've heard it's pretty spendy there.

They are driving a Ford F-250, Club Cab, possibly 1997, Quebec license plates, with a large truck camper bolted to the back and the brand name "Okanagan" in large letters stretched across the front.

Orvis greets their arrival with a wagging tale and a big grin. As you know, he has a thing for the French.

They are, perhaps, the happiest people I have ever met. They are almost on a par with Ron W. Bailey of West Seattle, Washington, who is actually and undoubtedly THE happiest person I know. And he's not even French. ("I'm Scots, laddie, dunna forget it…")

But the French, you know, love them, hate them, whatever sentiment you have for them, you do have to grant them one thing: They are French. There is nothing like it. (Orvis is smiling while I write this.)

Let's do a little geography and demographics review here.

France is a Western European country located roughly between the Atlantic Ocean and the Swiss Alps. Spain and the Mediterranean Sea in the south, Belgium and Flanders Fields in the north. A city named "Paris" somewhere in the middle. It is about the size of Oregon, which is thirteen times the size of Connecticut. There are seventy million or so people living in France, probably another five million outside of the country who consider themselves "French." They all speak a language (in one form or another) that they also call "French." It has words like "croissant" and "pomme de frite" that you may have heard. "Chevrolet," that's also a French word. As is "Pouilly-Fuissé." They drink a lot of wine there, and most of it is not from California.

Our French Friends speak many languages, and I am trying to teach them how to pronounce American English. They are having trouble with "Gatorade" and "Super Bowl," but we are working on it.

Ok, now that you've got the background, we can get on with our story.

A few years ago, I can no longer remember the exact year, but before I died of appendicitis and after I died in that car crash, maybe sometime in the mid-teens, say 2016 or so, I met Our French Friends in Los Barriles. One of those casual meetings around pickleball. The man was very athletic and a quick study (he's now, more or less, a professional pickleball player, coach, and teacher). The woman had other things going for her. She was super smart. Very artistic, good at languages, kindly and open-minded. Friendly and non-assuming.

We got to like each other very quickly. A few years later, they showed up unexpectedly at Surf Camp.

"*Bonjour, bonjour,*" I said, as they came through the gate, quickly exhausting my entire French vocabulary. "Welcome to Surf Camp. How did you possibly find us?"

"*Pas de probleme*," Our French Friends said. "We are French. We find everything!"

Which brings us (in a very circuitous and serpentine manner) to the crux of our story.

A couple of weeks ago, Our French Friends got lost.

They had been camped with us, or near us, during the winter season for the last two years. We appreciated the fine French cooking of the young man. The young woman made wonderful crepes. We began eating cheese for dessert. Speaking French at the dinner table. Speaking Spanish with a French accent. Watching old French movies with very bad English subtitles. It was grand fun.

Two weeks ago, they disappeared. No calls, no texts, no friend requests on Facebook. Were we being ghosted by the French? We began to wonder.

Then I found myself in a conversation with some Canadien friends. They said: "Did you hear what happened to those French folks?"

It was only days later that I did actually hear what happened.

Young and full of life ("joie de vivre," as the French like to say), this is how you could imagine Our French Friends. Young and foolish, as the old people say, this is how you could also imagine them. They decided to hike/backpack over the Sierra La Laguna mountains. About seventy miles, from near Miraflores in the east to Pescadero and the Pacific Ocean in the west.

The Sierra de la Laguna mountains are only about 2,100 meters tall at their highest (6,800 feet). But the range is steep and made up of several smaller ranges (Sierra San Lorenzo, Sierra San Bernardo, Pico Azurrado, Sierra Mata Gorda), and a couple of deep canyons (Canõn San Beatriz, Canõn

Cresta de las Chivas, Canõn Santa Cruz de las Sacrificio). It is rugged outback. Filled with rattlesnakes and scorpions the size of small automobiles, though that might be an exaggeration. There is no drinking water. Hot sun and swift wind blowing in from the oceans. Crumbling granite to walk over. Barbed backwoods trees and shrubs to crawl through. Scratchy. Itchy. With virtually no one to come save you if somehow you achieved the impossible: a cellphone signal to call home.

On the second day of their adventure, Our French Friends became lost. The "trail" they had been following disappeared into the steep box canyon of an arroyo they were traversing. They kept trying to go higher toward the crest of the mountains. Climbing the stony crumbles only to slide back again. Eventually, exhausted from hiking and almost out of water, they reached a saddle in the highest ridgeline. From here they could see the ocean. But between them was a cliff into a canyon, a steep descent through prickly bottle brush, and no trail to be seen.

It must be said the Our French Friends are in great shape. Athletic and toned. Young and strong. Determined and courageous. But given all that…well, at least they weren't stupid.

They turned back.

Well, partway back. They retreated back down the mountain to where they found a running stream. A ruined cabin. A large kettle that still held water. They spent a day boiling drinking water from the ground spring. Filling their various canteens. At night they huddled next to a fire and listened to the wildlife.

It was not pleasant. If you have ever heard the howl of hungry coyotes or the grunting, grubbing, root-twisting sound of wild boars searching for a meal…you might get the idea. They had nothing but a campfire to defend themselves. It was a sleepless night.

But in the morning did Our French Friends turn back toward Miraflores?

Pourquoi pas? Peut-etre sont-ils moins intelligents que nous le pensions.

Onward. At one point they were caught on the steep and narrow cliffside by a wild boar. Curling tusks next to a hungry snout. It charged by while they scampered up a nearby Palo Blanco tree. Death by wild pig? Almost.

Two ankle-twisting days later, they were limping along, hitchhiking on a dirt track that twisted through the ranchlands west of the mountains. Once again out of water. Still twenty miles from the ocean.

Eventually, they got a ride from dirt-bikers on motorcycles. They reached Mexico Highway 19 just north of La Tatanza where it ran close to the shore of the Pacific.

It took them several more days to return to Surf Camp. Orvis was relieved to see them. Also, they were carrying a good story.

Alive and still smiling. Happy. And very, very French.

CHAPTER TWENTY

Window Seat, Volaris Flight 783 to Mexico D.F.

My latest, biggest mistake (there have been lots of smaller ones lately) was telling Orvis that we were going to travel to the birthplace of Gabriel Garcia Marquez. It's in a tiny jungle town halfway up the Sierra Navarro de Santa Marta mountains along the Rio Aracataca. The locals call the town Cataca. It's in the Caribbean region of Colombia.

"Who?" Orvis asks.

"Garcia Marquez. His friends called him Gabito. Colombian/Mexican writer. Won the Nobel Prize for Literature in 1982. The father of "magical realism." Died in 2014, ten years before the Zombie Apocalypse."

Orvis raises his eyebrows. "Right. Another writer who taught you to make up weird things? Like the Zombie Apocalypse…"

"Absolutely. He's the one who practically INVENTED imaginary characters like you. Though I'm not sure he even believed in Zombies."

"Is that why he's dead?"

"Possibly. But I think it was old age that killed him."

Orvis does not want to go. Orvis wants to stay home and hang out with Our French Friends.

"Nothing doing," I say. "You are going to love it. Our first stop is a little place called Mexico City."

To try to increase his enthusiasm I give him the window seat on the jet airplane we take from Los Cabos to CDMX. It's his first time on a plane.

"What keeps us up?" he asks, as we cruise at 30,000 feet over the Sea of Cortez.

"High-speed air hitting the bottom of the wings. If you go forward fast enough, it stops you from falling. Pretty cool, huh?"

It's not long before we are flying over the outskirts of Mexico City. It's on the site of an ancient Aztec center (Tenochtitlan) in a lakebed between the peaks of two unpronounceable volcanoes (Popocatepetl and Iztaccihuatl). From the air you can see the megalopolis stretch out in all directions. No more lake. Just endless barrios. About twenty-two million people live here. The elevation is about 7,400 feet. Lots of air pollution. Enormous traffic jams. A very dramatic and young population of humans scurrying in all directions. Dynamic. Toxic and intoxicating. Mexican to the extreme.

Our first adventure is to take the underground metro from the airport to our hotel. Thousands of people packed into tin-can subway cars rumbling through dark tunnels at high speed. Everyone enveloped in their own catatonic cocoon of privacy and self-preservation. A few enterprising individuals trying to sell face masks to ward off the black death (air pollution plus Covid).

"Like zombies," Orvis says. "Only without the appetite for human flesh."

"That comes later," I tell him.

We are booked into the Hotel Isabel Catolica. My traditional residence in the downtown sector. Inexpensive and near everything. The Bellas Artes Opera House to the left, the Zócalo to the right. The Metropolitan Cathedral on one side of Independence Square, 500 years old, its towers canting from the vertical, the left-hand side sinking into the ground. All sorts of old churches and museums scattered throughout the downtown. It is a maze of commerce clogged together beneath a layering cloud of automobile exhaust. (It is a rare day when you can see the snow-covered tops of the volcanoes, only a few miles away.) After four days of intense crowds and amazing muralists (Rivera, Orozco, Tamayo, Siqueiros) my eyes are watering, my throat is raw, and I've developed a dry cough. We are ready for some tranquility. I look at the map.

"Coyoacán," I tell Orvis. "The place of the Coyotes. You'll like it there."

Our Mexican Friends (Marta and Emilio) have a small pension they let out in Coyoacán, just a few blocks from Jardin Centenario and Fuente de los Coyotes. This is possibly the most beautiful *colonia* (neighborhood) in Mexico City. Easy to get there by subway, but even easier if you call an Uber.

On the ride over, our driver seems rather withdrawn and taciturn. The map on his phone shows areas of deep red where the traffic is jammed up ahead. If you are trying to make a living driving in the traffic of Mexico City, it will undoubtedly turn you into a zombie. It takes fifty minutes or so to get to the center of Coyoacán (about six miles distance). The streets are choked like the air and it feels like we've died twice over. Another twenty minutes in the Uber and we too will be zombies.

But Coyoacán is an oasis. A compact neighborhood with the lush green Viveros de Coyoacán (park/nursery) to the north and the main campus of UNAM to the south (Mexico's National University). In the other directions, a scattered border of ancient churchyards and cool, shaded squares. Some of the streets are paved with rough cobblestones, their sidewalks split by weathering and bulging tree roots. Many of them are narrow, the street enclosed like a long hallway, the houses on either side having tall security walls that protect an inner courtyard. These walls vary in texture and color, brown adobe or rust-colored *ladrillo* (brick), grey stone with off-white grout lines, plastered concrete painted bright yellow or blue. Each house has a large doorway, big enough to drive a car through, with massive wood or steel doors that swing on stout iron hinges. Beside it, a much smaller human doorway variously decorated with a street number and an iron door knocker on its door, the face of a lion or wolf, or maybe an angel.

On some blocks or corners, you'll see a doorway or two that open onto a courtyard containing a cafe or bakery, a restaurant or sweet shop, or a bookstore selling *libros antiguos* along with "cafe Americano." There is a thriving central Mercado Municipal next to a picturesque square devoted on Saturdays to modern artists selling paintings from canvas booths. There are two central plazas kitty-corner to one another and a cathedral dating to the seventeenth century, all surrounded by multiple *churrerias* selling deep-fried, sugar-coated fritters—enough to clog your arteries just thinking about them.

At night, in front of the fountain of the two coyotes, there is a parade of various entertainers, from opera singers to mariachis. Each night an impresario with a bullhorn is hawking free theater, the Comedia del Libre, just down Calle Carrillo, family-friendly and the place we go every night to practice our understanding of Spanish. We try to laugh in the right places. It is quite a challenge.

Orvis immediately befriends Emilio's dog, a *perro pelado* (officially the breed is Xoloitzcuintli) named Dandi who is sleek and hairless and, from my understanding, quite the sophisticate. She tells him about a place he must see, and of course Orvis wants to take me there. It's about a forty-five minute walk. Halfway to San Angel.

The place is called Casa de Cultura Jesus Reyes Heroles. It's on Calle Francisco Sosa. A school of the arts built around the former residence of a retired Mexican president. An amazing brick mansion with a courtyard of meandering paths between tall and leafy rainforest hardwoods. Tamarindo and ficotura, Mexican plane trees with ten-foot-wide trunks, flowering oleanders and a jacaranda two stories tall. Just the landscaping is amazing, a jungle oasis inside tall brick walls, cool and shady in the harsh afternoon sun. But what Dandi told Orvis was that he had to see the two art galleries. There was a painting he couldn't miss.

The Casa Jesus Reyes Heroles now belongs to the city of Mexico, but it is not a museum. Not really an art gallery either. It is set aside as a place for classes, where any of the city's citizens can come and study the arts. Dance and sculpture, fine woodworking, watercolors, multimedia. There are teachers here and classes with very affordable tuition. It is freely open to the public.

Two of the largest rooms are set aside as galleries. The paintings currently hanging here are by a contemporary Mexican artist and they were all created in the last two years. During the pandemic. The artist, a man named Jose Esteban Martinez, must have been very, very busy.

And brilliant. Every one of his paintings is large and intensely colorful. They immediately become favorites. We wander through the galleries, each painting more whimsical and captivating. Then in the final room, there it is: the painting we have come to see. Dandi was correct. It was worth the trip.

The canvas is very large, two-meters-by-four, and it takes up most of one wall. Impossible to really describe. Crazy, vivid colors. A crescent moon sprouting shark fins. Blooming peyote cactus. A forest of green nopales. Flying angel dogs. A chef eating stars. Red palm trees. A bone with a bowtie. The painting is named "Los Perros se van al Cielo."

"The dogs go to heaven." And right in the middle of it, center stage, looking a little older but with wisdom in his eyes, is a perfect portrait of Orvis.

CHAPTER TWENTY-ONE

Xochimilco, Ciudad de Mexico, CDMX

The last thing I want to do is get into another Uber, so when Orvis suggests we visit the floating gardens of Xochimilco I tell him we will have to take the subway and then walk.

"Easy," I say. "We just take the light green line to Zapata and the tan line to Ermita and then the blue line to Xochimilco. Twenty-five stops. Then we walk to the Embarcadero."

"Sure," Orvis says. "That should only take us a few days."

Okay, so I'm cheap. The subway in Mexico City costs five pesos (currently about twenty-eight cents US). Orvis, being imaginary, rides for free. So it's going to cost us considerably less than one dollar to go there and back.

"Also," Orvis reminds me, "there are zombies on the subway."

"There are zombies everywhere. Mexico City was built on an island where the Aztecs cut out human hearts and offered them to their hummingbird sun god. Who knows what eventually happened with the rest of the bodies? They threw them down the steps into a big pile. After that I'm pretty sure they just ate them. Human bodies without the heart. Yum yum. Zombies love that kind of thing. So they feel right at home here."

"That doesn't actually make me feel any better about riding the subway."

Orvis's real problem is that he's been reading the guidebook. There is a massive section about Mexico City, and he pages through it every night. That's where he reads about Xochimilco. The floating gardens of the Aztecs.

Normally, I don't go for visiting tourist attractions. I'm not sure if it is my bad attitude toward other tourists (I call myself a "traveler," not a tourist, but really I am the same) or that I just don't like crowds.

There are some amazing things to see, I'm sure, but not if everyone has to see them all at once. Orvis, however, is new to traveling. He actually believes what he reads in the guidebooks.

"Xochimilco is one place where you get some feel for the ancient city and its waterborne commerce, thriving markets, and dazzling color. Rent any of the colorful boats and you'll be ferried around many kilometers of canals," he reads to me as I am trying to go to sleep. "Women selling flowers, fruit, and hot food from tiny canoes will paddle alongside you and offer their wares..."

"Don't believe everything you read in the Rough Guide," I tell him. "It's an English publication. They tend to get things wrong in the Americas."

He doesn't hear me because he's already asleep. He thinks we should get an early start to get over to the floating gardens, but I know better. It's rush hour in Mexico City between about 6 a.m. and 10 a.m.

The subways, which are normally crowded, are like canned sardines. In Mexico they call people from Mexico City "*chilangos*." It comes from the name of a little fish that once lived in the original Aztec lake. The subway during rush hour is like twenty-two million little fish squeezed into a sardine can. It is certainly something to be avoided.

"I'm going to sleep in," I tell him, but he is already snoring, his dreaming feet pawing at the floor like he is running through beds of flowers, flying from one floating island to the next.

Harsh reality will awaken the poor dog, but first it is the dog that awakens me. Seven a.m. Okay, give me a minute, I tell him. I don't bother to shower or shave. It won't do any good to be clean after about five minutes in the "floating gardens."

With surprising ease, we negotiate our way through the masses of zombies who are riding the subway. In fact, they are quite nice to us, pointing out twice that we missed our stop and are heading to the exact opposite side of Mexico City than was our intent. It all gets sorted out and soon we are standing in the parking lot of the "embarcadero." It is surprisingly empty, and I wonder if the floating gardens are somehow "*cerrado*."

It turns out that it is just a slow day at the swamp.

So, a short explanation. (Stop me if you've heard this one.) Sometime around 1325, a small group of people calling themselves the Mexica arrived on the shore of a shallow lake in the mountains of Central Mexico. There was a small island in the lake and their god (Huitzilopotchli) told them to settle down where they found an eagle perched on a nopali cactus while devouring a snake. Sure enough, they found it. The island was small and soon the Mexica (later called Aztecs) outgrew it. So they started to build new islands. Great engineers, they wove together mats of lake grass and dredged up the lake bed to put fertile soil on the floating mats and then there they were. Growing food and flowers on all the surrounding little islands. The city grew into a collection of floating islands that weren't really floating because the roots of the plants anchored them to the lake bed. In between the islands were canals.

Today, the lake has been completely drained and filled with city. The last remaining vestiges of the Aztec islands and canals are now only found in the *colonia* of Xochimilco. It's in the far southeastern part of the city. It's a famous holiday spot for Mexican tourists celebrating weddings, birthdays, or just a Sunday afternoon off work. The guidebook describes it as one ongoing fiesta after another. How lovely.

Or not.

Where the embarcadero meets the water of the canals, we came to a fleet of brightly painted but very funky flat-bottomed barges. They had names like "Yernanda" or "Claudia" or "Huiltzitzili." Next to each one was a boatman, a "barcadero" who looked pretty bored until they woke from their half-slumber and saw us walking along the little *malecón*. In a minute they were on us, offering to take us boating for a mere 600 pesos an hour (like $34 US). I looked at Orvis and saw immediately that I had no choice but to shell out the money and take my chances.

You wouldn't want to get wet in the canals of Xochimilco. You probably wouldn't want to eat the vegetables that are grown along the shores of the canals. Our guidebook said that in recent years the city government has tried to clean up the water and the surrounding pollution. But it is a city of twenty-two million. It's going to take about that many years for this place to return to any sort of purity after the humans die out.

We hired a short and animated pilot who name was Ernesto. We negotiated the price to 500 pesos because it was a slow day. He gave us a canned spiel about the canals and the flower gardens (no flowers growing in late February because it had been so cold) and said there were 180 kilometers of waterways in Xochimilco. That may or may not be true. He poled us along and spent most of the time yelling at other boatmen and crashing into the little flat bottom canoes that were trying to sell us soggy empanadas and cheap tequila. We bought two warm Coca-Colas that were in sealed glass bottles and looked safe to drink. We listened to scratchy mariachi music from bands of bad musicians who also floated by us in rickety barges. Ernesto poled us about two hundred meters in one direction and then another two hundred meters back to the dock. That was it.

Afterward, Orvis was pretty pissed off at the guidebook and I didn't blame him.

"Lessons learned," I told him.

But all he did was growl.

CHAPTER TWENTY-TWO

Rancho La Fortuna, Cabo del Este,
Los Cabos, BCS, MX

Two days after returning to Coyoacán, I receive a message that forces us to change our plans. We will not be flying to Colombia the following Thursday. Instead we will be returning to Los Cabos.

The message is simple: Fortunato has died.

This was not an unexpected event. Fortunato Burgoin Aripez, one of the patrones at Rancho Santa Aqueda, Rancho Dos Ballenas, and Rancho La Fortuna was (by rumor if not by fact) somewhere between ninety-five and ninety-eight years old. The numbers out here on the East Cape are not exact. In the eyes of the world, this is mostly explained by lack of education and good recordkeeping. The East Cape ranchos have traditionally been isolated, connected to the rest of the world by a rugged dirt track that is drivable only during parts of the year. It's a couple of days to town if you are riding a horse or donkey. The families here are traditionally insular and interrelated. When Fortunato was born, there was hardly any road at all. Of course all that has changed now, but the attitudes on the rancho seem to change less quickly. I suspect that this is as much from a specific desire to be ambiguous and mystical as it is from any lack of education.

The upshot is that his children do not know exactly when Fortunato was born. They do know, however, that he died last Wednesday.

The news comes to me through Fortunato's son Pedro. I have known Pedro since he was a boy, since before he became a wildlife biologist hired by the World Wildlife Fund to protect and nurture the sea turtles that nest along a thirty-mile stretch of the beach centered roughly at Rancho Cardoncito. Pedro has been protecting sea turtles here for about twenty-five years now. I have talked to him many times on the beach when he drives by on his forest-green quad, usually with a large cooler strapped to the back. The cooler does not contain cerveza. Mostly it carries baby sea turtles. He gathers them as they hatch, many times in the early morning before sunrise. He saves them from predators like seagulls and rancho dogs and humans driving four wheelers on the sand, going so fast they don't even see or hear the tires of their dune buggies crunching baby sea turtles. Pedro takes the new hatchlings to a sanctuary near Fortuna, and when they are healthy and well-nurtured, he releases them to the sea.

Pedro writes me a Facebook message. There will be a Catholic Mass, an open coffin at the rancho, and then nine days of prayer and mourning for Old Fortunato. I write back that I am currently traveling but that I will be there. At least for some part of it.

Of course I knew Fortunato for longer than I've known Pedro. When I was a young man, first settling in to spending the winters at Shipwrecks Beach (located between the ranchos Dos Ballenas and Cardoncito), I would see him every morning. I was building a house back in the desert with my former wife. Fortunato was the caretaker, hired to watch over the houses when we gringos were gone. He would walk the entire perimeter of the properties every morning. This, I think, is what kept him so healthy.

I was young and somewhat fit, and I would jog along the same route that Fortunato walked every morning. He thought that was very funny. Me running uphill, sweat pouring off my forehead, a grimace on my face. We could see each other from quite a way off. The sound of my heavy breathing mixing with the birdsong and the rhythm of crashing waves in the distance. When we would get closer to one another, he would start to smile.

I wish I were a good enough writer to describe to you the way that Fortunato smiled. He was a small man and he had a small face. He always looked old to me, even when he was only sixty, but he had the smile of a child. One side of his mouth would lift and the skin of his cheeks would wrinkle and he would close his eyes. All of this for one little smile. Just a grin, really. A happy grin as though he were telling a good joke to himself.

I would be running and I ran pretty slowly, and Fortunato would politely step aside and let me pass. When I was close enough, he would begin the smile, and then when I was within hearing distance, he would broaden the smile and he would say—yes, every day that he saw me running, he would step aside and he would say:

"*Rapido, rapido!*"

Faster, faster. He thought that was a pretty good joke. And he was right.

So I tell Orvis that we are going to have to return to Los Cabos and then back out to the East Cape because I feel compelled to pay my last respects to Old Fortunato.

He does not protest, as he sees that this is important to me. Also, he's been chewing on the guidebook and it has begun to quell his taste for traveling.

Circumstances being what they are, I make it back out to Rancho La Fortuna on the last day of Fortunato's funeral.

Most of the family is gathered there at Pedro's house. Fortunato and his wife Maria had at least six children (again, numbers are ambiguous here). Two daughters and four sons. I only know the sons, but it is his daughters who lead the funeral service. There is an altar set up outside the house with a temporary shade structure covering it, and there are folding chairs and an area behind for others to stand.

The altar is simple. A card table covered with a white sheet. Another white sheet hung behind it on the wall. Blue and white narrow silk banners hand-lettered with the names of the extended families giving condolences. There is a large, wooden-framed image of the Virgin of Guadalupe. Votive candles in glass jars. Two stands of funeral flowers on the floor beside the table, red roses on the left and white roses on the right. To the side, there is a green fan palm.

Set off slightly to the right center of the table is a photo of Fortunato in a black frame. He is an old man in the photo, looking all of his ninety-odd years. He's wearing a white caballero's hat, a blue-checked collared shirt. He has a goodly growth of beard, light brown and grey and then whiskery-white below his chin. His eyes are closed and he is smiling.

I stand in the back with the rest of the men while the sisters lead everyone in prayers. They are saying the Hail Mary in Spanish. A Mexican version that features the Virgin of Guadalupe, who came as a vision to a man named Juan who was Indio, not Spanish. It meant a great deal that the

Virgin Mary came to him and not some other. This is a very Mexican tradition.

But it is a very Catholic tradition that has them saying the prayer over and over and over and over again. They say it fifty times. We all join in at certain parts. It takes a little over an hour. I am swaying on my feet by the end of it. God, I am out of shape—an hour standing in one place and I feel like I'm about to fall down. I would make a terrible Catholic.

Then they sing "*Adios, adios, adios*," and finally we are released to sit.

I ask Pedro if I can take a picture and he says okay and then I go up to the altar and take a photo of Fortunato's photo. On closer examination, I see his smile is more crooked than I remembered. His cheeks are raised and there are lines around his nose and the humor of life has obviously gathered behind his closed eyelids.

I wonder what he might be saying to me, and then I hear his raspy voice. Not "*rapido, rapido*."

No, he is saying something else.

"You need to get more exercise," he tells me.

CHAPTER TWENTY-THREE

Puerto Agua Verde, BCS, MX

If I begin to question my own motivations, one of the first things I would do is question why I feel guilty about Orvis. I know it was a mistake, I knew it at the time, to tell him we would go to Aracataca. The whole thing about visiting the home of Garcia-Marquez was my fantasy, not his, but once I got him involved…well, I felt like it was my duty to follow through.

Which I did not do after we returned to Los Cabos.

The month of March was upon us, and if I was going to make good on my larger plans, it meant we had to start traveling north. It was necessary to return to Eugene before we could leave again. Of course I couldn't tell him this, because if I did, he would ask why and then I would have to divulge my larger plan. I didn't want to do that because then, I mean…what if it didn't happen? I'd be even deeper in the hole I had already dug with him.

So I told him about Agua Verde instead.

"It's up the coast about 250 miles," I said. "Before you get to Loreto. There is a funky road off the highway that cuts through the mountains and way, way down to a remote cove and an amazing beach."

Of course I had never been there, so I didn't really know, but I had always heard about it and I even read a novel about it (*Heaven on the Moon*), and I wanted to go there. So if I could convince Orvis…

"It's got to be great," I said. "The French people go there all the time."

"Do they take their poodles?" Orvis asked.

"I'm sure."

There is a green sign on the Transpeninsular that points to Agua Verde and says its thirty-one kilometers to the southeast. In about four kilometers, the pavement ends and there is a dirt road the rest of the way. It is not for the faint of heart. Do not go there. If it is raining while you are there you will not get back out. I warned you, so now you are on your own.

Of course you will disregard my advice and then you will see what I mean. We were driving the taco truck, which is as much a go-anywhere vehicle as you can have. I mean, within reason. We made it down the cliffside to the beach, but only because there was no other traffic and we had all afternoon. I drive like my grandmother. Even Orvis says that.

Our American Friend gave us directions to a beach he said was empty and pristine, and where he also intended to stay. Our American Friend is pretty savvy. He sent us a red dot on a digital map and said not to share it with anyone. We watched as the blue dot on our phone approached the red dot he gave us. When we got there, it was nowhere near where we were supposed to be. So much for red dots.

Instead, we found ourselves in the "town" of Agua Verde. Which means a rundown rancho or two. A restaurant with fish tacos (pretty good, considering) and a store that is constantly sold out of everything except stale potato chips. When you don't go there, like I told you not to, be sure to bring all your own food and water. Maybe even some extra stuff that you can give to the store so they have something to sell. If everyone did that, it would be a pretty good store, I think.

We couldn't find Our American Friend. So we pulled off on another funky cliffside road and drove a short way to Puerto Agua Verde.

This is a steep beach with hard sand and a place you can put a trailered boat in the water. When you don't come here, be sure to not bring your trailered boat. Anyway, we camped among the kayakers and stand-up paddleboard folks. As we were setting up, a huge ship pulled into the small harbor. She was a beauty. The *First Person Plural* out of San Diego, California.

Orvis watched from the beach as she lowered her anchor and secured herself for the night. The *First Person Plural* was painted blue and white. She gleamed in the late afternoon sun. Brightwork bright, teak rails oiled, stainless rigging shined. She looked a wealthy boat. Orvis was sure there were French people onboard.

He sat there while I pitched camp. I could tell from his demeanor that he was pre-disappointed. He wanted to be on that ship.

Who could blame him? She was a beauty. Mega-cruiser class. About 170 feet, stern to bowsprit. At least five decks off the water line. Swept-back bridge with plenty of free-board in the forequarter, a third-deck sunporch big enough to land a small heli, a fantail stern with a nice rounded swim platform. I don't know how she would do in the weather, but as a sunshine, calm-water cruiser, she was stylin'.

Orvis sat on the beach staring at the *First Person Plural*. It seemed he could taste the coq au vin or dorado el gusto they would be serving for dinner. It seemed he could smell the subtle French perfume of stewards (female and male) who would be serving unlimited desserts. He wanted to be on that ship, that's what his body language was saying.

"Okay," I finally told him. "Let's go."

He looked at me quizzically. Go where?

"C'mon. Out to the ship. It's not far. We can swim it pretty easily, and once we are there, what are they going to do? Throw us overboard?"

I should tell you that so far, Orvis had not shown himself to be much of a swimmer. One little bit of bodysurfing at Shipwrecks Beach, a little bit of riding on my paddleboard. Other than that, he was a beach dog. Not the sort that runs after sticks and tennis balls. The sort that sits quietly and watches the ocean. Looking for whales and surfing French poodles. Calm, collected, mostly dry.

But all dogs are natural swimmers. I mean they invented the dog paddle, didn't they?

I shimmied into my wetsuit top, lightweight 2 mm neoprene with the words "New Haven Swim Club" printed on the front. In a minute we were in the water, a bit chill, but I warmed up quickly and it was pretty comfortable. The boat was farther out there then I thought. By the time I was hanging onto the grab bar of the ship's swim platform, I was breathing pretty heavily. Certainly not ready to swim back.

"Ahoy!" I shouted. "HELLO THE SHIP!"

Before anyone answered, Orvis was there beside me. With one hand on the rail I took the other arm and helped lift him up onto the swim platform. He stood up and shook himself off. Right into my face, I might add, so that I was blinking away the saltwater when a steward appeared above the stern.

"Hello," I said. "Permission to come aboard."

The steward: a fit. young, well-muscled woman in a white shirt, blond hair back in a ponytail, a look of "who-the-fuck-are-you" on her face.

"Permission denied," she said. "Let go of the ship."

"But we swam…" I started.

"Release your hands from the ship NOW," she said. With that she raised her right hand, in which was a huge orange pistol. It was not a handgun, exactly, but I'm sure it fired a flare that would burn off what remained of my facial hair, not to mention my skin.

"Wait a second," I said. "We are swimmers in distress—by maritime law you are required to assist…"

She cocked the pistol.

Just then Orvis barked. He has a very distinctive voice. More of a woof, woof, than a bark, bark. With a bit of a rolled rrrrrr growl at the end of it. It gave the steward pause before she fired.

Which paused everything for a couple of heartbeats, which was long enough for another head to appear at the stern. Which for some happy circumstance was the head of the captain.

And what a captain she is. Capt. Emily Percotti out of Laguna Beach, California. Every inch of five foot three. I'm going to say 120 pounds at the most. Long thick curls, auburn in color, slightly gray with that sort of graying that makes women more beautiful as they age. Wrinkles around her eyes, which I later learned were hazel-green in color.

"Get off my ship," were the first words she said. "Now."

I immediately let go of the rail. You did not hesitate when Capt. Percotti gave an order. I mean, not even for a second. But as I was treading water next to her ship, she let me explain.

"We were wondering…" I began.

It was a pretty long story, and it was only when I started to go under that she had the steward climb down onto the swim platform and pull me out of the ocean.

"Rest up," Capt. Percotti said as I sat there shivering. "The tide is going out and it will be a longer swim back into the beach. Also, with the sun setting it will get dark quickly and you know how the sharks are at nighttime."

"Sharks?"

"The small, young ones mostly. Pretty hungry at night, but not discriminating. They bite at almost anything that moves."

"But…"

"I think you can probably make it if you start now," Capt. Percotti said. By this point, she was standing next to Orvis and scratching his ears. She was so lovely. Orvis was eating it up.

"And your dog can stay. We wouldn't want anything to happen to him, would we?"

CHAPTER TWENTY-FOUR

Aboard the First Person Plural,
Agua Verde, Loreto, BCS, MX

For the purposes of this story, the luxury yacht *First Person Plural* is owned and operated by the same syndicate that owns the *San Diego Union Tribune*, a newspaper with a circulation of about 150K that is part of Tribune Publishing (also owning the *LA Times, Chicago Tribune*, etc. etc.), An old friend of mine is on the board of directors of this media corporation, and she owns a beach-front house near Shipwrecks Beach. I won't use her name. But that's not what got me on board…

"Wait," I said, as I sat there getting cold on the swim platform of the *First Person Plural* (FPP). "You're going to throw me to the sharks?"

"WOOF!" Orvis said. Like he was enjoying it. Like he was encouraging me to jump overboard and leave him with Capt. Percotti.

"They only take little nips at first," the captain said. "A couple of little nips and then they leave you alone when they find you aren't really edible."

"Hold it. Isn't there some maritime law about this? Something about sailors in distress, like you have to save them or something?"

"Yeah, if you had a ship. But you are a swimmer, so

actually, once you touch my ship I can put you in the brig for trespassing."

I looked at the water. I looked at the sun setting behind the crumbling cliffs. Fish were starting to feed, making little jumps that disturbed the calm surface of the harbor. Hungry fish.

I made a snap decision. "Okay, I'll take the brig."

"Yeah, well, we don't really have a brig," Capt. Percotti said, "We usually just hand people over to the cartel and they take care of things."

"What cartel?" This was getting ridiculous. The shark waters were looking more inviting. Mexican cartels? The guys that cut off your johnson and leave your body hanging there on the highway overpass? No way.

"Hold it a second," I said. "We have a lot in common. I know people."

Orvis looked at me quizzically. Capt. Percotti paused for a moment in her fond petting of his head.

"For instance, I am personal friends with Nick Hernandez, rockstar at large."

Everything stopped for a moment. In the distance I could see a flock of twelve pelicans skimming the surface of the quiet waters. A heron was ankle-deep at the edge of the bay. Planets were appearing in the sky, first Venus and then Jupiter right below.

"You don't say," Capt. Percotti said.

"Yes, THE Nick Hernandez. I beat him at horseshoes just a couple of weeks ago. Lead singer for the reggae band Common Sense. Old school. You may know his hit single, "Feed them to the Sharks."

Did I just hear myself say that?

"Nick Hernandez? Common Sense? From Laguna Beach?" Capt. Percotti was frowning now. "I went to freaking high school with Nick Hernandez. Laguna Beach High, class of 1985. He was a complete fuck-up. One of those high school guys I wished I had never woke up with."

"You slept with Nick Hernandez?"

"What a screwup. But he was a pretty good singer. I thought he died of a tequila overdose?"

"No," I said. "But he's still trying."

This seemed to cheer her up. "Well, why didn't you say so…You know Nick Hernandez. What a small world."

"Yep. He's my personal friend. Has a little dog named Dread. He's building a house near me at Shipwrecks Beach. Still blowing his brains out playing music up in LA."

I was smiling. Orvis was wrinkling his eyebrows at me. Capt. Percotti was shaking her head. She was such a lovely person when you got up close.

"Also, I should mention," I said, "I'm a travel writer. I've got a pretty famous little thing I write. It's called "A Journey With…"

"A travel writer AND friends with Nick Hernandez?" Capt. Percotti now stood up from where she was petting Orvis. She motioned to the steward to open the little watertight hatch door in the transom. She took a couple of steps and was up on the aft deck and then she motioned Orvis to follow her. He was wagging his little wet tail as he climbed up onto the deck.

The steward then closed the side hatch. I was left standing on the swim platform.

Before they went into the galley, Capt. Percotti turned and looked back at me. Such a lovely profile. A smooth pert nose, clean line to her eyebrows, a slightly dimpled chin.

"I was fibbing about the sharks," she said. "They'll eat just about anything. Even you."

"Hold it! What about Nick Hernandez and the travel writing?"

"Nick, yeah, that's for sure somebody I would rather forget. Thanks for bringing THAT one up. Ugg. The things you do when you are young…"

The water was kind of cold. I didn't really notice, though, because I was swimming like crazy. Twirling my arms around, kicking my feet. I sprinted the 200 yards to the shore. It felt pretty good when I was standing there on the beach. Panting, trying to catch my breath. Happy to be on solid ground.

Then I remembered Orvis. My faithful dog.

That son of a bitch.

CHAPTER TWENTY-FIVE

Playa Pelicano, Agua Verde, Loreto, BCS, MX

Conspiracy theories abound these days. Just before I left San Jose del Cabo, I met a guy from Staten Island, New York. His name is Mike the Greek. He's a retired fireman, getting stem cell treatment in Cabo. He said:

"Well, you're from Oreeegonn, huh? Did you ever see Bigfoot?" (He was speaking Brooklyn, a weird American dialect.)

I looked at him quizzically.

"You know he's real, right? They call him Nonesuch."

"I think that's Sasquatch."

"So you DO know him?"

"Yeah…I mean no…but…well, if I see him, I'm sure I'll know it," I said. "He's pretty famous."

Mike the Greek nodded. Like we were both confirmed in our belief of Bigfoot. Then he began: "I saw them set the explosives to take down the World Trade Center. You know…the night before 9/11…"

Anyway, I really liked Mike, even though I didn't actually agree with anything he said. But I bring it up because the next day on the beach at Agua Verde, conspiracy theories were bounding up and down the beach like stray rancho dogs. The word was that the big luxury yacht in the harbor was owned by a Russian oligarch who had just bought up most of the town of Puerto Agua Verde and all the beach around it. He had been seen buzzing the beach in his helicopter. I didn't tell anyone I had gone out there and met the captain. And being Ukrainian, I wasn't about to defend any Russian oligarchs or try to correct any false conspiracies, so I just said:

"Yeah, they kidnapped my dog."

Which wasn't strictly true. As far as I could tell, Orvis was in love with the ship and was staying out there on his own accord. No kidnapping, but maybe he was being "rescued."

Anyway, I heard from some tourists that a guy who fit the description of Our American Friend was camped out on another beach a couple of miles away. So I packed up the taco truck and prepared to go seek him out. He's one hell of a guy. And he has his own satellite dish with high-speed internet (thank you Elon Musk, now please go away). This makes him a pleasure to camp with.

So I got all packed up and hopped in the truck and what do you know, trotting down the beach, here comes Orvis.

I rolled down my window. Orvis stood next to the truck, looking up at me.

"What happened?" I asked. "Was the foie gras too rich for your taste?"

"The boat is filled with Russians," Orvis said. "Fat old guys with cigars and young women with fake breasts. Capt. Percotti is on her last cruise before she hands the whole operation over. I guess they bought the ship and half of Mexico."

So much for debunking conspiracy theories. Believe what you will.

I put a towel on the passenger seat and Orvis got in, still wet from the ocean. The last we saw of the *First Person Plural,* she was lifting her anchor and starting her engines. When the taco truck climbed up along the cliffside and back up to the headland, we could see she was already on her way. I'm sure I'll never see Capt. Percotti again, but I hope she lands on her feet. What with those hazel eyes and everything…

It's a rough road down there at Agua Verde, and at the next turn we made, there was a sign that said "Stop! Go back! You'll Never Make it!"

But I thought I recognized the handwriting of Our American Friend. So we proceeded.

Twenty minutes of white-knuckled, nearly impassable road later, we were parked on the beach next to him.

"You found me," he said. His dog Tessa was standing beside him. She was very glad to see me.

We had about three days to kill before heading north. It could have been longer, but that's how much food and water we had. Plus, I had to sleep in a tent on the ground and that always makes me antsy.

Smile.

On the second day, I felt like I had to have a talk with Orvis.

"You know," I said, "I'm just sayin'…if I were an imaginary dog…I would fall in love with Tessa."

He refused to look at me. But I was not deterred.

"I know, I know what you are going to say. You're going to say that she is a black Labrador. A retriever. They are not known to be the sharpest tacks in the junk drawer. Granted, but she's different."

"Not French," Orvis said. "Not even close to being French."

"Actually she is an English Labrador. Purebred. And she doesn't bark. And she doesn't swim. And have you ever seen her chase after a tennis ball? No, you haven't. Because she won't."

"She chews sticks," Orvis said.

"Brushing her teeth," I replied. "She is one heck of a dog, that's all I'm saying. Very smart. Very polite. The kind you want to bring home to the family."

Of course, all of this was lost on Orvis. He remained stoutly devoted to finding the French poodle of his dreams. All I could do was sigh when I thought about it. Tessa was a fine dog.

Our American Friend is a native of Oregon. He grew up flyfishing on the Deschutes River and currently owns a cabin on the banks of the Sandy. His dad, now deceased, was a hunter and gatherer and a trial lawyer in Portland. He hunted trout from the stream, pheasants and grouse from the sagebrush. He raised and collected hunting dogs. But Tessa was bought from a breeder in Nashville to be a home dog. He liked English Labradors. He bought Tessa as a puppy shortly before he died. So I guess you could say Tessa is a rescue dog. Our American Friend rescued her from his father's estate.

At the time of our meeting, Our American Friend was not my Facebook Friend. Things being the way they are, we actually started our friendship OUTSIDE of Facebook or any other social media. I say this not because it is unique, but just to point out that he didn't really know about Orvis.

Orvis is not someone you just meet on the beach. Nor is he someone whose presence is that easy to explain.

Okay, so the long and short of it is: I guess I was in the mood for falling in love. Springtime and such. First there was Our British Friend. Then there was Capt. Percotti. Now there was Tessa.

I mean, if Orvis was going to be so aloof, I didn't see any reason I had to be.

We were having a great time at Playa Pelicano. Please don't ever go there. Very picturesque. Flights of pelicans cruising the shoreline. Fish jumping in the light of gloaming. Stratified cliffsides to the west that glowed in the morning sunlight. Campfires at night with roasted onions, *salchichas* on the grill, baked sweet potatoes in the coals, melted chocolate on sugared biscuits.

"Some life," Our American Friend remarked.

On the third day, we were buzzed by a helicopter. Maybe the Russians noticed the Ukrainian flag on the roof of the taco truck. Would they send in the mercenaries? Condemned prisoners with ancient guns, released to become cannon fodder? Supersonic cruise missiles to take out our solar panels?

"We need to head north," Orvis said. "Back to America. Home of the free and the brave and the surfer babes of Southern California."

"What do you know of surfer babes?" I asked him.

"Not nearly enough," he answered. "And what is a Pineapple Express, anyhow? Tessa says there is a Pineapple Express heading to California. Sounds delicious."

"I think it is a river of rain," I told him. "But I'm not sure."

"Well, let's go find out," he said.

And we did.

CHAPTER TWENTY-SIX

Denny's in the Twilight Zone, I-5 Corridor, Central California, USA

I told Orvis that it was going to be a long drive home. He nodded when I said that, but I think he did not really grok what I was talking about. Two days after we started, two long days of driving ten hours or more, we reached the International Border and crossed into the United States of America.

"Well," I told him, "we are about halfway home."

The border is usually a snarl of traffic and long lines waiting to cross while various poor people come up to your car window and try to sell you stuff. The last time I crossed was at the beginning of the Covid pandemic and they were trying to sell masks and toilet paper. This time it was back to wet burritos and votive candles of the Virgin of Guadalupe. I didn't buy anything.

In fact, we were hardly in line at all. We made a wrong turn (taking the advice of Siri) and got into the VIP/Express lane. You have to have a special sticker to use this lane, but once you are in it there is no backing up. It's a $5,000 US fine to use the lane without the sticker.

I know this because the border guard, a fine middle-aged gentleman named Fred, told me this. When I told him that Siri had sent us this way...

He looked over the top of his glasses and handed me back my passport.

"Sir," he said, "Siri is a phone."

What could I say? He had a point.

He told me if I ever got into his lane again, he would personally shake me upside down until $5,000 fell out of my trousers.

Then he let us go through.

"That was easy," Orvis said.

Sunshine and breezy in Southern California. We took a circuitous route around Los Angeles and ended up late in the day intersecting with Interstate-5 north. Siri told us it was 967 miles to Eugene. She did not explain that a winter storm (the heretofore mentioned "Pineapple Express") was quickly bearing down on us.

Darkness and Rain came at about the same time. Ugly rain, in large doses, spraying up from the mudflaps of speeding eighteen-wheelers. Dark clouds that made the night darker than mere darkness. I plugged along for a couple of hours and then I had had enough. We pulled over somewhere. There was an exit into oblivion. A blurry Motel 6. A Denny's restaurant with lights that seemed to oscillate in the night. I wish I could tell you where we were, but...

The clerk at the motel was not a happy person. She was old and Indian and grumpy. Possibly had ingested alien seed pods earlier in the night. There was no hot water at the motel, she informed me.

And no heat in the rooms. Special discount she said. Seventy dollars a night.

"I'll take it." I was not going back out on the interstate, that was certain.

We shivered into the room, Orvis not being accustomed to the cold. We got our own blankets and pillows out of the truck. It was pretty miserable and water was still falling from the sky, like endless rain into a paper cup. Slithering wildly as we slip away across the universe.

"Let's get some dinner," Orvis said.

Back out into the flooding parking lot, slithering wildly over to the Denny's.

It seems like every restaurant now has a sign just after you come in through the door. It says something along the lines of: "We are experiencing a time of staff shortages. Please bear with us. We appreciate your patience and are thankful for your patronage."

The sign here said: "You Have Entered the Twilight Zone."

Orvis didn't get it. I thought it was pretty funny. Well… at least at first.

I wish I could describe our waitress. But her face keeps morphing in my mind. It's like a dream. You are one moment kissing your old girlfriend from high school and the next moment she is your Aunt Thelma and SHE is trying to kiss YOU. You wake up trying to get that image out of your head.

Our waitress was lovely. Well, I think. But her face kept changing. Most of the time she was laughing. She was all by herself and the restaurant was crowded. At least the section they had open. The section that was closed…well, that was another place entirely. I'll explain that after I tell you about the cook. Just one person in the kitchen, I think. We only saw part of him? her? it? A very long and very hairy arm coming through the kitchen slot. Maybe some grunting or groaning to accompany it. Six, maybe eight fingers on the hand? Passing the plates piled with food. Food? Sandwiches melting into the plate. A hamburger with half a bun (the part on top). French fries that seemed to be still moving. Fresh?

"Wow" Orvis said. "This is some place."

But it wasn't really THAT odd. Not until the folks sitting in the closed part of the restaurant started acting up.

"Don't worry about them," the waitress told us. "The state troopers drop people off here all the time. That homeless girl with her homeless dog? She's here almost every night. Constantly calling 911."

Yes, we could hear her on the phone talking to the 911operator. Nice and loud.

"You have to send someone," she said. "I feel threatened. My life is in danger. I think the aliens have infected my dog. He's just not the same dog anymore. I'm almost afraid of him now. Afraid of my own dog! Do you know how horrible that is? My OWN DOG!"

Her voice echoed through the Denny's. The other diners were looking down at their plates. No one said anything. The waitress came back out of the kitchen with two plates of food. Hamburgers with the buns tortured and mutilated by the grill. A melted cheese sandwich with bacon hanging out of the side. Uncooked.

We looked at each other as the waitress put the plates down in front of us. She smiled. Her face had turned into an old lady. Then it turned back again into a lovely young waitress. Enjoy your meal, the young waitress said.

Weird beyond weird. We were looking at each other and then we looked out the window next to our booth. The homeless dog was there staring at us, right up against the window. Weird on weird. He turned around and scratched at the sodden grass, a little drier under the eave of the building. He squatted and began to poop. Right there, three feet away.

I put my sandwich down. I had gobbled half of it and now I lost my appetite. I tried hard not to look at the backside of the homeless dog, and then the window turned into a mirror and I was looking at my own self sitting there and Orvis sitting across from me. At first glance, I looked a lot younger and Orvis was just a puppy, and then as I continued looking my face got old. Very, very old, and Orvis turned all gray and then...the mirror turned into a window and the homeless dog was kicking grass and dirt over his pile of...

I can't go on describing this...it is just too weird. We eventually paid the check and walked back to the hotel. When we got there, the taco truck was parked in front of our door. The number of the room was 126 but now it said 767.

That was exactly how far we had to drive to get home to Eugene.

I didn't sleep that great. I kept tossing and turning and seeing the homeless dog pooping in my dreams, only the stuff coming out was not poop, it was...

Like I said, I hardly slept at all. I'm pretty sure Orvis was up all night. In the morning he said to me:

"Man, this is weird. Like, very, very weird. This is SO weird, man. You've got to start writing this all down."

CHAPTER TWENTY-SEVEN

Eugene Depot, Eugene, Oregon, USA

It has been quite a chore trying to teach Orvis to use my phone as a camera. I have a hard enough time using it myself. I thought we had it all worked out, but then we went down to the train station to make some portraits before leaving on the next leg of our trip, and well, I had to get a lovely passerby to make the photograph.

Orvis can't be trusted. He likes to chew on the phone. So you won't be seeing much of me on this next part of the journey. Not a great loss, I realize. I've never been very photogenic.

We were glad to be home after the ordeal of making it back to Eugene. A good check-in with family and friends, a few days rushing around to pay bills, get visas, set up a plane flight. An armful of guidebooks from the thrift store. A couple of railroad maps of western Europe. Before long, we were boarding a bus to Seattle. A short visit there and we would be on a nonstop flight to Istanbul.

I didn't tell Orvis where we were going. In point of fact, I didn't know myself. I had the future outlined for about two weeks. Some days visiting the Seattle Moisture Festival. A small apartment rented in Cihangir (a neighborhood in Istanbul). After that? Wandering through the Greek Isles? A passage through Athens and Piraeus? I knew I had to be in Paris by about April 30. London by May 2. But even all of this was just an estimate. We could end up in some limited variety of anywhere.

This is how I like to travel, at least when I am in charge of only myself (and an imaginary dog, who, despite his attitude, had no choice but to follow me faithfully). Flexibility has always been the key to my travel philosophy. Keeping the unknown close by. No more than a day-and-a-half away.

Easy to say. Easier if I don't have to try to explain it to anyone, especially a reluctant dog.

We had the luxury of coming back to our friend's farmhouse in the River District of Eugene. It's rugged and plush. A warm kitchen, a large upstairs bed, plenty of space away from the vagaries of a cold March springtime. Ice rain. Hail stones. An occasional sunny day. It's all beautiful if you can sit in front of a woodstove and watch it through the window. I remind myself every day that I am blessed to not be homeless. It's one great thing I have figured out in this lifetime: how to keep a roof over my head.

Orvis does not see the need to leave Eugene. Honestly, I tend to agree with him. It's a calm, lovely place. Enough of a city and not too urban in its vibe. People still say hello when they walk by each other on the bike path. There is a very good chance that your catalytic converter will stay attached to the underside of your car when it is parked in the driveway. The worst that will happen is that your bike will get stolen if you don't lock it up properly. That's bad, I know, but it's not a life-or-death mugging. It's not carjacking or armed robbery at the corner store. Those crimes may be coming soon, but for now, Eugene is a good place.

And I have no good explanation to share with Orvis as it disappears in the rearview mirrors of the Bolt Bus as we pull out of town. Why are we leaving? Do we need more traveling time to be happy? Isn't life interesting enough just sitting in the warm glow of our own memories and thoughts?

Orvis has the window seat again and we are right behind the driver, who is wearing a black hoodie and speaks in a Los Angeles slang probably centered around the neighborhood of Watts.

From the moment I hand him my bag, the driver has referred to me as Moneyman Mitch. I should have covered the Patagonia patch on my jacket. He has entirely the wrong impression.

"What, my man," he says, "they call you M&M on the streets, right? MnM, that's your street name. Made of Money."

"Right." I say. "I've got over $12 US sewn into the lining of my jacket. If you get me safely to Seattle, some of that can be yours."

"Too bad," he says, as he shakes his head. "I'm not going to lie to you, Mitch. I'm only going as far as Portland."

I look over at Orvis, who is still looking at safe little Eugene as it disappears behind us. The unknown is ahead. I know it is going to be weird.

And that's how our new journey begins. My thoughts are not about what adventures there might be to come. No. I'm just thinking: "Gosh, I hope we make it back."

Is that too much to wish for?

CHAPTER TWENTY-EIGHT

*Moisture Festival, Broadway Performance Hall,
Capitol Hill, Seattle, Washington USA*

The Saturday night show on the first weekend of Moisture Festival is sold out, so it is lucky that Orvis doesn't take up much space. I've been gifted a seat next to the videographer and I scootch over to let Orvis sit half on the armrest and half on my lap. It looks a little odd, but only in my imagination.

Orvis has never been to a Vaudeville/Varieté show. I've never been very good at explaining what exactly that means. Vaudeville? Varieté? And even if I could, I would not be able to tell him what we are about to see tonight.

"You should like it," I say. "It will be weird."

The Moisture Festival, which few folks outside of Seattle have heard of, has been happening for almost twenty years. I had a very small part in making it first happen and now many years later I am still treated as royalty by my extended Vaudeville family. At the door to the theatre we are greeted by the executive producer (retired) and the Chief of Artist's Liaison. They usher me to the Green Room (backstage), where I can leave my bags. On the way, we meet several performers who are my old and interesting friends. If Orvis was the sort of dog that noticed these sorts of things, I think he would be impressed.

The history is a bit murky, but I believe that sometime in the late 1970s, there was a small movement to revive vaudeville. This was a type of variety theater that was very popular once upon a time and perhaps was wiped out by television and motion pictures. Among the crew that began the revival were acts like The Flying Karamazov Brothers, Artis the Spoonman, Tom Noddy Bubble Magic, the brilliant clowns from Pickle Family Circus (Bill Irwin, David Shiner), Mildred Hodittle, The Royal Famille du Caniveaux. The shows were a mixture of oddness and music, physical comedy, aerial acrobatics, juggling, mime, clowning, and magical illusion. It was (and is) live entertainment at its best.

The Moisture Festival became a thing because it made itself into a showcase for these sorts of acts. It was a paid gig for many performers who were living on a string and a prayer. Over the years it cultivated an audience, until it was almost always sold out. It had a funky but wonderful venue in the warehouse of a brewery in the Fremont neighborhood of Seattle. Built on a shoestring by a handful of hardworking producers. And it was a success.

Of course, like much of live theater, it was set back and nearly obliterated by the pandemic.

But now it has made comeback. Moved to a "real" theater house on the north end of Capitol Hill.

The Moisture Festival shows, in my humble opinion (and believe me I have seen A LOT of vaudeville), presented some of the finest acts and the best variety of the New Vaudeville genre. Every show that I have been lucky to attend has had many good acts and at least one or two FANTASTIC performances. I was never disappointed.

But I didn't know what to tell Orvis. So I told him nothing.

I let him find his own surprise. By the midpoint of the show, I think he got the message. We had been entertained by the series of oddness. The man juggling hacky sacks with his feet, the spinning web-walker in a black and white leotard, the ribald song writer ("If I had a copyright on the f-word, New York City would make me rich"), the aging quick-change magicians (old-school Las Vegas), the fake-German pandemic survivor who did too much exercise in his Brooklyn apartment (I was driving me out of my mind, so much, muscle"), and then, right before the break:

Duo Breathless. Ukrainians trained in classical ballet. But then taking that to a performance of dance, acrobatics, and contortionism. Its own brand of beautiful weirdness. Almost unbelievable what they were doing to their bodies. Gasps from the audience and then a standing ovation.

Intermission. Orvis thinks the show is over. He is already in awe from his first experience of live theater.

"That's vaudeville," I tell him. "You never know what to expect."

Old friends in the audience stop by to say hello. I do some reminiscing. Orvis is looking at me with a big question mark on his face.

"Are we going home now?" he says.

"That was only the first half of the show," I tell him.

His jaw drops. Really? Already exhausted by a little weirdness? No way.

"Hang in there, pal," I say. "Usually, they save the really special stuff for the second half."

I watch as his eyes go wide. Vaudeville will do that to you.

CHAPTER TWENTY-NINE

Bakrac Sokak #10, Cihangir, Beyoglu District, New City, Istanbul, Turkey

The very first meal that we share in Istanbul is at a breakfast cafe up the hill from our flat right next to the Galata Tower. It is a spinach omelet served with a slab of fresh goat cheese, a generous side of hummus, a plate of tomatoes, cucumbers, and olives, two slices of fresh artisan bread, drinking water in a sealed glass bottle, and a tall glass of hot Turkish tea. It is more than delicious. I do not share it with Orvis. He is off making his own discoveries. Instead I am joined by my new friend Yusuf.

Yusuf is the Uber driver who picked me up at the airport and drove me all the way to the other end of the city (where I had erroneously given him the incorrect address for the flat I am renting). I am renting from a man named Betal and he told me the flat was near the center of Istanbul, across the Golden Horn from the Grand Bazaar, but somehow I confused the street name and numbers. Poor Yusuf had to drive me into a very questionable neighborhood out near the northern industrial district. To his enduring credit, he did not abandon me there. Together we got in touch with Betal (who speaks perfect English, as Yusuf does not) and in a rapid-fire Turkish conversation they worked it out. I got into the flat very late after an eleven-and-a-half-hour flight from Seattle. Without Yusuf, I would have never arrived at all. I thought the least I could do was buy him breakfast.

Yusuf and I have a bit of a challenge communicating. I do not speak Turkish. Not even a few words. A young man on the plane taught me how to say: "Thank you very much" by using the words: Tea, sugar, and crème. Tea-sugarcreme. If you say that, it is a gross approximation of *Tesekkur ederim*. Also: "Hello"— *Merhaba*. And "How are you"—*Nasilsin*. The always useful *Fiyati ne kadar* (How much does it cost) and the indispensable *Lavabo nerede* (where is the restroom).

I wish I could tell you that I have mastered those five little phrases, but truthfully, they fly right out of my head whenever I am pressed to use them. Yusuf and I communicate with our smartphones. It is a slow and tedious process, but we smile at each other a lot and order a nice tall latte to finish off our meal. After we say goodbye (*Gule gule*) and "See you again soon" (*Yakinda tekrar gorusuruz*), I finally start to wonder what has become of Orvis.

It turns out he is nearby. Right across from the entrance to the tower. He is sprawled out in a sunny spot on the warm marble steps of a bank building. He has joined the great confederation of The Sleeping Dogs of Istanbul.

Heading east at about 650 miles per hour, we passed through ten time zones on our flight. We left at 6 p.m. in the evening and landed about 6:30 p.m. the next day. My internal clock said it was 8 a.m. in the morning. Of course, Orvis slept like a baby. I watched four full-length movies and possibly dozed off for a couple of fitful hours. I tried to sleep after we got into the flat. The effort was futile.

This led me to a 5 a.m. adventure on the middle of the Galata Bridge with the early fishermen. More on this soon.

I tend to walk the city when I can't sleep. I walk and I try to chat with folks, but of course I can't because I speak no Turkish. So mostly I just look at them and smile.

So far, Istanbul is a very friendly city. An ancient crossroads and a two-way gateway between Europe and Asia, it has always been one of the great cities of the world. There is no reason to think that this has changed. If it reminds me of any other city, that would be Rome, where you can walk the streets getting easily lost and finding a new treasure around every corner. I am staying in the New City. This is across the long, river-like inlet known as the Golden Horn. There aren't a lot of new things where I am staying. An old crumbling flat in a neighborhood of steep streets and funky cafes. Nearby mosques cut into the hillside. A steep downhill walk to the edge of the Bosporus Strait. The Galata Bridge, where I like to chat with the fishermen.

Orvis has taken to the city in his own great manner. In every square he finds a group of Sleeping Dogs. They do not seem to be bothered by the noise or the traffic or the tourists making photos. They do not seem homeless or hungry or in any hurry to do anything but lie around and sleep. They do not bark. They do not sniff each other. They do not notice when Orvis sidles up in his own gregarious manner and settles in beside them. They are very good dogs, or at least indifferent ones.

I know that at my age it is going to take me a few days to adjust to the time change. A great science-fiction writer once said that when you fly across time zones you tend to leave your soul behind you. It takes a while to catch up.

Back up at our flat, sometime after midnight, I finally am able to fall asleep. Soon I am dreaming of cumulous clouds drifting across the heavens above the Marmara

Sea, the domes of blue-tiled mosques rising above me, the smell of cardamon spices, strong coffee, a sweet lilting voice coming from a slim woman, her head wrapped in cashmere scarves with her eyes lined with kohl mascara. Is she asking me if I would like a guide for my stay in Istanbul?

Honestly, I don't know. Even in my dreams everyone is speaking in Turkish.

CHAPTER THIRTY

Mid-Span Galata Bridge,
Above the Golden Horn, Central Istanbul

Insomnia has its value if you can embrace it. In the very early morning I leave Orvis sound asleep at the foot of the bed and venture out into the streets of Istanbul. Even the strangest of cities seem safe to me at 4 a.m. The junkies and thieves have mostly given up by then. No one is out wandering. It is too late for the bandits and too early for the garbagemen. Stores and cafes are shut and secured. Streetlights are fluttering after a long night of surveillance. There is no one out and about. Except me.

There is a misty gloom coming off the Bosporus Strait. My flat is up on the Galata Hill, a few blocks northeast of the tower, so my walk is mostly downhill. It seems every time I leave the apartment, I take a different route through the meandering streets. New alleyways appear, new sets of steps connecting new streets with small and intriguing cafes (closed) that I think I will one day visit. A Turkish glass of tea, a latte with the Turkish flag outlined in steamed milk. But Istanbul is like a magic book from a Jorge Luis Borges short story: You can never find the same page twice. I know that I will search endlessly and never find this street again. It will evaporate with the morning light and never look the same.

My secure point of reference is the foot of the Galata Bridge on the New City side of the Golden Horn. If I can find my way back here, I know that I am not lost. There is virtually no traffic at this time of the morning. As I walk out onto the span, I am too early for even the first of the fishermen. I have the entire bridge to myself.

The Golden Horn is actually the estuary of the Alibey and Kagithane Rivers. It is about five miles long and 2,500 feet at its widest, which is just east of where I am standing. There is about 100 feet of water below the bridge. Normally, the bridge is filled with automobile traffic. A tram line runs down the center. It is noisy and crowded with pedestrians, fishermen, tourists, old men selling boxes of stolen perfume to indifferent old women.

But at the right moment, the golden hour of quietude sometime before the first gleam of twilight, it is calm and peaceful. I lean on the steel railing that spans the western side of the bridge and look down into the moving water. The flow of the rivers hits the stream of the narrow Bosporus strait as the ocean of the Black Sea flows to the south toward the Marmara, exhaling, and then with the motion of the moon, beginning to change direction as it inhales. I like to lose myself in the flow of water underneath bridges, and this is a perfect place for that sort of thing. I'm transfixed there for a period of time, and then I begin to hear the Call to Prayer.

The thing to understand about Istanbul is that it is not only geography that makes it into such a worldly crossroads. It is where the fictional boundary of the European Continent meets the equally fabricated border with Asia. One continent almost touching the other, separated by only 700 meters of seawater.

Historically, a famous spot for trade and commerce. But also a crossroads of religious thought.

To the north and west, the world is mostly of Christian tradition. Followers of the prophet Jesus Christ. To the south and east, the world is Muslim. Followers of the Prophet Muhammad (peace be upon him).

In 1453, Istanbul was stolen from the Christian Romans and conquered by the Muslim Ottoman Turks.

Christian churches were turned into Muslim mosques. The city became devoted to Muhammad. A couple of crusades later, it was returned by warfare to the Christians. After that it went back and forth a few more times. Today, it is currently part of the nation of Turkey, where freedom of religion is guaranteed in the constitution. That said, Istanbul is mostly Muslim.

The Muslims have a fantastic devotion to prayer. Five times a day, they are advised to face Mecca (a city in western Saudi Arabia), fall to their knees, and offer praise to Allah. There are no set times for these prayers. The time of prayer changes daily with the season. This is why in every mosque there is a muezzin, a singer who recites the call to prayer (adhan) from high atop the minaret. Only now it is done with loudspeakers, and the actual muezzin is singing into a microphone. He sings: *Adhhadu an la ilaha illa Allah…*"

The first call to prayer (Fajr) is very early in the morning. On the day that I stood on the Galata Bridge, it was at 5:09 a.m.

From the bridge, you can see the domes and minarets of fourteen mosques. In the early morning, with no traffic on the bridge, you can hear the call to prayer from at least six of them.

When the muezzins sing, it is both eerie and organic. It does not start at one time. It seems that the speakers from the complex of Suleiman the Magnificent go off first. A high and musical echoing in the distance. It seems to wake the rest of the city. Soon the other mosques begin to join the phrasing. It is like the most joyous of howling. Like a group of devout coyotes have found each other in the desert. Each one encouraging the next to sing out in the nighttime.

Honestly, I have hardly ever heard anything more inspiring. It almost makes me want to go to the mosque (the nearest one is at the south end of the bridge, Rustem Pasa Mosque), take off my shoes, cover my head with a taqiyah, and fall to prayer. Of course, I would not know what to say. Or how to pray. Would Allah forgive my ignorance?

I decide not to risk it. I'm content to listen to the prayer-calling as it echoes around the modern city. This is a seminal moment, almost as though I can hear Muhammad (may peace be upon him) himself extolling me toward a virtuous life.

The call to prayer happens five or six times a day. Most of the time, you can hardly hear it because of the traffic noise. The devout calling to Muslims drowned out by the hawking of modern commerce.

This is the modern world.

I take my time walking back to the flat. The sun is slowly rising into an overcast day. I find Orvis still sleeping on the bed. I go over and shake him a little, try to wake him up. He yawns and rolls over, lifts one eyelid, sees me, and then closes it back up.

"You missed it," I tell him. But he is already snoring.

CHAPTER THIRTY-ONE

Misir Carsisi, Sultanhmet, Old City, Istanbul, TK

On the *sehir meydani* below the entrance to Topkapi Palace, desperate old men are selling plastic amber worry beads to whomever they can *ikna* to buy them. For those who speak no Turkish, they write the price in ink on their wrist and then offer it as a notepad. Mostly, it is impossible to read their handwriting, which allows them to charge double the normal price. When one man begins to make a sale, two others crowd around and try to offer the same beads for less. Or maybe for more. They are great at identifying gullible tourists with ready cash.

My Kurdish friend Hamid, who owns a small textile shop on Bogazkesen Caddesi in the New City, says it is easy to spot Americans.

"Especially the ones from the West Coast,' he explains. 'They all wear a little label over their left breast. It says: "Patagonia."

Hamid lived in Portland, Oregon, and Berkeley, California. He likes to sit and drink tea with his customers. Nearly every day, he sells a restored carpet to someone not living in Istanbul. It is a thriving business in a city with 16 million people and 5,000 carpet shops.

"Istanbul has always been the center of trade." he tells me. "Everyone is selling. Everyone is buying.

"Merchandise is everywhere. But most of it is junk."

The landscape bears him out. I take a tour with Orvis through the Grand Bazaar and the myriad of streets and alleyways surrounding it. All kinds of junk in little booths and storefronts. Stuff from all over the world. And nothing has a price on it. It is a shopper's paradise. Or hell. I spend days looking for a cashmere scarf and a small shoulder bag. The problem is that there are ten thousand choices in 500 shops. I'm completely overwhelmed.

I'm afraid I'm not a very good tourist. When someone asks me to buy something, I immediately say no. When they ask me where I'm from, I tell them with an unpronounceable grunt that I'm Ukrainian. This usually puts them off.

Now if I could just remember to tape over the little sign on my chest that says Patagonia.

Orvis had enthusiasm for the Grand Bazaar, but it only lasted about an hour. He enjoyed the Spice Bazaar better because they gave out free samples of "Turkish Delight," little multicolored candies coated with crushed pistachios. Here's a travel tip for you: Carry three different hats in your bag. Then wander through the Spice Bazaar, changing hats periodically. The pastry dealers won't recognize you and you can get enough free samples to make up a substantial afternoon dessert. Orvis thinks this is a pretty good scam. I see it as just another manifestation of my terrible addiction to sugar.

It is not really tourist season in Istanbul. Cold and wet with a very chilly north wind blowing down from the Black Sea. It is fine when the sun shines, but there has been a pretty good drizzle most days. Typical early spring.

But that is not to say that the streets and shops are at all empty. Istanbul is a very vibrant city with a population of stylish and sophisticated folks who crowd the restaurants and cafes. There is so much life going on. Passionate conversations. Lots of long thin Turkish cigarettes to be smoked over cups of thick, sweet coffee. Obviously, they did not get the memo about lung cancer. It may shorten their lives, but it does not seem to diminish their enthusiasm.

Orvis is especially enamored with the sleeping dogs.

"Who taught them how to relax?" he asks me. "They are awfully good at it."

I have no answer. We are at one of our favorite cafes in Cihangir. It's around the corner from our flat, at the center of a five-way intersection. There is a small sunny plaza next to an old marble fountain. Every day that we go there we see at least three dogs fast asleep on the stone patio in front of the cafe. I'm no expert, but these are not small dogs. I'm guessing some sort of refined German shepherd mix. Bred to be mellow, is my guess. Nothing seems to wake them.

This would perhaps not be unusual until we have further explored the city and found similar sleeping dogs in every district. Up at the huge, enclosed courtyard beside the massive doors of Suleymaniye Camii (a spectacular mosque built by Suleiman the Magnificent), there is a calm dog sleeping quietly on the steps. Down at the bustling market in front of the Sirkeci Gari (the old train station where the Orient Express once stopped), right there in the middle of the crowd, lies a shaggy Belgium Mal Shepherd, his paws crossed, sleeping with his eyes open, oblivious to the lunchtime crush. And then in the Galata neighborhood, at the top of the steep hill where the cobblestone streets meet in the circular plaza at the base of Galata Kulesi (a stone fire tower, 205 feet tall, a landmark of the New City), three dogs of very mixed heritage are sleeping in front of the old streetcar that serves as a ticket booth for those who want to climb the tower. Across from the booth, at one of our favorite restaurants (Guney Galat), two dogs are sleeping in front, and when we pick a table on the terrace, I sit down and am not surprised to find another shepherd mix fast asleep under the table.

Orvis is very impressed. He thinks that these dogs have a superior life. Living in a beautiful thriving city, all the excitement of international cuisine, foreign languages, the hills, the seaside, the amazing architecture; how exotic, how stimulating.

"To be able to sleep through all that?" Orvis says. "Now THAT is some kind of accomplishment."

Well, from a dog's point of view, I guess I would have to agree. But I can't help but think: What would it take to wake them all up?

Orvis doesn't have an answer.

"I don't think we want to be here if it happens," he says.

CHAPTER THIRTY-TWO

Galata Bridge, Golden Horn, Istanbul, TK

Most days, our favorite thing is to go down to the bridge and hang out with Mister Yuhrkuk while he drops his line into the Golden Horn and fishes for anchovies.

Mister Y (as we call him) is Armenian. He retired from the company he worked for a few years ago and now he likes to go fishing every day. He is wearing a gray wool skullcap and a black hooded waterproof jacket with the words "OZEL GUVENLIK" printed boldly on the back. I think this is cool until I find out later that it just means "private security."

Mister Y has quite a hook to his nose. He keeps his bushy gray mustache in a droopy Turkish style and most days has a gray stubble of a beard on his cheeks and chin. I wonder about this. I think some days you have to shave, right? It can't always be the same gray stubble, can it? Or do they have special razors that just leave the stubble? Mister Y does not look like he owns a special razor. But I could be wrong about this. I do not have enough Turkish to ask him for an explanation.

But I can ask him about the fishing.

"*Balik isirir mi*?" I ask him "*Begun ne yakaladun*?"

He doesn't have a clue what I just said. My Turkish pronunciation is not even close. I'm reading it off my smart phone. I have to have him look at the words on my screen.

"Oh, oh," he nods his head, then shakes it a little to one side. "*Begun lufer tutuyoruz. Ama cok kucukler.*"

It takes awhile, but eventually I get the translation. The fishing is so-so. A few anchovies and some cinekop (blue fish), but they are small. He thinks the fishing is bad because of the *denizanasi*.

Denizanasi. I look at the phone. The word means jellyfish.

The day before, when Orvis and I came in on the ferry from Anadolu Kavagi (a small village up near the Black Sea), I noticed that there was a bloom of jellyfish caught in the eddy of the ferry dock and stirred up by the wash from the boat traffic. Now, looking down into the water from the rail of the bridge, I see that there are clouds of the invertebrates throbbing and floating in the currents. It is hard to know what causes them to cluster and reproduce into swarms. It wasn't that long ago that the waters of the Golden Horn were too polluted for almost all sea life. Centuries of human civilization had made the estuary into a sewer. In the 1970s, a massive program was undertaken to remove the polluting industries, dredge away the toxic mudflats, and restore the water quality. Since then, the air and water of the Golden Horn have returned to something almost acceptably clean. At least you can catch small fish from the bridge now.

As we are watching him, Mister Y feels a small tug on his line. He takes the fishing pole from the simple wooden cradle that he has made to hold it on the handrail. When he pulls the line in, we see he has a very tiny silver fish hooked on the end of it. A six-inch-long anchovy. He takes the fish off the line and plops it into a plastic bucket. There are about six other small fish swimming in the bucket water.

"Good if you eat them fresh," he tells my phone. "Grilled over applewood with peppers and onions."

Lezzetle, he says, smiling and puckering his lips. Delicious.

There is constant foot traffic across the bridge, and for the fishermen, it is almost like gathering in a pub or coffeehouse. People stop by all the time. Lots of smoking and laughing. The wooden cradles holding the fishing rods do all the work and it is mostly just standing around and watching to see if the tip of the rod moves. Occasionally they pull in the line and replace the bait with another tiny piece of frozen shrimp. Other than that, it's just another day out with the guys.

Walking back across the bridge toward the Galata Tower, we see a small crowd of men gathered around a guy sitting on a bucket. I edge my shoulder into the group to see if I can tell what it is all about.

The man is very old and balding and he's wearing a brown wool suit jacket that is shiny at the elbows. In front of him he has a cardboard box turned over so that the bottom of it becomes a small table. On the table there are four white cardboard tubes. The tubes are identical. They are sealed at the ends. Three of the tubes are empty. In the fourth, there is coarse sand or pebbles. He shakes the tube, and you can distinctly hear the pebbles rattle. He shakes the other tubes, and you hear nothing. Then he puts the tubes flat on the cardboard box, manipulates them quickly with his fingers, and then lays them out side by side. You now have to guess which tube has the pebbles.

Of course, before you get to guess you have to put a 200-lira banknote down on the box next to the tubes. You guess right: he gives you back the 200 with 200 more. You guess wrong: he takes your 200.

The action is fast and furious. Men stand around him and watch him quickly twirl the tubes, shake the one with the pebbles, shake the other ones, and then put them down on the box with a twist and a move of his fingers, one tube over the other, one tube diagonally on top, all the tubes together side by side on the box. A man reaches in, puts money down, and grabs a tube to shake it. Nothing. Loser. Another man reaches in (second try, you put down 400 lira). He takes a tube and shakes it. Nothing. Two tubes left. Now you have to bet 1,000 lira.

The men are furiously chattering. The man with the tubes has got a constant monologue going. C'mon suckers, he is saying, see if you can beat me.

The men standing around look at each other. No one wants to risk it.

The man barks at them and quickly grasps the tube on the left. He shakes it. There is a distinct rattle.

The men are laughing and shaking their heads. They knew where it was. Well, maybe. Quickly, the whole game starts over again.

Orvis is fascinated. We stand watching the man for several minutes. Orvis is sure he can actually smell where the pebbles in the tube are. He is sure he can defeat the old man.

"Give me some money," he whispers. "We can make a fortune."

I watch while the men keep playing. It goes very, very fast. The chatter is continuous and I don't understand a word. Sometimes they win, but mostly they lose. The old man sitting on the bucket has a fistful of lira notes. The inside pocket of his suit jacket is also filled with money.

I've got about four 200 lira bills on me. I was going to buy lunch and maybe some roasted chestnuts from the venders up on Taksim Square. Maybe a loaf of bread from the Migros grocer across the street from our flat. Two hundred Turkish lira currently translates into about 10 US dollars.

Orvis is sniffing around and then he looks up at me.

It is tempting to see if he can outwit the old man. Heck, it's only ten dollars.

I edge my way into the inner circle and the old man looks up at me.

"*Ne oyanmak istiyorsun*?"

I think he is asking me if I want to play. He shakes the tube and I hear it rattle. He shakes the other tubes. Nothing. He carefully puts them all down on the cardboard box. I'm watching very carefully.

Orvis is sniffing. He looks up at me. The third one from the left.

I can't believe I'm going to do this, but I take 200 lira from my pocket and put it down on the box. The men standing around me go quiet as I reach down to pick up one of the tubes.

When I grab it, I can already feel that it is empty.

The old man smiles at me and takes my money.

"*Tekrar deneyn*?"

As it turns out, I do not want to "try again." As we are walking away, Orvis is staring straight ahead and shaking his head.

"How did he do that?" Orvis says. "I was completely sure. I watched his every move."

I find myself smiling. I tell him, "It's the magic of Istanbul."

CHAPTER THIRTY-THREE

Aya Triada Kilisesi, Near Taksim Meydani,
New City, Istanbul, Turkey

Orvis found a free copy of the Qur'an in the lobby of the Karamustafa Pasa Cami, which is our local mosque. It's a beautiful domed structure with the usual four minarets that looks over the Bosporus, just a few blocks to the southeast of our flat. I like to go there in the mornings, when it is clear, to watch the first rays of the sun as they hit the golden tips of the pencil-shaped towers and the inverted crescent moon and spheres, also golden, of the Islamic symbol on the apex of the dome. Orvis wonders if it is real solid gold up there on the roof and I tell him it is probably just gold paint. But I don't know that for sure. Religions around here don't seem to spare any expense. It could be real gold.

We go to the mosque very early on Easter Sunday. It is so early, in fact, that we were still able to make the sunrise service at the Orthodox Christian Church (Aya Triada Kilisesi) which is only a few blocks in the other direction (northwest). You would think that we live in a pretty religious neighborhood. But at that time of day, there was hardly anyone in either place of worship.

In the Christian church, it is the holiest day of the year. This is the day that Jesus came back from the dead 2,023 years ago, give or take. According to the New Testament, he only came back for a quick hello, but his disciples were very impressed and they made a big deal out of it. So all these years later, we still celebrate this "resurrection," and all over the world, kids are eating chocolate Easter eggs. Honestly, I don't think this is what Jesus had in mind. But I don't know that for sure.

What I do know is that the story of Jesus has inspired some incredible architecture. The Aya Triada is a very beautiful church. It is ornate, with gold filigree woodworking on every wall. There is a central dome with the icon of Jesus looking down on the faithful. Four other arched transepts meet the central dome, and they each have sweeping bands of gold and blue ribbons painted into their ceilings. Icons of angels fill the intersections of the domes. At the front of the church, separating the chancel from the nave, a three-quarter-height wall of columns and transoms, sectioned by more gold filigree into shallow window frames that are holding more detailed icons. A gold arch leads to the altar, and within its upper curve there hangs a sunburst emblem of golden rods surrounding the image of the Holy Trinity.

Above the arch, an icon of St. Basil, also framed in gold.

On Easter Sunday, it is a working church and the priests and monks, even at this early hour, are going about the liturgy. A bulky young man, wearing eyeglasses and a short black beard, is dressed in a golden robe. He takes the thurible, a burning incenser on chains with bells attached, and shakes it across the altar. He then marches up and down the aisles, blessing every corner of the church with the smell of burning frankincense and rosewood. The thurible bells ring each time he shakes it. With each shake he recites a very quiet prayer.

There are only twenty or thirty people in the church. The ceremony seems very overdone for so small an audience, but it fills me with calmness and awe. One of my earliest memories is of a priest with an incense burner blessing the coffin where my grandmother, Anna Wascow, lay at her funeral. It was in a Ukrainian Orthodox Church in Ansonia, Connecticut. I was about four years old. The memory of the priest and the incense has outlasted any other interest I've had in organized religion.

Of course, the reason there are not more people at this Easter Sunday service is because, according to the Orthodox Church, it is not Easter Sunday. It is only later that I realize this. The Orthodox Easter is still two weeks in the future.

This becomes apparent only when we wander down past Taksim Square along the avenue Istiklal to the Catholic Church (St. Anthony of Padua), where the Roman Catholics are crowding the doors and spilling out into the street. Ten thousand or more worshipers here and they are not here for the Easter Bunny. Today is THEIR Easter Sunday. For sure. They are here because Jesus the Christ has risen from the dead, just as he has for approximately the last 1,990 years. Or so the story goes. No one really knows who moved the rock sealing off his tomb, though they suspect it was God. God moved the boulder and brought Jesus back to life (after he was crucified by the Romans, yikes!) and created the whole Christianity thing, which gives some people a lot of hope.

Good job, God.

Believe what you will, but the churches and the mosques of Istanbul are nonetheless impressive. Orvis and I spend a lot of our time exploring them. We sit for hours one afternoon in a tiny corner of the Hagia Sophia, gazing up into the vastness of its dome, 185 feet tall and over 1,500 years old. Built as a church by the Roman Emperor Constantine in 537. Transformed into a mosque in 1453 after the Ottoman Turks conquered the city. For many decades it was simply a museum open to the public, and then in 2020 an authoritarian Turkish government turned it back into a mosque. But whichever force of humankind wants to define it, the Hagia Sophia (Holy Wisdom) is a wonder of the modern world. Even when it is filled with tourists.

Orvis and I don't get very far into our study of the Holy Qur'an. Much of it doesn't make any sense to our modern minds. The Prophet Muhammad (peace be upon him) was certainly a man of wisdom and humility. But many of his words don't seem applicable to the world as we currently experience it. The Qur'an seems a lot like the Bible or the Torah. They were helpful when first written, but possibly need some updating.

And this is what Orvis points out to me. He asks, "Why did they build all these huge buildings? It seems like more than anyone could need for a little worshiping."

He has a point. The prophets didn't need churches. Buddha, Moses, Jesus, Muhammad, they did not find God/Allah in a temple. They found the divine in nature. Under a tree, on the mountain, in the desert and in a cave. This is where they spoke with the oneness of God. So why should the rest of us expect to find our creator in a mosque, a synagogue, a cathedral, or an ashram? Shouldn't we be looking in the forest? Perhaps in the mountains? Maybe out on the ocean somewhere.

I'm sure there are good theological answers to this question. Orvis and I do appreciate the wonderful buildings that have been constructed in the name of God. They are wonders of human achievement. Built for other humans.

Great places to go and think about Allah and where you might find him.

And they smell good too.

This is something that Orvis points out. When we are leaving the Easter service at Aya Triada, the smell of the incense clings to our clothes. It feels and smells like we have somehow been purified. Like we did our duty to say hello to God and Jesus, said a little prayer to the homeless children of the world, put in a good word for world peace.

It's still early. The shops along the Istiklal Caddesi are still closed. Just a few coffee shops are beginning to open. Up on Taksim Square, the morning light is beginning to hit the marble stone front of the Taksim Mosque, another huge dome, minarets tipped with gold, the sun giving it a rosy glow. It is just after the dawn call to prayer and men are coming down the steps, most of them dressed in black and grey, a white kurta and a dark skullcap. For most people in Istanbul, Sunday is not a special holy day of the week. Not even on Easter.

"We got time," I tell Orvis. "Let's walk over to the old city and have a cup at that cafe we like."

"Great idea. The one with that delicious hot chocolate," he replies.

Yeah, chocolate, I'm thinking. That is really the true modern reason for Easter.

Good job, Jesus.

CHAPTER THIRTY-FOUR

Cafe Amelie Galata, Staircase 17,
Muyyetzade, New City, Istanbul, TK

On our last day in Istanbul, we are hoping to reunite with Our Friend From Palermo. She is a photographer that we met on the boat coming back from the Black Sea. We have made a tentative plan to meet in the morning at our favorite cafe. This would be Cafe Amelie Galata. It is a tiny place built into the hillside next to a landing on the crumbling concrete staircase that leads up the steep hill from the foot of the Galata Bridge. Orvis is hoping she will make our photo next to the weird and wonderful street art we found after getting lost the other day.

On this particular day, Friday, we were searching for a *tornavida* (screwdriver) and a pair of *kerpeten* (pliers). These were things we needed to unlock a washing machine that had stolen most of our clothes. It's a bit of a story. But it has a happy ending.

It was still early in the morning, a grey and drizzling Bosporus morning when the weather is almost deciding to rain and then it does rain and rains hard. So hard we decide to buy an umbrella, the purchase of which (300 lira) causes it to stop raining. A cheap fix in Orvis's mind, but he never pays for anything anyway.

Over in the Old City around the Bazaar neighborhoods, the shops are mostly open-air booths. All manner of tarps and awnings are rigged to keep the rain off the merchandise. The water runs down the hillsides in a gutter cut into the middle of the narrow streets. It drips off the roofs and onto the tarps and pools in the low spots and leaks slowly onto the sidewalks. When it is cold and early it makes a pretty miserable scene, and we really had no idea where to find a hardware store. Finally we stuck our head into a shop selling knives and swords. Sign language and a few words of Turkish got my point across. The knife-seller shook his head but smiled and gave me directions to a shop around the corner.

"Twenty meters *duz git, sonra saga git*," he said. Twenty meters straight, then take a right.

Of course we could not find it. But a little more wandering among the dripping roofs, and there was a man just opening his hardware booth. He was very nice, though still yawning and taking down his tarps. He sold us the tools. Thirty for the screwdriver. Seventy for the pliers.

It was on the way back to the flat to assault the offending washing machine that we happened upon the most unusual art display. My legs were getting tired, so we decided to hop on a trolley car. Orvis loves buses, trollies, and the like. I'm a little Covid-weary about public transport, but what the hell. The rain had started up again. This gave me a certain satisfaction about the umbrella purchase. And in my self-satisfied internal glow, I stopped paying attention and we missed our stop. Which took us into unknown territory.

So we were walking back to the flat from a different direction.

A little side note here about Istanbul. It doesn't show on the maps or in much of the tourist videos, but Stamboul (as

Agatha Christie liked to call it) is a very hilly city. And the hills can be very steep. And the streets sometimes are not streets at all. Sometimes they are staircases.

I had a pretty good idea of how to get back to the flat, but not by any what-you-would-call "direct" route. It was kind of trial and error, which is the way I mostly travel. We were down near the ferry docks. Any route we chose was going to be uphill. This is an area of industrial suppliers. Places selling marine hardware, electrical fixtures, plumbing supplies. Old buildings with commercial space on the ground floor. Flats and lofts up above. Gritty in a commercial way. Artistic in another way entirely.

We turned into an alleyway, and there was a staircase going steeply uphill. A few steps in and we noticed it was also an art gallery.

All of the shops in this part of town have massive security doors. You've seen these kinds of doors. They are heavy corrugated steel and they roll up like an American garage door. Many times in urban environments you will see that these doors are splashed with graffiti. "Tagged" by miscreants with cans of spray paint. On this particular alleyway staircase, with the shops lining either side of the narrow corridor, the security doors were painted with colorful portraits of contemporary celebrities and famous artists. Amazing portraits painted onto the corrugated steel, which gave them enough distortion to look weirdly animated.

Salvador Dali stared crazily from behind Vincent Van Gogh. Marilyn Monroe looked ravishingly vulnerable with red lipstick and a black halter top. Michael Jackson with blue eyes and bleached skin. Frida Kahlo with a Turkish nose. Al Pacino looking twenty years old. Madonna with blond hair. Maradona and the Hand of God. Charlie Chaplin, surprised and worried. And my favorite: a superwoman photographer, purple hair, blue fingernails, red lips, holding a film camera to her right eye with a wild expression and shooting directly up the stairs.

"Wow," said Orvis when he saw her. "She's something else."

"Yeah. We really should show this to Fluvia," I said, referring to our photographer friend.

Well, it was raining and we didn't spend that much time in the alleyway. I wanted to get home to attack the washer. I figured that we could come back. Maybe even bring Fluvia with us. It sure could make some interesting pictures.

It is probably obvious what happens, right? A few hours later, after recovering our clothes and fixing the washing machine, we immediately wrote a note to Our Friend from Palermo and told her about the alleyway. We even made a plan to try to take her there. Then we went out to find the alleyway so that we would know exactly how to get there.

Guess what happened down there in the commercial district?

That afternoon, the sun came out and all of the shops opened. What did that mean? Well, it meant they rolled up their security doors.

I swear, we walked up and down that district for six hours trying to find the alleyway. Orvis was sure we had found it several times, but the art was nowhere to be seen. I thought we were lost. I thought we had dreamed it. I knew it was around there somewhere.

Which is when we eventually returned to the Cafe Amelie Galata. We sat outside in our favorite corner, next to the portrait of Audrey Tautou, the French actress. She also has an umbrella. We had to chase a cat out of the other seat so Orvis could sit down. We were both a little discouraged.

Then it dawned on me.

"The doors have disappeared because they are rolled up!" I exclaimed. "The art goes with them. It's only there when the shops are closed!"

Orvis looked over at me in wonder. As though he could not believe that I was so brilliant.

"Duh," he said.

I felt a cloud pass over my thoughts. "But what if Our Friend From Palermo shows up and the stores are still open and there's nothing to show her?"

We sat in silence for a good while. I ordered coffee for me, hot chocolate for Orvis. We ate a Napolitano de Paris. Soft on the outside, creamy on the inside. The cafe cat returned and eyed us suspiciously.

"We will just have to take our chances," Orvis said.

Which is exactly what we were doing two days later as we sat in the very same cafe waiting for our friend. In the interim, we had reconnoitered the alleyway of art, found it again after the shops had closed, and were confident we could find it one more time on this, our last day in Istanbul. But it was early Monday morning, and we didn't know when the shops would be rolling up their doors.

I was looking at my watch, nervously drumming my fingers on the table. Orvis was having a stare-down with the cat. Then my phone vibrated. A message from Our Friend in Palermo.

I looked over at Orvis. Both he and the cat turned to look at me.

"She's not coming," I told them. "She needs to do something else before she flies back to Italy."

Orvis sighed. The cat looked at us with something between contempt and annoyance.

"Well, at least we're off the hook," I said.

The cat narrowed her eyes, blinked slowly, turned her butt towards us and walked off into the shadows of the cafe.

See, like I said, it has a happy ending.

CHAPTER THIRTY-FIVE

Aboard the Night Train to Bulgaria

Honestly, I would have no clue why the train is stopping a few miles from the Bulgarian border in the middle of the night if it weren't for my bunkmates. Ahmed is a Kurdish Turk doing his graduate work at the University of Leipzig. He speaks Turkish and German. Ryker is from Berlin; he's creating an East European railway website. He speaks German and Bulgarian. Jesspers is an environmental activist just returning from two years at an ashram in Uttar Pradesh. He speaks Bulgarian and English.

The conductor speaks to Ahmed. Ahmed speaks to Ryker. Ryker speaks to Jesspers and Jesspers speaks to me. After all that, from what I am given to understand, there has been a landslide and the train cannot continue into Bulgaria. We all have to get off. They are going to put us on a bus.

From my reckoning, it is 1:30 a.m., though I'm not exactly sure what time zone we are in.

I should start this part of the story by saying that I have always had a romantic and unrealistic relationship with trains. It is my preferred way to travel. I first toured Europe on trains in 1973, when a three-month student Eurail Pass was within my financial reach. I went everywhere. I did lots of train travel in India, where you can stand between the rail cars with the door half open and watch the sun rise through the mists covering the Punjabi plain. I trained through Western Ukraine from Lviv to Zakarpattia Oblast under the watchful eye of a matronly conductor with a whistling samovar that served black tea. I even traveled once from San Francisco to New York on the Amtrak, three days of back-wrenching insomnia as I tried to sleep in my seat.

Of course, all that happened in my younger days. Now most travelers go by airplane. It's fast and ofttimes cheaper. (Istanbul to Paris, $99 on Ryanair; 289 euros if you can find a train route. There is no longer any Orient Express for this route.) The airports and the airlines have taken over international travel. It's sad, but not unexpected.

I like trains because you can see the countryside. I like trains because you can talk to people. If you are in a sleeper car, you can even get to know them. Four folks sleeping together in four narrow bunks lining a six-foot-by-seven-foot compartment. It's not like an airplane. Here you just have to talk to each other.

Which is how I found myself trying to explain, in English, through multiple translations, what I was doing and why I was traveling with an imaginary dog.

"Zis dog you have, is not a dog?" Jesspers asked.

"No, no, he's a dog alright. He's just imaginary."

A flurry of foreign words circled the compartment. Then Jesspers turned back to me.

"Zis imaginary? It means he is not real. But still he is dog?"

"He is real in my mind," I said.

"And he travels zwith you?"

"Yes. He's quite enjoying himself, actually."

I looked up into the corner where Orvis was curled up, sound asleep among the pillows in the luggage rack. I hoped he wasn't hearing this.

There was some conversation between Ahmed and Ryker. Then a question passed through Jesspers.

"It is good to have dog," Jesspers said. "But why not real dog? Maybe poodle. Small, easy into the suitcase."

The word "poodle," even spoken in a Bulgarian accent, made Orvis's ears twitch. He lifted his head and opened his eyes for a second, but went back to sleep.

"I like just having him in my imagination," I said. "It makes a better story."

This got translated. They all looked at me.

"It's supposed to be humorous," I said.

The translation made the rounds. Now they were smiling. They were all young. They smiled at me with that sort of indulgent smile you might give your Uncle Max the third time he told you the same not-funny joke.

Which made me wonder: Had I turned into Uncle Max? That old guy with the stale imagination destined to retell the same tired story about the imaginary dog and their trip through Eastern Europe?

Was I trying too hard to be "interesting"? It was something to think about the next time I tried to explain my relationship with Orvis.

We set up the bunks after that and all tried to sleep. Then the Turkish conductor woke us to get off the train, get on the bus, get herded through customs, get on another train, get stopped at the border by the Bulgarians who took our passports, cleared through customs again, set up the bunks again and then try to sleep again. I got maybe three hours of shut-eye and then the grey skies of a Bulgarian morning greeted me through the window of the train.

I swear it felt like I had been here before. It felt like the Soviet Union all over again. A countryside of rolling hills with clusters of birch trees. The landscape almost greening in the spring but not quite there yet. Houses near the tracks with dilapidated red-tile roofs, stucco cracked and falling off the walls, mud driveways. Cracked asphalt roads quickly turning to dirt in the distance. Small train stations deserted because the train did not stop there. Fields of weeds, too wet to be plowed for planting.

I know that train routes do not usually take you through the best parts of towns and cities. It's what I like about this kind of travel; you get to see a little bit of the underbelly of a place. Bulgaria, on first impression, looked poor and very rural. A land of lasting peasantry. With my tattered hat and my pushed-in Slavic face, I was going to blend right in.

It took a few hours to reach Sofia. This city of about 1.5 million is the capital of Bulgaria. It has ancient Roman roots, Neo-Byzantine architecture, a thriving software industry, and a ski resort just south of town.

I had rented a room in the central district near Vitosha Boulevard (which some guidebooks call "the Champs-Elysees" of Sofia, though that is stretching the metaphor by one or two magnitudes.) The train station where we arrived was on the other side of town.

(Quick note: Bulgaria uses the Cyrillic alphabet. In fact, it was invented in Bulgaria in the ninth century by the Preslav Literary School. It has lots of different characters and symbols that do not appear in the Latin alphabet. I don't read Cyrillic, or Bulgarian for that matter. In other words, there was a lot of signage that I could not read. In the more modern parts of the city, like the subway, the words are also written in English. So study up on your Cyrillic Bulgarian if you plan to visit. Or just ride the subways.

When we arrived, we were, of course, immediately lost. A young man we met on the train (Luke from London) ran into us at the ATM machine. Also lost, he had the advantage of two things: a very positive tech-savvy attitude and a smart phone with an EU SIM card. I gave him the address where I was staying. He repeated it into his phone and shaaaazamm, we were on the road. The beginning of a half-hour walk. We were conveniently accompanied by a little blue dot that moved with us on his phone. I bought him breakfast on the way. We both looked at Sofia with the same thought. Why did we come here?

Because at first glance, Sofia does not look that great. It looks like it is still scarred by communism.

The tall, crumbling, Soviet-style apartment blocks. The parks that have become repositories for stark socialist-realism sculpture. To a Westerner, it all looks vaguely Russian. Shivers of the Cold War seem to linger in the shadows.

Then we saw the woman on the street corner.

She was buried in pigeons. A poor old woman wrapped in a blanket, a handmade wool cap on her head. She was sitting in a wheelchair with a handful of breadcrumbs in her lap. The pigeons had her surrounded. Dozens of pigeons. Flitting about, flocking to her, crapping on the sidewalk. She was enthralled with the pigeons. Like they were her only friends. Like the rest of the world had left her behind somewhere in the 1950s.

We stood for a few moments and watched her. People walked by and gave her coins from their pockets. A small boy gave her a small bag of birdseed. She just sat there underneath the pigeons and kept smiling.

I didn't want to say anything to Luke, but the woman looked just like my ancient Aunt Thelma, long-deceased, who used to kiss my little-boy face and smell like old onions. Somehow this was not at all comforting.

Orvis noticed the change in my expression. He could feel it happen as I slowly deflated.

"Welcome to the past," he said.

I made a quick photo and we turned away. A few blocks to the west, we came to an old trolley car, clanking as it went along the boulevard. It was painted pale green and faded red with a white stripe down the middle. Bulgarian colors. But it looked old and worn-out. A classic or a relic of the last century? We paused as it passed us, almost in awe of our own time travel.

"Let's keep walking," Luke said, glancing down at his smartphone. "We're almost there."

Really? I thought to myself, I wonder where we are going?

CHAPTER THIRTY-SIX

Tsar Samuel #3, kv. Vitosha, Sofia, Bulgaria

I have always contended that international travel tends to open one's mind. The world is filled with a billion new perspectives. There are as many different ways of looking at life as there are lives to look at. As you travel, it becomes very apparent how small and cloistered our lives can get. How we can succumb to our prejudices, narrow our field of vision, become intellectually limited by our own point of view. I think international travel is a remedy for this. I think it can change a person. Or, for that matter, an imaginary dog.

It was understandable how Orvis reacted to the streets of Istanbul. These are streets ruled by cats. The dogs are asleep. The cats are famous. In our neighborhood, Cihangir, the cats were movie stars. Subject of many documentaries. Obviously, they had an attitude. (I mean, what cat doesn't?) Orvis did not like the cats of Istanbul. It is one of his shortcomings, but, hey, we all have prejudices.

This is why I was so surprised that after a couple of days in Sofia, he told me he wanted me to meet his new friend.

We were extremely fortunate to be staying in a fifth-floor apartment with Our Bulgarian Friend. She grew up in a small village down near the Macedonian border, but spent several years in the USA getting her graduate degree in computer science. Now she is a mental health professional designing self-help phone apps. She loves living in Sofia. She speaks fluent English. Her apartment is sparse, in an old Soviet-era building only a few blocks from downtown. There is no elevator, just eight short flights of steep stairs. She gives us a set of keys and leaves for work. I make Orvis his own imaginary copy. I don't want to be huffing and puffing up all those stairs every time he has to go out to do his business.

In Sofia the neighborhoods are interesting. There is a central district surrounding the Alexander Nevsky Cathedral. It is mostly lined with government buildings and cultural centers. The Ivan Vazov National Theater, the National Opera of Bulgaria, the National Parliament. It is very imposing and posh, golden roof domes, granite columns, statues of war heroes. But just a few blocks in any direction, the city becomes mostly residential. Long blocks of cookie-cutter apartment buildings, four or five stories tall, with square balconies set symmetrically with white-framed windows, slanted tile roofs, mostly stuccoed concrete and sometimes crumbling, steel security doors on the ground floor. Sometimes a small coffee shop or grocery is wedged into the corner. These are communist buildings, for the most part. Part of the great socialist revolution. A few of them are in better shape than others. None of them are aesthetically pleasing.

Our Bulgarian Friend lives in one of these buildings. It is in the Vitosha district, seven or eight blocks from the National Palace of Culture. It is across the street from the Church of St. George, which stands in the center of a cracked asphalt plaza, a very modest kids' playground on either side, a plywood hut outside the main entrance selling long, thin votive candles to hopeful worshipers. Saint George is part of the Bulgarian Orthodox Diocese. The church is not in great shape. Some of the stucco is becoming separated from the bricks on its north side. There are roof tiles missing from one of its domes. The inside could use a good scrubbing. Decades of incense, candle smoke, and human sweat have darkened the gold-trimmed icons that line the altar. The marble floor is worn and hollowed out from the foot traffic through the inner doors. Some of the stained glass has been replaced with plywood shutters. The years have taken their toll on St. George.

It is right outside the church that Orvis meets Rasputin.

Rasputin is a Siberian house cat. Until recently, he had been living in the rectory next to the Church of St. Nicholas the Miracle Maker, which is a very beautiful and stunningly well-kept mini-cathedral built by Tsar Nicholas II in the 1880s. St. Nicholas is Russian Orthodox. It is next to the Russian Embassy.

Rasputin is a Russian cat, though he was born in Romania and came to Sofia as a kitten. In the fall of 2022, he had to leave St. Nicholas under suspicious circumstances.

"They were trying to poison him," Orvis tells me, "because he was opposed to the war in Ukraine."

Currently, from what I gather, Rasputin (it's pronounced RasPUteen) is hiding out from the Russians. He's been living at St. George's in the plywood shack that sells candles.

"I thought you hated cats?"

"This is different," Orvis says. "Wait till you meet him."

Well, personally I like most cats, though I don't necessarily trust them. So when Orvis invites Rasputin to have lunch with us, I have no objections. Though I wonder if he speaks English.

"Don't be silly," Orvis says. "He speaks cat."

I look at him like he can't be serious. Who speaks cat these days? I thought it was a dead language.

"No sweat," he says. "You don't have to say anything. Just pay for lunch."

Which is how I end up sitting across the table from a large cat at Sushi Max Vlahova over on Ulitsa Gurgulyat, a couple of blocks south of the church. It was the only place Orvis could find that had fresh tuna. I guess Rasputin has pretty high standards.

After we polished off a few nigiri (two tuna, two yellowtail) Rasputin settled back into his chair and told us his story. He had been living for the last six months under the plywood candle shed in front of St. George's. It had been a cold winter for him. He was forced to eat mice and pigeons. You could see the aristocratic part of him shudder when he told us this.

"Pigeons are terrible," he complained. "They taste like chicken."

While he was living over at St. Nicholas, life was very posh. The ambassador's wife had adopted him. He would come over from the cathedral for a late dinner. Nothing but caviar and blue fin tuna.

"You know, the good stuff," he told us. "And sardines from the Black Sea. She loved to open the cans for me. We spent the winters next to the samovar. When his excellency was out on some diplomatic mission I would sit in her lap. Purring. She loved to hear me purrr. It aroused her. She would pleasure herself while I sat at the foot of her bed. Pretending to sleep, but all the while…watching…"

Orvis looked over at me. I cleared my throat.

"I think that's a little too much information," Orvis said.

Rasputin came out of his self-absorbed reverie.

"But then that evil one, whose name I will not say, has to start this stupid war."

He was referring to the war in Ukraine. The unmentionable one is V. Putin (pronounced PuTEEN), President of Russia.

"The ambassador's wife, she is a pacifist. Half her family is from Ukraine. She convinced the ambassador to send a private protest to the president. Two weeks later they are recalled to Moscow. I beg her to take me with. But she does not speak cat."

It turns out that Rasputin never hears from the ambassador's wife. Despite all the propaganda coming out of the Kremlin, he becomes staunchly opposed to the war. As far as he is concerned, it has tragically disrupted his supply of tuna, caviar, and Black Sea sardines. He is shocked when the priests at St. Nicholas conduct prayer vigils to support the Russian troops. The Russian Orthodox Church is squarely behind the government's invasion of Ukraine. Rasputin is disgusted. At night he sneaks into the vestry and sprays his urine on the cassocks. Eventually they lock him out of the sanctuary.

"They send a new ambassador, but his wife is tall and thin like string bean. I think maybe she is anorexic, and allergic to cats. She tells the housekeeper to feed me outside on the stone portico. It is low-grade. Food for pets only. I let the squirrels have it."

I can see why Orvis likes this guy. He is over the top. Even for a cat, he has a vastly superior and self-absorbed attitude.

I have no great love for Ukrainians, Rasputin said, they tend to smell like old onions. But war is not the answer just because people smell bad.

Orvis leaned over to him and whispered to be a little careful, nodding toward me. "His grandparents were Ukrainian and he's buying lunch."

Rasputin looked across the table. His eyes were little slits, and I could almost feel myself being hypnotized.

"There is much more I can tell you," he says, gazing at me intently. "But first, perhaps, we should order more sushi."

CHAPTER THIRTY-SEVEN

Malashevtsi Road Flea Market, Lavandula 45, Sofia, Bulgaria

Orvis tells me that we could certainly spend the rest of our trip, one boring day after another, making photos of churches, mosques, synagogues, and Roman ruins. There is plenty of that stuff everywhere, he contends. But let's find something interesting. Let's find something real.

So I ask Our Bulgarian Friend where the "real" people hang out. She immediately says: The Malashevtsi Flea Market.

So far, we have stayed in the central part of Sofia. Cafes and restaurants on Vitosha Boulevard. A walking tour of the Alexander Nevsky Cathedral, the archeology site at Serdika (circa 26 BC), the Rotunda Church of St. George, the Soviet Sculpture Park on Ulitsa Lachezar. It has been mostly sunny and we have been mostly walking. But then we discover the subway system.

It is a very modern metro (opened in 1998), and it is really an outstanding work of design and engineering. It seems meticulously maintained. Each station we visited (admittedly we did not see them all) is its own unique work of art. Polished granite floors, sweeping arches of steel and glass, mosaics of words and images that relate to the individual stop and the history of the city. There is virtually no graffiti. There are no stinky corners where skinheads and drunks go to take a piss. It is safe and well-lit and it is buried very, very deeply underground. (They had to do this to get underneath the ground level of archeological significance, so as not to disturb undiscovered ruins.)

We loved riding the subway. The turnstiles worked with any modern credit card (chipped). It cost about 90 cents US per ride but caps off at a total of four euros per day ($4.40). Easy and lovely. We spent hours just riding around, especially if it was raining up above. It took us to all kinds of interesting places.

That is the contrast of Sofia, and probably of Bulgaria as a whole. It is part of the European Union and the North Atlantic Treaty Organization, giving it stability and relative peace. This means that though it is far to the east of Europe, it is rapidly becoming more integrated economically into the more wealthy western parts. It is an ongoing process. The subway is a good example.

One day we took the M3 Green line out to its last stop: Hadzhi Dimitar. The location (supposedly) of the New Bulgarian University. We expected to come up from the underground into a neighborhood U-district. Typically a place of bookstores, cafes, and cheap restaurants, a Starbucks, a Costa Coffee, maybe a British-style funky pub (the "Cock and a Bull," or "Fox and Hound," or "Gandalf's Closet," something like that…). Off somewhere in the near distance would be a campus of new concrete office buildings, lots of glass, brick-and-mortar classrooms.

A modern escalator took us up to street level. We walked out of the metro and there was nothing around but a field of grass. To one side, a single brick duplex was being built along a wide boulevard. To the east we could see some apartment buildings, a big-box grocery store, a kiosk where people were waiting for the bus. To the west, open fields, some high-rise Soviet apartments in the distance. As we stood there wondering where the university might be, a man came by, going slowly uphill on the wide asphalt road. He was driving a wagon with big rubber tires. It was being pulled by an aging horse. The back of the wagon was filled with potatoes.

Sofia is a mixed bag. The good part is that it is very original. Most of the architecture goes back to the late 1940s or earlier. The neighborhoods are not gentrified like so many western cities. It is mostly middle-class and mostly affordable. There is little air pollution and not much traffic.

The bad part is that it probably won't last.

So we took the Metro as far as we could out toward Malashevtsi Road. It was still a ways from the last stop, so we had to spring for a taxi. The driver spoke very little English, but like every other taxi driver I met on this trip, he seemed to have a brother or a cousin or a friend that was moving to San Francisco. I tried to warn them all that San Francisco is not what it used to be, but mostly they didn't want to hear me. America was the promised land as far as taxi drivers are concerned. Streets paved with gold. Travelers with pockets full of money. Ready to be fleeced.

The Malashevtsi Flea Market was free and open to anyone who wanted to spread a blanket on the ground in either of the two big parking lots and offer their junk for sale. And by junk, I mean, you know, real junk. Any manner of anything. Lots of old clothes that looked like the rejected items from Salvation Army. Lots of new stuff in packages that had fallen off a truck somewhere. Plenty of old books (most everything in Bulgarian or Russian), cheap wristwatches, well-worn shoes, bicycles and bicycle parts, tools and old tires, copper pots and stainless-steel frying pans, many old samovars, radios, cassette decks, CD players…it was what you might call a mega garage sale. But Bulgarian-style.

We searched and searched (and Orvis is a great search dog) but we could not find one single thing to buy. We only had a couple of 100 lev notes (about $45), and we were in no position to negotiate over someone's lack of change. I had blown out my sneakers in Istanbul and was somewhat looking for a new pair of cheap walking shoes, but trying them on? In this crowd? With no place to sit? Not a pleasant experience.

Ok, Orvis did find one thing that he liked.

There was a guy selling World War II memorabilia in a corner of the market where men had set up tables and a makeshift booth cover. Weird stuff, like an original Nazi helmet, an SS armband, some shell casings from a mortar round. A well-worn hardbound copy of *Mein Kampf*. Then photographs of Third Reich celebrities. Hitler. Joseph Goebbels. Next to that, some Soviet stuff. Hammer and sickle patches. A Soviet flag. Red star metals from the Communist Party. I stood there and was actually shocked by this collection. Mostly people were ignoring the man's display. Walking past without making eye contact.

Orvis didn't really know what he was looking at, but one thing caught his eye. There was a nicely framed portrait to one side of the table. It was a portrait of a soldier, a general, looking off into the distance, dark swept-back hair, a thick black mustache, red patches on his collar, a single star medal pinned to his chest. He looked strong. He looked heroic. In some ways he even looked kind. The image was colorized, which made it seem antique. The frame was gilded in gold paint.

"Wow," Orvis said. "That's cool. Great old photograph. What a good-looking dude. He seems like a nice man."

"We are definitely not buying it," I said quietly. "That's a portrait of Joseph Stalin."

Orvis was oblivious and certainly not attached. He has no memory of the last century. He just shook his head and went on to the next booth. I backed away slowly from the man's table. I didn't want him to see the fear and displeasure that was racing through my heart. I felt like I had been bitten by a spider.

I finally spent the coinage that was jingling around in my bag (probably about $3) on a sausage and a roll from a very nice couple who had set up a barbecue at the entrance to the flea market. It was good and I gave half to Orvis.

Then I spent a fortune on a taxi to take us over to the nearest subway station.

It seemed like the safest way to get us back home.

CHAPTER THIRTY-EIGHT

Somewhere in Serbia

For a reason that I cannot fathom and do not have the patience to investigate, the authorities have closed the train route from Sofia to Belgrade. This is the normal route of the Orient Express, which, as I have said, no longer exists. Perhaps there has been a murder? A landslide? Spring snow drifts higher than an elephant's eye? A strike by railway workers in Serbia? We instead decide to take the Florentine Bus. It goes from Sofia to Florence, Italy. We will take it as far as Zagreb.

It is a very modern, high-tech autobus, built by Mercedes in Germany, with four drivers, three of whom are surly; the fourth is involved in selling black-market cigarettes to the passengers. He seems happy.

There is something I must say about (and to) my pal Rick Steves, who has become (deservedly) famous for his books and videos about travel in Europe. Good job, Rick, but how come you never mention that everyone smokes?

Do they not have lung cancer in Eastern Europe?

Okay, whatever. The bus is about half full, some backpacking college kids from Sweden, some wrinkly Babushkas from east Bulgaria, an old guy with a gut that looks just like my Uncle Joe Tuzik (deceased along with Aunt Thelma). What is it with bus travel? It's just like being on a plane, but lower and slower. People are all facing in one direction, toward the front, and no one is very friendly. Just like on an airplane. When is the last time you made a new friend on an airplane? I guess maybe in first class. Those folks seem happier. Maybe it's the champagne.

Luckily, there are large windows, very clean, and the panoramic view of the landscape passing by at about ninety kilometers per hour. The weather is getting quite spring-like now, and the fields and forests are lush and greening. Cumulous clouds are piled on the horizon, some of them dark over the southern part of the Carpathian Mountains. Our route skirts the mountain range and flows through a wide area of rolling hills, little towns tucked into the folds of the landscape next to a river or stream, brick houses with red-tiled roofs and a clock tower somewhere in the center, usually across from a small church. I only see this from a distance, so I can't tell what the villages are really like, but from the highway they are picturesque.

We have to do the usual two stops at the international border. Passports checked twice (each country wants to know if you are coming or going). About two hundred cigarettes get smoked when we have to leave the bus. Orvis and I stand off to one side, not that we feel like exceptionalists, but both of us have sensitive lungs and his nose does not like the smell of burning tobacco. It is getting on towards evening when we pull off the highway in Serbia. I'd like to tell you where we are, but I do not have a clue and no one is talking much, at least not in a language I can understand.

Of course, the bus drivers have a deal with the owners of the restaurant. Everyone gets off and they lock the bus so you can't get back on. We are in the middle of the countryside. A sign in Serbian (maybe) says: "Nowheresville…"

For some reason, there is a Turkish flag flying. Did I go in the wrong direction? It is a mystery that remains unsolved.

I have two clues that I'm not going to eat in this restaurant. The first is that there are ashtrays on every table. The second is that the restroom is behind a turnstile that will only let you through if you pay at the restaurant. I'm thinking about going out and pissing on their flag, but I don't want to get arrested in Serbia. Instead I go out of the restaurant and head uphill on a country road where I can relieve myself in the forest. Orvis and I need a little stretch anyway.

The road goes up around a bend and I walk past a yard that is strewn with junk. Dried-up plants in ceramic pots. A tattered umbrella looking forlornly folded into itself. Parts of a tin roof leaning against some rusted patio furniture. There is a little peeling painted sign in English that says: Snack Bar. The place looks closed and abandoned, as does the boarded-up motel that is behind it. I slip through an opening in a chain-link security fence, find a thirsty beech tree, and express my freedom by relieving myself in nature.

It is when I am zipping up my fly and turning around that I notice someone is watching me from the back window of the abandoned restaurant.

Oh well. Like I've said: I am not a good tourist.

Back on the legal side of the chain-link, I am walking down the road to the parked bus when I hear a voice call out. It is a man up the hill behind me. He is waving his arms and calling to me.

I look down at Orvis. He looks up at me and smiles.

"Busted," he says.

The man gestures for me to come back up the hill. I turn around and slowly walk toward him.

He is a tall man and thin. He is dressed in gray wool trousers, a white shirt with the sleeves partially rolled up. A gold wristwatch. About my age, maybe a little bit older. His shoes are brown leather loafers, well worn.

I won't attempt to tell you what he says. Probably it is in Serbian. I'm not even sure. He may be telling me I have to pay him for peeing on his beech tree. But he isn't shouting, he is actually being very nice. With gestures he motions me back up the hill.

I look at Orvis. He shrugs one shoulder. Why not?

It turns out the man's name is Yakimuz Balik and he owns the "snack bar" that looks so abandoned. We follow him past the junk in the yard through a wood-and-glass French door that opens into the main dining room. I'm ready to excuse myself and run, but it is quite a surprise.

A perfectly beautiful homespun country inn, Serbian style. White tablecloths, red place mats. Hand-built wooden chairs with hearts cut into the back splat. Happily worn red cushions on all the chairs. Houseplants hanging everywhere. A beamed ceiling with hanging lights made from green wine bottles. The floor made from wide planks of old-growth pine, grooved and scratched from hard use, but polished clean and varnished heavily so that it shined. The place looked well-loved. It looked well-used. It even looked appetizing.

And it was totally empty.

The closest language we shared was German, of which I know perhaps twenty-five words.

"*Das ist gut*," I said. "*Du hast essen*?"

He laughed and then he said, "*Bitte nehmen sie*."

So I took a table and he handed me a menu that was in tiny letters, in dim light, and even if I could read it without my glasses, which is not possible, I wouldn't be able to because it was in Serbian, written in Serbian script (something between Cyrillic and Latin), and it had seventy-five items on it and I didn't have a clue what they were. So I ordered a hamburger.

"Hamburger," I said. It's just about the same in all languages. "And a beer. Whatever's local."

He came back with a bottle of Kick Ass Billy. It was pretty good. A little too hoppy, but…

Fifteen minutes later, he brought out a huge plate that had the largest hamburger that I had ever seen. It was easily ten inches in diameter. It had a loaf of round bread cut in half horizontally sandwiching it. Also a pile of potatoes cut in quarters, deep-fried, topped with mayonnaise.

It would take me days to eat all of this. Then I would die of a heart attack.

But it was pretty good, and I kept eating and smiling and thanking him. We tried to do a conversation, me using very bad German and my smartphone. His daughter was in the kitchen cooking, and she came out to join us. Just three in our little family, me sitting and eating, they standing nearby, watching.

When I had gone through about half of the burger, I just had to stop. I ate a couple more slices of potatoes and then pushed the plate away. It was just too much.

The daughter looked disappointed but took the plate away. The man, whose nickname was Goran, smiled and presented me with a bill. It was for about three dollars.

Of course I had no Serbian currency (the dinar, about 100-to-1 USD).

I smiled. I showed him a handful of euros, which was all I had. He frowned.

Then he said in perfect English: "Don't you have a credit card?"

It turned out he had grown up in Pennsylvania. Near Philadelphia. But the cost of living was too much for his family.

"We couldn't afford to live in America anymore. Everything too much. Just the cost of cigarettes! You know what they charge now?"

I didn't, but I kept quiet. He came over and sat down across the table from me. I could see now that his teeth were yellow.

"It's impossible. We love Serbia. Glad to be back with the family. America is nice, but not for us. Why here cigarettes cheap. You can smoke all you want for almost nothing…"

He took a pack out of his shirt pocket. It was black on one side and had a photo of a diseased lung on the other. He offered me one.

"No thanks," I said, getting up. "I have to catch my bus."

Orvis was waiting outside. I gave him the last half of my hamburger.

"Let's get out of here," I said.

CHAPTER THIRTY-NINE

Gunduliceva Ulica 11, Zagreb, Hrvatska (Croatia)

I do not know how I managed it, twisted into a pretzel in the bus seat, but they had to wake me from a sound sleep when we reached the Hrvatskan border. Orvis never woke up at all, completely comfortable in the window seat next to me. Dogs have it made when it comes to sleeping.

So I was the last person off the bus and at the end of the line for passport control. The lines of sleep on my face must have made me look even more Slavic than usual, because as soon as I came to stand behind her, the woman with the penultimate place in line turned and started talking.

I did not know her language. It was probably one of three or four I heard on the bus. Let's just say, for arguments sake, that she was Serbian. She was going on about something. The bus drivers? The rain? The fact that my face was twisted into a puzzle? I tried to interrupt, but it was not possible. So I stood there and looked down at her and smiled.

I have a firm belief that no one is responsible for their body type. Tall, slender, short, wide, dark, light, whatever. You get what you come out of the womb with. It's preprogrammed, and you are not responsible. There is beauty everywhere. However…I also believe that a human should be taller than they are wide. Even just by a little bit. Being wider than you are tall points to a bad diet and a lack of courage to change. Really, it means that you don't give a fuck…

Ok, who am I to say? That was a little harsh. This woman was four-and-a-half feet tall and six feet wide, but heck, I didn't have my glasses on so maybe it was just an optical illusion. Anyhow, she just kept talking until exhausted and short of breath, which is when I said:

"Do you speak English? Just a little bit? I'm an American and we only speak English. It's part of our charm."

She looked at me. She said "No Eeenglishhh." Then she paused, reconsidered, and said "*Poco. Poco poco.*"

Which pretty much answered my question.

Our conversation was saved by the movement of the line. She was up next, and she sure gave it to the customs official. He was still shaking his head when I gave him my passport. Then he smiled while he looked at my passport.

"Where are you from?" he asked.

Which I thought was an odd question, as he was looking at my passport.

"USA," I said. "You have my passport, right? I'm from the United States of America."

He smiled again. Then he said, "Are you sure?"

"I'm pretty positive," I replied. "I'm from Eugene, Oregon, USA. It's on the West Coast. North of California. We call it the Pacific Northwest. Big trees. Lots of rain."

He smiled. "One more time, where?"

"USA," I said.

He smiled and laughed a little. "I just wanted to hear you say it again," he confessed. "It's the accent. I love it. Just like in the movies."

Then he handed me my passport and I got back on the bus.

I twisted myself back into a pretzel and fell asleep thinking I was going to like Hrvatska.

CHAPTER FORTY

Zagreb Cathedral, Ulica Tome Bakaca, Upper Town, Zagreb, Croatia

Orvis loves Zagreb. We are staying in a beautiful room, ensuite, hosted by an amazing woman who I will call Abigail. Her apartment is in the heart of Zagreb, a fourth-floor walkup with marble stairs and imposing tall doors on every landing. She lives on the top floor, which is actually a half-floor under the eaves, and our room is tucked under old wooden beams set at angles to the ceiling. Everything else is modern, a writing desk in one alcove, a queen bed in the other, and a balcony that opens up to a view of the chestnut tree growing in the back yard. Even the weather is good. Sunshine and thunderstorms. Like I said, Orvis loves it.

We landed at the bus station (finally) at 2:30 a.m. on a Wednesday morning, with no idea where or how we were going to get to Abigail's place. She is a saint and had agreed to stay up and wait for us, but I had no idea it would be this late (or early) and I could not warn her because my phone will not work without the internet. Luckily, there is a twenty-four-hour cafe at the bus station. I ordered a mineral water and stole their wi-fi. I was too chicken to actually call her and talk on the phone (as I have no Croatian), so I texted her in English. She was awake and waiting. Saint Abigale. She told me to avoid the taxis at all costs (meaning they would clean me out at this hour). So I called an Uber.

Another fantastic Uber driver, another quiet drive across a dark city. It was after 3 a.m. when we got up to the fourth-floor flat in Central Zagreb. Orvis went straight to sleep. That dog gets more sleep than anything. I read a few more pages of *Murder on the Orient Express*, and passed out just as Hercule Poirot found the knife.

I'm old now and I don't sleep much, so by 7:30 we were up and wandering. The city is still quiet, morning sun hitting the roofs of the buildings in the upper city, a few shopkeepers out hosing down the sidewalks in front of their display windows, cleaning the glass of their storefronts. A short line at the bakery, a pretty good chocolatine, a pretty good Americano latte, a pretty good dog that just wanted to keep walking.

So we strode across the Lower City through Ban Jelacic Square, stopped to throw a coin in the Mandusevac Fountain (hoping no one noticed that it was Bulgarian), and then a narrow side street uphill to the Kaptol and a stone bench in front of golden angels facing the Cathedral of the Assumption of the Blessed Virgin Mary. I finally got to sit and eat my pastry and drink cold coffee. Orvis was fascinated by the activity going on so early in the morning.

Just a slight mini-history of Zagreb to orientate you. Two hills with a creek running down the middle. The taller hill, with a steep backside to the east, is where the Catholic priests built the cathedral (circa 1120) and a monastery, with a big wall around it to keep out the vandals and Visigoths (it didn't work). On the west side of the creek, merchants and craftsmen and a distant King Bela IV of Hungary (circa 1242), who said you can have a tax-free zone if you build your own wall to protect yourselves from vandals and Visigoths (it also didn't work). The church side called Kaptol. The merchants' side called Gradec. All the lowlands surrounding the hills: the lower city. Now imagine a few centuries of fires, earthquakes, floods, droughts, invading Huns, Turks, and Communists. Everything rebuilt many times. The creek paved over, bridges become tunnels under new buildings, the dividing lines get filled with restaurants, coffee shops, and little stores selling refrigerator magnets that say, "I heart Croatia."

Okay, been there, done that. Right?

But this morning they are setting scaffolding to rebuild the top of the cathedral, and both Orvis and I sit there in fascination as we watch them. Tall cranes with extra extensions lifting sections of aluminum bridgework way, way up in the sky, all the way to the top of the towers, and setting them into brackets bolted to the top of the church. It makes my knees shake just looking up and watching men in safety harnesses swinging between the church steeples. And then someone has to climb up there for days on end, cleaning, repointing, and refacing the stonework. Orvis is amazed.

The next thing we know, there is someone standing beside us, equally amazed. His name is Damir Koboevic. I know this because there is a little blue laminate hanging from his neck that I later learn is his city license to be an official guide. On the badge are his name, his photo, and the words "Turisticki vodic."

"Earthquake damage," Damir says to us in heavily accented English. "Constantly to be repaired."

He is a small man with thick glasses and intelligent eyes. He lives with his mom and dad in communist housing (*stanovanje po Titu*), because he lost his job as a structural engineer when the economy collapsed a few years ago. It wasn't a tragedy. He didn't much like sitting in front of a computer doing calculations. So he took night courses in English. Passed the required history tests to become a city guide and bought new walking shoes and a leather shoulder bag, where he keeps brochures in five languages. He would very much like to be our guide. It can be a small donation. Pause. Or even cost-free.

"*Trebam vježbati. Engleski za amerikance.*" (I need to practice my American English.)

"Your English is good," I tell him, "but I don't really want a guide."

Damir looks very disappointed. I feel Orvis step on my foot with his heavy front paw.

The morning sunshine, which has already painted itself onto the front of the Zagreb Cathedral, is just reaching the top of the old fortifications that surround the back and sides of the church. The pointed cones of the wall towers are tipped in weathered red tile, and the sun catches a bit of its glow on the roofline. The walls are very old and slightly crumbling and they need work, which is why the cathedral is closed and a cadre of working men in hi-viz overalls are busy constructing the scaffolding. One of the church spires, which barely survived the 2020 quake, is sitting on the ground to the left of the cathedral. The other spire was completely destroyed.

During Communism, they used very cheap stone to repair the sides of the cathedral, Damir explains. Now we are using good limestone from Italy. Travertine. It is very expensive. Many people contribute.

"I'll tell you what," I say, as I feel Orvis starting to chew on my left shoelace. "Why don't we meet up tomorrow and you can take me on a tour?"

Damir smiles. "Tomorrow I must take care of my parents. They are old communists. Saturday is the day for shopping."

"All day? Maybe in the early evening? I have to leave for Paris on Sunday."

Damir smiles. "Evening tour a little bit more. But for Americans I will make the time."

"Go USA," I say.

He laughs. "Then tomorrow we meet at 1600. Here or at the fountain?"

"The fountain," I reply, "in case I need to find extra money."

He coughs a little and laughs. He thinks I am being funny.

CHAPTER FORTY-ONE

The Museum of Broken Relationships,
2 sv. Cirila I Metoda St., Near St. Mark's Square,
Upper town, Zagreb, Croatia

It is our last day in Zagreb and we have time before we go to meet Damir at the fountain, so I ask Orvis what he wants to do. This is always a mistake.

Before he can answer, I tell him that what we SHOULD do is take the #12 Tram up to Maksimir Park and then walk all the way up the hill to Groblje Mirogoj (Mirogoj Cemetery) and spend the afternoon wandering between the ornate arches and 300,000 gravesites, many of which are dead writers and poets with clever epitaphs.

Like: "No one knows the last words he said/But now the famous writer's dead/Those years he worked were all mis-spent/For now his books are out of print."

For some reason, Orvis thinks that would be a little bit depressing. So he suggests that instead, we ride the funicular to the top of the Gradic embankment and stop in at the Museum of Broken Relationships.

"Great," I say. "That sounds like A LOT of fun."

He is not good at catching my sarcasm. We end up walking across Jelacic Square and then take a right up Tomiceva Street, tripping over the cobblestones, to the foot of the Zagreb Funicular. Which is out of service.

"The Museum of Broken Funiculars," Orvis quips.

So we start walking up the stairs. It's only about six flights, but this leaves us just about at the top when the clock strikes noon. In Zagreb this means they shoot a cannon from the upper gallery of Lotrscak Tower. Yes, every day at noon for the last 146 years or so. That might be an exaggeration. It might only be 145 years. Either way, the cannon is loud with sparks and gunpowder. I mean, the real thing, excluding the cannonball (hopefully). It hits us completely by surprise and I have to catch Orvis by his scruff just as he is about to sail over the handrail and plunge down into a dense thicket of hawthorns and laurel and English ivy (invasive). A small cloud of gun smoke drifts over our heads. I can't really hear him, but mostly read his lips when he says:

"Looks like the cannon is still working."

My hearing is just starting to come back after we reach the viewpoint at the base of the tower. There is a photoshoot going on. A handsome groom and his beautiful bride—he is wearing a tuxedo, she is in a white wedding gown—appear to be buying souvenirs from a kiosk as several photographers surround them, trying to stay out of each other's frame. We give them a wide berth and head up the lane, where it is only a few steps to the doorway that takes us into the Museum of Broken Relationships.

I honestly did not want to spend the seven euros it cost to get into the museum. I guess I don't really believe in Broken Relationships. I tend to see them more as Transformed Relationships. They come and they go and they don't really end, not even if you really want them to. Every relationship is always part of you somehow and somewhere and at some level, however buried and hidden. What are we without our past relationships? Empty vessels of non-memories. But try to explain this to Orvis.

So I paid the entrance fee and we spent a couple of hours wandering through the museum. It consists mostly of stories, some funny, some sad, of unusual ways that people have ended their love affairs. I particularly liked the one where the woman runs over her own cell phone with her car so that she won't be constantly looking for text messages from the guy who left her. The exhibit is the actual phone. That is something I could see myself doing. But I tend to hate cell phones anyway.

Orvis didn't really get it. He liked the one where the guy steals his ex-girlfriend's underwear so he can sniff it beneath his pillow every night. He thinks this is funny and gross, but feels it would probably smell pretty good after a few days. But you know how dogs are; they like to smell each other in that special way. Was this worth seven euros?

I guess so, because Orvis came out of the museum thinking about relationships, and the first thing he asked as we were making our way up the street toward St. Mark's Square was: "What about us?"

"You want to know about our relationship?" I said. "True, unconditional love, as long as you behave yourself."

He stopped in the middle of the street. I knew when he looked at me like this there was no use pulling on his leash. Luckily, there was no traffic.

"Dogs are very much into relationships," Orvis replied. "We love to be loved."

"Doesn't everyone?"

"Humans tend to make it too complicated," Orvis says. "It's all confused with conditions and expectations. Likes and dislikes and who gets what and who wants what and cell phones crushed under the car tire. You'd be better off just enjoying each other. A couple of sniffs should do it. From then on, it's just about true love."

"What you are saying, I think, is that we ought to love one another the way we love our dogs."

"What I'm saying is that you should love one another the way your dog loves you."

Which was something to think about as we wandered farther away from the Museum of Broken Relationships. Sometimes it takes an imaginary dog to let you know you are on the right track. Unconditional love directed first and foremost at yourself. A state of mind where nothing, really, can ever be broken.

At the top of the hill, we came to the cobblestone plaza to the west side of St. Mark's Church and the view of the colorful roof tiles that form the pattern of the city's coat of arms. It's all very picturesque and symbolic, but like so many other old buildings in the city, it was mostly covered by scaffolding. There was a lot of rebuilding going on. But it was Saturday, and no one was working.

So we went down the hill toward the south and east through the Stone Gate, stopped to say a prayer to the painting of Virgin and Child (the miracle of its existence closely secured behind a thick wrought-iron lattice) and turned onto Tkalciceva Street (filled with Zagrebians eating lunch at outdoor cafes, drinking little saucers of coffee next to large tankards of beer). I wanted to buy bread and cheese at the Dolac Farmers Market. I needed to sit and rest and try to prepare myself for the evening tour with Damir.

But first there was a statue of St. Christopher with a lance, on his horse. He stood in a circle of fresh tulips at the base of the Talachcic stairs. I've always loved St. Christopher, the patron saint of safe travels. But my favorite part of his legend is that (like many saints) he was most certainly imaginary.

So I stood with my dog and handed my phone to a nice young woman who made a photograph of the four of us guarding the tulips. It was me, Orvis, St. Chris, and his horse.

And honestly, when I glanced later at the photo, it was quite a bit out of focus. The only thing that looked real was the horse.

It didn't matter to Orvis. He was going to be happy anyway. He happens to love horses.

"Well, you are lucky to be a dog," I told him. "Lucky to be a dog.

CHAPTER FORTY-TWO

Mandusevac Fountain,
Ban Jelacic Square, Zagreb, Croatia

Every story is some kind of legend these days. Since we started making up facts everything is true to someone. I guess that leaves a lot of leeway for a professional storyteller. Which can be fairly entertaining if you don't take things too seriously.

Damir tells me that once there was a thirsty Knight in Arms. He rode upon his horse, coming into the clearing where there was a spring bubbling up from the ground. Though he was very thirsty, he apparently wasn't thirsty enough to get off his horse. So he called to a fair maiden who happened to be wandering by, as fair maidens did back in those days. Her name was Manda, though it is unclear how he knew that. Perhaps all local girls were called Manda back then. She was very beautiful, as by definition, are all fair maidens. Anyhow, he called out in the local dialect of the time: "*Zagrabi Manda*!"

Which, as we all know, means: "Manda, scoop me some water!"

The rest is history. The fountain that now sits over the spring is called: Mandusevac (Manda's Water). The city is called Zagreb (Scoop me Some). But alas, the name of the Knight is forever forgotten. Perhaps he should have gotten off the horse and taken Manda in his arms and, you know, "zagrebbed" her. Poor forgotten Knight. He was killed in battle the next morning. Something in the water gave him the trots and he was caught with his armor down.

Ok, so maybe I've embellished the myth a bit. It happens. There was a huge amount of information imparted to me that evening and I may have mixed some of it up. Damir, in my humble opinion, was speaking too fast.

Perhaps he thought that I was paying him by the word.

I tried to slow him down by interrupting with pertinent questions. Like: "Have you seen my imaginary dog? He was around here somewhere."

To which he answered, without pausing: "Croatia is about the size of the American state of West Virginia."

"There are about four million Croats living in Croatia. And an estimated three million more living outside the country."

To which Orvis then asked: "How many are living in West Virginia?"

I hadn't seen him there, standing beside us next to the French taco shop. I knew that his next question was going to be: "What is a French taco?" So I preempted him and said to Damir:

"By the way, what is a French taco?"

"We now use the euro, but for centuries, the currency of Croatia was called the kuna," He replied. "After the small weasel (marten), whose furs we traded. "

He took a one-euro coin out of his pocket and flipped it over. On the reverse side was carved the head of a marten with rounded ears and a stout Slavic face. The kuna.

"Now we will turn up this hill on Ulitsa Radiceva, which is one of the oldest streets in Zagreb. It will lead us to Muzej Mucenja. The Torture Museum."

And that was the way our evening unfolded. Lots of good questions, a few good answers, a great guide and a good dog. By the time we reached the Gric tunnels hidden under the Bloody Bridge on a side alleyway behind the base of the funicular, I was ready to collapse in a corner and wait for the bombing raid to be over. The tunnels stretched in three directions, connected by four other tunnels used as air-raid shelters and a subterranean shortcut to Strossmayer Promenade, where we walked back uphill past the Lotrscak Tower and finally sat down next to the great Croatian writer Antun Gustav Matos, who was apparently seized up by writer's block one lovely spring afternoon and still sits there wistfully gazing out over the city. I had lots of good questions to ask him, but being cast in bronze, he, like Damir, was short on answers.

But I did find out that from this point, we had another two full hours left in our city tour.

"Well Damir," I said, "I'd love to…but you know, traveling with a dog and everything…I think we better stop for now and get something to eat. Can I buy you a taco?"

"You need to: "Feed the Dog?" he said.

I think he thought this was a cute American expression, something like "Water the tree," or "Bleed the lizard." He pointed to a sign that said: *Javni Zahodi*. Public Toilets.

"Great," I said. "Then let's just get a beer. And some pretzels. The giant ones with mustard."

"I know a very good place for Americans," Damir said. "It has good Croatian beer (Karlovacko) and *kranjska kobasica*, which is really Slovakian, but we too love it here in Zagreb. Also, you can buy Bud Light, but it is expensive."

So with the evening light fading over the Lower Town, we watched our distant reflection in the glass office towers of Vanjska Poslovna, the outer business district. I could see the horseshoe of parks and palaces that encircle the main train station, and far to the east, the last bit of sunlight hitting the top of Maksimir Stadium, where the national team played its football matches. A lovely little city in a lovely little country.

"Then, after a snack," Damir told us, "we have only a few more stops. The Museum of Chocolate, The Museum of Mushrooms, The Cannabis Museum, The Museum of Illusions, The Museum of Hangovers, and then finally the Grand Museum of Imaginary Dogs, which is the approximate size, I looked it up, of the American state of Rhode Island."

He smiled brilliantly at me, and I saw him glance around to see if Orvis was listening. When he was sure that my dog was not anywhere too near, he leaned in toward me and whispered:

"I created that last one with my mind only. Don't tell the dog. I think he might be getting bored. So I want to spice him up."

"Ok," I said. "But I don't think he's ever been to Rhode Island."

Which left a very quizzical expression on Damir's face.

True confessions here: We never made it to the end of the tour. I bought a couple of rounds of beer and then happily passed out in a red leather booth in the back corner of Papa's American Bar, underneath a red, white, and blue caricature of Elvis Presley and Tom Cruise flying a two-seater F-16 Falcon. Finally, Damir loaded me into an Uber. I paid him twice the going rate and he told me for sure next time he would take me on the FULL tour; just call him anytime I was in Zagreb.

“Sure thing,” I said. “Are you certain you don’t want to come with us to France?”

“I would,” he said. “But I’ve heard it is twice the size of Colorado.”

Which left us both with something quite unnerving to think about.

CHAPTER FORTY-THREE

Chantilly de Patou, Paris, France

Personally I could have skipped Paris altogether. The beautiful little boutique hotels we used to stay in down near St. Michel are now 350 euros per night. You need a reservation eight months in advance. And you still have to turn sideways to fit into the hallway bathroom. When I first came to this city, we slept in the all-night telegraph office (PTT), on a bench in the Tuileries, and under the bridges with the bums (*les coucheures des dirt*). And we still quickly ran out of money. Fifty years later, I'm quite well off. Which in Paris terms, means I get to sleep in a plywood box.

I don't mean this in a metaphoric way. Our first night in Paris, we literally slept in a six-by-six-by-seven-foot plywood box on the fifth floor of the Joe 'n Joe Hotel at 93 Avenue Paul-Vailliant-Couturier, Gentilly, Paris. It cost only ninety euros. Well, let me correct that: It wasn't actually IN Paris.

To understand this, you would have to know a little bit of the layout of the City of Light. Think of it like this: With a stick, you draw a circle in the sand, a little bulgy on the top, a little flat on the bottom. Through the circle, from the bottom right, draw a curving line that is a bit off-centered to the left, dividing the circle by about one third and exiting left bottom. The line of the circle represents two congested, four-lane superhighways called Le Peripherique. The line through the circle is a river: La Seine.

It's nothing official, but if you live within the circle, Parisians consider you living in Paris. If you live outside the circle, you live in France. The river flows from east to west. On the north side of the river, you are on the Rive Droite. If you are south of the river, you are Rive Gauche (Left Bank). There are a couple of islands in the middle of the river (Île de la Cité, Ile Saint-Louis) one of which has a pretty nice church currently being rebuilt after a fire (Notre Dame). There are many, many bridges (Pont Neuf, Pont au Change, Pont Marie, Pont de la Tournelle, and maybe forty more). The river flow is contained by concrete and stone embankments. Generally there is a pedestrian walk down next to the river and one up on the embankments. In central Paris, there are wooden booths along the upper path that open up into little shops that sell books and artwork and various little trinkets like miniature Eiffel Towers.

The real thing, the Eiffel Tower (La Tour Eiffel), is a very, very tall steel structure with four legs that sits on the south bank where the river makes a big curve to the south. It is pretty famous. There is a big security fence/wall surrounding it. Crowds of tourists pay twelve euros to get past the security fence and then another twenty euros to climb the tower and another million euros to take an elevator to the top. That is all a bit exaggerated. You can also have dinner at Le Jules Verne restaurant. He was a famous French sci-fi writer. You can have lunch at his restaurant for only five million euros, but you need to make a reservation forty years in advance. It's great if you are adept at time travel.

So you get the idea. There are also some famous streets like Rue de Champ de Mars, Rue Bonaparte, and the ultra-famous Champs-Élysées, a big boulevard running downhill from the Arc de Triomphe, where you will find the very famous American restaurant, "Five Guys." You can get a double burger with cheese there for only fifteen euros. But the lines are astronomic to get in. Like from here to Pluto.

Well, to get back to our plywood box.

Really, it was just a plywood box. They had divided the hotel rooms up into tiny cubicles stacked on each other. It was raw plywood with a plastic-covered mattress on a plywood platform and one coat hook on the back of the door. Modern conveniences included a place to plug in your phone charger and LED lights along the ceiling. No windows, but a slot in the wall that looked out on the plywood hallway and a tiny plywood sliding door so you could say hello to your neighbors three feet away. Even Orvis thought it was a bit claustrophobic. And that wasn't just in his imaginary imagination. To top it off, it wasn't even IN Paris. Quite a bit outside Le Periph. But you could get a train into town.

So you see, there were good reasons why I would normally avoid Paris.

Of course, with Orvis tagging along there was no way we were skipping Paris. It's like he had dreamed about it his whole life. Perfectly coiffured poodles on every corner. Young women in stockings and short skirts riding black bicycles while wearing high heels and holding an umbrella. Surly waiters in white aprons on break behind the Cafe L'Opera, smoking cigarettes and complaining about the government. The City of Lights twinkling in the April rain. Cue the accordion music.

Ok, so I'm a little jaded about Paris. It has become such a tourist mecca, it is now hard to visit without running into the crowds of bucket-listers. But even with that said and acknowledged, it still has its charms.

We left our bags at the plywood box and managed to negotiate the subway through malfunctioning ticket machines to someplace downtown, possibly Les Invalides. We walked along the river, grey threatening skies overhead, no sign of protestors or strikers or any other of the bad things we had heard about on the evening news. Hunger and loneliness finally got the better of us, and we climbed from the river and into the city near Ile Saint-Louis. In the near distance we could see the Cathédrale Notre-Dame, very impressive with its roof taken off and a totally world-class set of scaffolding surrounding the east side.

"Wow," Orvis said, "Get a look at THAT. Let's go see the scaffolding."

It truly is one of our favorite parts of any European city. So we skirted along Saint-Louis and took the Pont Neuf over to Île de la Cité, and there in a narrow alleyway we heard our first Parisian music.

Just a couple of blocks from where they were rebuilding the cathedral, a man sat in a doorway with his cat on his shoulder. He nodded to us and the cat looked closely at Orvis, and then everyone relaxed.

Honestly, he looked just about as poor as we are and yes, quite as rich too. A gray beard, a tattered beret, a metal chair with a well-worn cushion. He seemed like a man, just like ourselves, who had slept under bridges, was satisfied with a loaf of good bread and a hunk of good cheese, and would laugh when we told him about our plywood box for ninety euros. There were just a few other people wandering through this narrow street, and I think he was there more for the acoustics than the tourist trade.

He started playing. At first it sounded like that old standard Bal-musette or "La Vie en Rose," but then it morphed and morphed again and no doubt he was improvising, making it up as he went along and looking over at us enjoying the French tableaux from where we were standing across the narrow street. It was pure pleasure for everyone listening, including, apparently, the cat, who settled, still as a statue, on his shoulder.

I wish you could have heard him play. The music went right into the essence of everything good in the world. Mournful and melancholy, with highlights of happiness, grace, and that *je ne sais quoi* that defines and describes the lovely tragedy of being French.

I stood and I listened. Orvis smiled up at me with his "I told you so" look and I felt myself falling in love all over again, despite the plywood box and the crowds of tourists.

With Paris.

CHAPTER FORTY-FOUR

Cafe Les Deux Magots,
Place Saint Germain de Pres, Paris, France

Orvis is insistent that he wants to go to the park where Hemingway ate the pigeons.

"I don't know what you are talking about," I say. "And in that instance, neither did he."

"It's in his *memorie*," Orvis says, "*Prove-able Feats*. I saw a YouTube video."

There is no educating the young these days.

"It's called a memoir. Hemingway's book was *A Moveable Feast*. It was 80 percent bullshit, by the way."

"No, no, you're just another jealous writer. It's a great book, especially when he has the baby named Bumby in the carriage and they are poor and hungry, so he takes him for a walk in the Luxembourg park where they strangle pigeons and eat them for lunch. How cool is THAT! Lots of pigeons. Free lunch every day."

"Such a bunch of lies." I tell Orvis. "Hemingway was never that poor. His wife had a trust fund and he was getting paid for being a journalist for newspapers back in the States. 1924. Paris was very cheap back then. Twenty-one francs to the dollar. A loaf of bread cost less than two francs. Hemingway had a very active imagination when it came to creating his own myth."

"Well at least you two have THAT in common."

He is saying this because we are sitting in the Cafe Les Deux Magots and I am staring at the menu, trying to decide if I want to spend thirty euros on the "Petit Dejeuner Hemingway." They say it is a full-on breakfast, but this is Paris and the last people to trust are the waiters. It's like trusting a taxi driver.

There is a tradeoff going on here in my mind. It is early morning, and a steady cold drizzle is shining the streets. I left the umbrella I bought in Istanbul on a train or a bus, or somewhere I can't even remember. I left my suitcase in the foyer of the apartment at Neuilly-sur-Seine, because we can't check into our tiny room until 3 p.m. So there is time to kill, and I do have my travel notebook and a new pencil, but if I sit here taking notes and only order chai latte while the place fills up with tourists until there is a line out the door...well, you can imagine the heart-stopping looks I am going to get from the garçon and the maître d'. My heart's not that strong to begin with.

I have to eat, anyway. But thirty euros?

Of course, there is an intense irony at work here. The whole reason that Les Deux Magots (and across the Rue St. Benoit, Le Café de Flore) is so amazingly crowded with tourists is that exactly 100 years ago, men and women like me sat there and tried to sketch or write stories, or just drink themselves to death while they created modern art and literature. Without the fame and fortune of all those artists and writers (you know the list: Picasso, Fitzgerald, Stein, de Beauvoir, Sartre, Camus, Dos Passos...) the cafes would probably no longer exist. They would now be storefronts, like the leather goods place on the other side of the street selling Louis Vuitton handbags for 2,000 euros.

I still don't quite understand how people like my waiter (who becomes very nice to me once I order the expensive breakfast) or the busboy, or even the maître d' and the manager (a small man with a pencil-thin mustache and a white-red-and-blue lapel pin), can afford to live in Paris. Perhaps they live somewhere out in suburbia. Perhaps that is why they look so discouraged when the red and yellow Big Bus Paris drops off thirty Asian tourists at the corner. I can't blame them. Asian tourists don't normally leave any tip at all. In my notebook I write, "Paris: city of beauty, wealth, and the romance of poverty."

It is not long before we give up our spot and are back out in the rain. From the street, I look back through the window to see the waiter clearing my table. He looks up with my tip in his hand and sees me on the street and gives me a little nod with the ten-euro note slipped between his fingers. It's not exactly a thank you. Just more of an acknowledgment that he's worth it.

I don't have any great desire to walk over to Jardin du Luxembourg, with its manicured English Garden and its ornate French Garden and the classic Senate building and the statues and the fountains and etc. etc. It's looking like the rain is going to back off—a stack of grey clouds are still piled up on one another in the sky to the west, but the overcast seems to be breaking into puffs of cumulous and it looks like most of the rain has drained out of the sky. I steer Orvis over towards the river by telling him that I'm going to show him where all the famous backpackers in the early 1970s slept under Pont des Arts.

"It was very chic," I say. "You could wake up in the morning and piss in the river while you had a pretty good view of the Rosette Window in Notre Dame Cathedral. We even pitched a tent. It was great until the gendarmes made their rounds and rousted us."

As I am saying this, we are walking north on Rue Bonaparte, and as we come to the intersection with Quai Voltaire, we hear the familiar sound of a police car, with its blue lights flashing as it comes towards us around the Champion curve on Rue de Seine. EEEEEEE-YOU EEEEEE-YOU EEEEE-YOU…There is nothing like the distinct sound of an emergency siren in Paris. They must get all the police cars together each week and tune the sirens so that they are at just the right pitch to get your attention but not irritate too much. This is probably because they use them all the time. Even for small emergencies like the Chief Flic has run out of cigarettes and the traffic is bad between here and the corner Tobac. Flash the lights, turn on the siren. EEEEE-YOU EEEEE-YOU EEEEE-YOU.

Yes, there is something about life in Paris. Even the police sirens have a certain elegance.

Along the river boulevards there is now a designated bike path, and the Parisians have embraced it in the usual Parisian way. Driving through the core of the city will be banned this year, and the electric bike has become the go-to vehicle. With the guidance of its progressive mayor (Anne Hildago), 900 miles of new bike lanes have been created. So if you want to commute and you don't want to break into a sweat: *Voila*! *Velo electrique*! These are beautiful little pieces of design and technology produced by the best French bike-makers, and they are superb. Moustache, Lapierre, Gitane, Peugeot, EVEO, they all have made the transition and their bicycles are works of art. As we are walking past the Académie des Beau Arts, going to cross the Quai Malaquais to the river, we watch the morning commuters pedal along the bike lane. Is it possible to look chic and elegant in high-viz? An early walk along the Seine and you will see that it is more than possible: It is a new fashion category.

We walk by a woman sitting astride a white Lapierre. It's a step-through with the battery concealed in the side tube and the motor on the crank, with the entire underside sealed in a graceful curve of machined aluminum. The woman is wearing a mid-length gray skirt, black stockings, leather low-cut boots. Over a grey cashmere sweater she has a tasteful vest of high-visibility orange nylon; etched into the fabric is a crosshatch of reflective glitter. She is also wearing a Bouclier bike helmet, about the same matte grey as her skirt, and she has the visor pushed up so we can see the expression on her face. Focused, determined, oblivious to her own *elegance naturelle*.

Over by the river, we climb down to the lower pathway and walk upstream toward Notre Dame. I am amazed that when we reach Pont Saint-Michel: there are actually some tents pitched under the bridge. Modern, ripstop nylon, colorful tents, five or six of them. Out of the rain.

They look at least as comfortable as our plywood box.

I am tempted to go over and see if anyone is actually sleeping there. I want to ask them how much it costs. Could this be the affordable way to see Paris?

I mean, it can't cost more than, say, fifty euros a night…

CHAPTER FORTY-FIVE

Toilettes Publiques, La Tour Eiffel,
Arrondissment 7, Paris, France

Our next adventure takes a little explaining.

It goes back to Bulgaria, a little variety shop on Vitosha Boulevard in Sofia, my last day in the city. Part of my ethos of traveling is to find a trinket or small piece of apparel from the places I visit that will somehow evoke my experience of the place. Many times it is not the item that inspires me to make the purchase, but the person or place from which it comes. Out of thousands of pashmina scarves in Istanbul, I bought one because it came from a tiny obscure shop on a dark forgotten alleyway that was owned by a young woman. She was so happy I walked into her store. I figure that happiness rubs off on the scarf and will go directly into the heart of my friend in Eugene when I give it to her.

In Sofia, I had found nothing to inspire me in this way. The tourist shops were filled with rose-water products, t-shirts that said "I (heart) Bulgaria" in English, and wooden eggs that nested into one another with the faces of peasant girls painted on them. On that last night, I was walking home and on impulse decided to duck into one last store. There was nothing to buy, but this was where I met Daniel Ayodele.

Ayodele is from Nigeria. He was in the shop with his wife, who was buying souvenirs. Like me, they had traveled from Istanbul. Unlike me, he was very tall and very handsome, and he had a big bright smile that lit up the room. He was dressed very well. In fact, all of the Africans that I met on this journey were dressed to the nines. With Ayodele this meant tasseled black loafers with black linen pants, a gleaming white shirt (recently ironed and starched by the cleaners), and a well-fitting, dyed-in-the-wool, three-quarter morning suit jacket the color of charcoal chalk. When he shot the cuffs, you could see his cufflinks with little ebony stones set into the silver. When he shook my hand and introduced himself, he smiled and nodded with a set of perfect teeth unstained by any tobacco products.

Of course, Ayodele spoke perfect English, and like a dummy I remarked on this. He said:

"Yes, yes. When the colonialists came to Nigeria, they took everything from us (smile)...but left us with good English. Now we are using their language to try to get some of it back."

Sometimes when traveling, if you keep your mind open, you can become fast friends in a few moments, and that was how it went for Daniel and me. We stood in the warmth of the trinket shop (it was cold and blowing as night fell on the streets of Sofia) and smiled at one another while his wife bought souvenirs. He was very happy to meet an American, and I told him I was fascinated with Africa and wanted to someday visit Nigeria. This is when he handed me his card and said to please contact him if ever I would like to have a guide to his country.

"Where do you go from here?" he said.

"First to Zagreb and then on to Paris."

"Ah Paris…" Daniel shook his head. "So many tourists. But if you turn up at the Eiffel Tower, you must meet my brother Patrice. He can be your guide. I will tell him you are coming."

Of course you know, right? That he said this last sentence in perfect French. A Parisian accent. And of course, it follows that I understood it very imperfectly. He had to say it twice and then repeat it in English.

"For sure," I said. "I will make it my mission to look for Patrice."

Then he gave me his card and we said our goodbyes, and honestly, I don't know if I will ever see him again.

But on my third day in Paris, I wrote to his email (Daniel Ayodele) and almost immediately got a message back that Patrice would meet me at a cafe (La Fontaine de Mars) at 1400 the next day.

Which would be my last day in Paris.

So that is the background that brings us to the afternoon that I met Patrice Agweugbo on the Champ de Mars with the Tour Eiffel rising against a sky of scattered showers, as reflected in the vast mirrored windows of the Grand Palais Ephemere. I could not believe that he was the actual brother of Ayodele, because he was short and rotund and his teeth were stained yellow and I think he had too many *pain au chocolat*, and much too much steak frites, and possibly an aperitif before lunch. He was dressed in wrinkled pants and red converse sneakers, but over it he wore a lavender-and-peach sport coat of some shiny synthetic fabric that caught the light and twisted it in so many ways that you could not look closely at him for too long a time without getting dizzy. He was very young, possibly twenty, with his hair cut young, you know the style, with a tight, curled afro on top and then the sides shaved to the skull with sort of a lightning bolt etched into the back, above the nape of his neck. He shook my hand, and his grip was disconcertingly limp. I'm afraid I might have broken something with my gregarious American handshake.

We did not go into La Fontaine because it was packed with tourists, and so I bought him a cappuccino and a baguette at Gustav's Patisserie and we wandered through the greenery, headed more or less toward the Trocadero across the river. We talked about life in Paris while the coffee quickly worked its way through my sixty-eight-year-old digestive system.

Paris, he said, was spectacularly expensive for anyone from Africa. But it was also a city of unlimited opportunities. Easy to make money here. Almost as easy as spending it.

Honestly, I was only half listening to him, because the espresso was working its way through me rather quickly. I needed to find a bathroom.

If you have been to Paris, you will certainly recognize this next description.

In the city proper there are, scattered at certain locations, (you can find an app or guidebook that tells you where) little square structures that the French call *Sanisettes*. They are automated toilets, which means they clean themselves after every use. When there is a green light on the control panel, you push a button and a door slides open. It reveals a commode and a little sink. You step inside and the door automatically slides shut. You take care of business and then you push a button on the inside, and if the toilet thinks you have completed your toilette successfully, it will slide open and let you out. Then it slides shut again, and on the inside you can hear it cleaning itself. (I don't know what goes on in there, but there is a pause of a few minutes before the green light goes on and the next person can open the door and use the bathroom.) Depending on what you do on the inside, the whole process takes anywhere from two to five, or even ten, minutes to cycle through.

It is very efficient. And very French. And very, very slow...

In places where there is a concentration of tourist traffic, like the Tour Eiffel and the Champ du Mars...there are far, far too few *Sanisettes* and far too many folks who just had an espresso at the cafe and forgot to use the bathroom. Picture long lines of people dancing the "I-gotta-go" jig or standing very, very still while they clench their lower digestive tract.

I tell Patrice that in preparation of my personal need to void my bowels, we better get in line NOW.

So there we are: two new friends standing in the *Sanisette* line, chatting away about the prospects of making money in Paris, talking about his desire to live in San Francisco, talking about America, Land of the Free and the Brave, and the old men like me who have trouble holding their bladders. Yes, picture this: the Eiffel Tower rising in the background, Patrice and I standing in the toilette line, the line moving extremely slowly as the automated cleaning system meticulously does its job, one person after another, some couples going in together and REALLY taking their time. I'm severely concentrating on holding on to my self-respect (no poop in the travel pants please), and Patrice is chatting away about being an entrepreneur in a world of opportunity...

IT TAKES FOREVER to get to the front of the line.

When we are finally there, Patrice is standing ahead of me. I am about to ask politely if I can go in first, and he says:

"For you, my new American friend, I will demonstrate that Paris is a city of opportunity. I will show you how to make instant cash…perfectly legal instant cash in euros…"

Before I can say anything, he turns and faces the crowd of people who are now behind us in the line for the toilet. He raises his hand and waves it back and forth. Then he shouts:

"*Attention!…ATTENTION. Mes braves gens. Qui a besoin d'utiliser les toilettes? Tout le monde? Oui! Je suis en première ligne et je vendrai ma place pour dix euros….*"

Immediately, from the back of the line a woman steps out and raises her hand and rushes forward to where we are standing. She hands Patrice a ten-euro note. The green light comes on at the door to the toilet, she pushes it, steps inside, and disappears as the door slides shut.

I am left there, speechless, as Patrice pockets the money and steps out of line.

Say what you will, but that was a pretty clever move to make some fast cash. In my very limited experience (I have only ever met a few dozen West Africans), they are a very brave and creative bunch of humans. I stood there trying to hold my bowels and shaking my head as he did this. People in line behind me were laughing. Eventually, the woman came out of the toilet, looking very relieved, and I waited patiently as the *Sanisette* cleaned itself. I would have gladly paid ten euros to not be in my current state of distress. Luckily, I got in there just in time.

We spent about another hour together, talking mostly about how hard it is to come to America, and then Patrice had to leave. He had to go to work. He washed dishes in a Moroccan restaurant somewhere in the Marais. We shook hands and his grip seemed a lot tighter this time. We said that we would meet again, but that was very doubtful.

I think we both knew this, but as he left, I smiled at him and nodded my respect.

"Next time," I said, "you are buying the coffee."

CHAPTER FORTY-SIX

Aboard the Eurostar, Gare du Nord to St. Pancras International Station (Paris to London under the English Channel)

L'Orvis can hardly contain himself as we come through the connecting tunnels of the metro station and arrive at Gare du Nord to catch the Eurostar.

Orvis loves trains, and subway cars, and bicycle taxis, and I think he would even like a horse-drawn carriage if we ever make it to Central Park. Orvis loves to look out the window at the landscape. He loves to see himself moving.

I tell him that the Eurostar is not going to be that exciting, because it is only a couple of hours and about thirty minutes of that is in a dark tunnel underwater. He doesn't exactly catch the significance of The Chunnel. Or how you used to have to take a boat to get from France to England. Boats make him seasick. Trains make him peacefully go to sleep.

Which is very fortunate for me. I deposit him in the luggage rack above seat number 67A, coach 1954, on the 10:35 train to St. Pancras International, London, England. Seated, incidentally, next to a very attractive woman from near Goteborg, Sweden, currently living with her husband in Lausanne and even more currently about to become Our Swiss Friend.

The last twelve hours had been very trying and had effectively made me lose some of my faith in our fellow human beings. I might tell that full story sometime, but it involved pickpockets from Madagascar, a demand for all the money in my pockets, and a bevy of six young men who stood too close when they surrounded me.

They were standing so close that they heard, very distinctly, L'Orvis as he growled a very incisive warning. The man who was holding my wrist and telling me he was going to "take me to Afrika" said:

"*C'etait quoi ce bordel*?" (What the fuck was that?)

The other men looked around. We were on the steps coming down from Sacre-Coeur up on Montmartre, and the evening was falling into a gray darkness. We were surrounded by tourists and there was plenty of noise, but they definitely heard L'Orvis when he growled the second time and let out a short, threatening bark.

"It is my ghostdog," I said slowly and distinctly in English. "He thinks you are standing too close."

The six of them looked around and surveyed the ground, but they could not see L'Orvis.

"Generally he doesn't bite," I said. "But honestly, we've never really been in this situation before, so I'm not actually sure what he will do. I should warn you: His teeth are very sharp."

Right on cue, L'Orvis growled again. The Madagascans, looking like they heard a *musongo* (they can be a very superstitious folk), stepped back. I walked away, down the stairs, gingerly checking my pockets to see if I still had my wallet and the wad of euros inside my coat. It was all fine. The young men were already seeking out easier victims. I felt L'Orvis walking beside me.

“Good job,” I said. “You can be a real dog, sometimes.”

“I wonder what Madagascans taste like?” he replied.

Of course he was joking, that’s just the kind of imaginary dog he is, but it sure was handy to have him around. It was the only time on the trip so far that I’d felt the least bit threatened. And it was from a group of East Africans. This did not make me feel so good.

So we walked back to our little room in Neuilly-sur-Seine and I tried to get some sleep, and then in the morning we boarded the Eurostar. After one look at the passenger sitting next to me, I knew that our luck had changed.

It will embarrass her if she reads this, but Our Swiss Friend dazzled me from the start. She had Icelandic blue eyes, blond hair pulled straight back, a perfect face of youthful wrinkles, an intelligent forehead, and a quiet voice that spoke in at least four languages. How I found the courage to talk to her, I will not know in this lifetime or the next. Why she decided to talk so openly with me, well…like I said…we were just lucky.

(Later in our train ride together, I told her L’Orvis was sleeping in the overhead. The thing I really liked about Our Swiss Friend was that she believed me.)

Much has been written about the idea of intimacy between strangers. But until you have the experience, it seems like nothing more than some fantasy in a romance novel. You can keep your mind out of the gutter—I am not talking about physical intimacy, like having sex in the WC or making out in the darkness of the Chunnel (I’m sure all of that has happened, but none of it to me). I am speaking here of true emotional and psychological intimacy, of how you can find yourself telling a stranger things that you would have trouble sharing with your closest, longest, friends.

The creation of an almost instant rapport, a trust, a joy, a friendly and interesting conversation that passes through hours of time as though it were mere passing moments of a very happy, but too short, lifetime.

This was how we met, Our Swiss Friend and I. We found ourselves smiling until it hurt.

Obviously, I'm not going to say what we talked about. The subject matter didn't mean that much but was embraced by the way we said it, how we learned about each other and the empathy we shared for each other's situation. Even now when I write about it, there seems a most plausible explanation: I am making this all up.

However, I'm not that good of a conjurer.

L'Orvis slept through almost the entire train ride from Paris to London. Of course Our Swiss Friend wanted to meet him, so I had to wake him up shortly after we came out of the Chunnel and were speeding through the countryside of Southeast England. When I introduced him, I was very amused that he was struck speechless. Our Swiss Friend gave him a little scratching behind the ears and petted the top of his head. L'Orvis seemed rather stunned, actually.

We said our goodbyes on the platform at St. Pancras International. She was going to meet an old university friend and I had my own rendezvous to attend at King's Cross Station. We had traded contact information and promised to stay in touch, and I knew how unlikely that really was, but still, I could not help but smile. I gave her a big awkward American hug and felt the smoothness of her slim architecture under her coat. She put her bag down for a second and leaned in and kissed me twice, one kiss on each cheek, and I caught the very most intimate scent of her fragrance.

Then we were off to our separate lives.

While we were walking across Euston Road toward the main entrance to King's Cross, L'Orvis looked up at me and shook his head, as though he were having trouble understanding.

"Who was that woman?" he said.

"She is Our Swiss Friend," I told him. "We happened to sit together on the train. That's all."

"That's all?" he said. "She is the most beautiful human on the planet, don't you think? That can't be all..."

Whereas I found myself smiling broadly again.

We walked over to King's Cross, and I took a couple of photos of the British logos fluttering in flags all around the lobby. Big advertisements for the coronation of King Charles III, which would happen next Saturday. I received a text message and then I turned around and there was the love of my life walking right toward us.

L'Orvis was stunned. He didn't know she would be meeting us. I had wanted to surprise him.

Our British Friend walked right up to us, her handy red backpack rolling behind her. We dropped our bags and gave each other such a hug I thought it would never end. She kissed me straight on the lips, bent down and picked up L'Orvis, and hugged him too.

Such a bright and wonderful smile.

"Welcome to England," she said.

CHAPTER FORTY-SEVEN

I understand what your first question will be, and I will tell you from the start that I have no answer.

You will ask me: How did an unassuming, nearly homeless young pup from Fossil, Oregon, who took his name (Orvis) from a tattered catalogue of fly-fishing gear that was left next to the seat of the outhouse behind a thrift store on East 3rd Street, become the sophisticated, fully grown dog-about-town who entered the Old City, London, with the name L'Orvis (pronounced Looorrrveeeese) after a short stint of chasing French poodles in the City of Light, Paris, France?

And what will I say? I don't know. It just happened.

Honestly, there is no predicting the future moves of an imaginary dog.

You might say that I am a bad pet parent. I let my dog be free to change his name? What will I allow next? A change of sex? Maybe even a change of species? Where will it end…?

All very good and completely unanswerable questions.

But let's take this ONE thing at a time. Orvis now wants to be called L'Orvis. What harm can it do?

It is not like he is changing all that much. I certainly feel the pain of parents who are, in the modern world, forced to accept the morphing of their children. From Jane to Jim, Heloise to Hank, Fred to Felicia. It's got to be difficult and confusing in this gender-shifting new paradigm. But it's not like their child is becoming, say…a pony. I mean it's not THAT bad (yet). I think to myself: What if L'Orvis went off the deep end and decided to become, for instance, an imaginary dolphin? He certainly is smart enough. What would I do then? It is hard for me to imagine traveling the world with an imaginary dolphin. Just the thought of it makes me seasick.

So I decide to accept this small change without much comment. I will call him L'Orvis if that's what he wants. Though I have to point out to him that people are going to probably mispronounce it and call him LORvis.

"It's L'Orvis," he says. "Lorveeeeesssse."

A losing battle, I think. But whatever.

To her credit, Our British Friend, who is also semi-fluent in French, takes the change in good faith. She actually loves his new name. The old name kind of confused her. Was he a member of the famous fly-fishing family in Vermont? Did he sell high-end hip boots?

"Negative, *ma soeur*," I told her.

Our British Friend only smiled. She took us from King's Cross Station on a short train ride to Chislehurst, where we had the great fortune to be roomed and boarded by her very wealthy relatives who have a beautiful house on White-mouse Lane. Our stay was further augmented by the fact that her relatives (a beautiful older sister and her surgeon husband) were on vacation to Bali for ten days. We had the house to ourselves. Wow! What a score. For once, L'Orvis had his own room. And I had a little privacy.

My original plan was to stay in London for a few days to observe and write about King Charles III and the festivities surrounding his coronation. I knew that the crowds would be daunting, but I did not calculate that they would also be British to the core. I suppose I thought that as soon as I crossed the English Channel I would be in a country where they spoke my language. Known worldwide as the "English" language. Well, what I was really hoping for was something a lot closer to American English. A language I could mostly understand. No going, luv. We're prickin' the King's English here, mate. Fuck off and die if you won't be grokkin' it. That's the God's Own Truth.

What's so hard about peace, love and understanding......?

We rode a double-decker bus with no driver on the top and a driver on the bottom who told me where we were going, but it made absolutely no sense because I couldn't understand a word he said. But the view was outstanding and we ended up on Portobello Road...or was it Brick Lane...or St. James Park...or Trafalgar Square...Piccadilly Circus...Paddington Station...Kings Road....Giles Meade... Butcher Gale Grove....perhaps Pentridge Street on the way to Calypso Gardens...

Ok, I had no idea where we were going or where we went. It was all over the place. I bought a docker's hat from a woman on the street at Brick Lane and a shirt that says, "Stumper Fielding Bicycles, Portobello Road, London." I did not buy any British Flags, though I was handed several free ones when I agreed to subscribe to the Times of London. I had them send it to: The Peace and Love Institute, 1212 Abbey Road, Fisthanded, London, UK. It was as good an address as any.

We were luxuriously wined and dined by Our British Friend. Home-cooked meals in the Whitemouse Lane house. A short walk to the Cock n' Bull Pub for a pint and a sing in the early evenings. We took in a play on the West End (something called "To Kill a Mockingbird," though I didn't quite get where the bird came in. It was more about Southern incest and blaming everything on the black guy. Typical American theme.), and trod through excellent art museums, with a particularly amazing curation at The Tate surrounding the historic transitions from expressionism to impressionism to dadaism, right on up to pre-post modernism. Pretty much covered all the isms. Made Picasso look like he was standing on the shoulders of giants when he wasn't getting laid by his nude models. Fascinating stuff. Really. Quite.

About four days of this and we were all rather exhausted. I had planned to stay until the coronation one week hence, but it was just too much fun. We collectively decided to train back on up to County Norfolk, where Our British Friend was born and raised and where her Mum still had acreage and a house built from car-stone: The Old Rectory. A haven for weary travelers who don't mind pulling weeds in the garden. Just a short skip, hop, and jump from the King's Estate at Sandringham. Perhaps we would watch the coronation from his backyard. I mean, if he couldn't be there to enjoy it, there was no reason for us to waste the lovely spring sunshine falling gracefully through the leaves of giant plane trees in his Deer Park. Or was it Pheasant? I don't know, they certainly shot something there in them olden days of yore. It's right out the backyard from Mum's house. No crowds to speak of.

It was not difficult to tear L'Orvis away from the streets of London. He was expecting something much more gritty and Dickensian. Poor lads picking pockets at Tower Bridge. Witches whirling curses from the smelly banks of the Thames. But it was all so very gentrified. A clean, modern city where no one can afford to live.

But still, they do live there and they speak a foreign language. You can get around on The Tube. Buy Portuguese pastries from the sausage carts outside Old Scotland Yard. There is the London Eye and The Shard and The Gherkin. The Tower of London. The clock called Big Ben. The museum called Albert and Victoria. The Royal Geographical Society. The British Museum and the British Library.

All built of stone and glass and bricks made in Brickton.

Honestly, L'Orvis and I, and especially Our British Friend, were all very glad to be aboard the train heading north. It took us first through the backside of inner London, crumbling brick townhouses backed up to the tracks, row houses fronting on the stalled traffic on the A5203, right along to Finsbury Park and the Emirates Stadium, which is as close as I came to seeing an Arsenal football match. Yes, that's my team, for better or worse, worse since Thierry Henry left, but getting better with Sako, Odegaard, Martinelli, Jesus, and Xhaka all scoring in double digits this year. Yes, they got their asses kicked by Manchester City (but who didn't), and they came in second place (well done, lads), but they are still all champions to me.

And then the train burst into the countryside. Rolling green hills and meadows sparkling in the lushness of English Springtime. What a compact and vast country it is. People everywhere, but still lots of greenery and stone villages. I fell asleep near Cambridge and woke at Kings Lynn. Mum's caregiver was there to meet us, and Our British Friend took us home.

Finally, I felt blessed to be in England. Even if my imaginary dog now had a French name.

In a few days there would officially be a New King. Master of Organic Farms and not afraid to save the world from Climate Change. There was still hope.

Even L'Orvis could feel it.

"Let's see what's out there," I told him.

CHAPTER FORTY-EIGHT

The Old Rectory, West Newton,
Sandringham Estate, Norfolk County, England

When we finally reach The Old Rectory, Mrs. M is in the garden sitting room watching the telly from her easy chair, with a beautiful bucolic view out the double glass doors into the backyard, where the muntjacs are eating their way through her English garden. Monty Don is on the telly and he is explaining how to grow an ornamental flower patch that is "pest resistant."

Mrs. M, who is currently ninety-four but leaning heavily toward ninety-five, has the slight weakness of muttering to herself, but her opinions are as strong and vivid as any thirty-year-old and she has sixty years experience and more to back them up. She has lived at the Old Rectory for sixty-four years at the time of this writing. Which is pretty good for someone who is still an American citizen.

"I wish he would tell us how to get rid of the deer and the damn rabbits," she says. "I think those nasty muntjacs have made themselves a nest over in the west corner under the lilac trees. I'd shoot them myself if I had a gun."

(She actually does have a gun, but her children are reluctant to tell her its location.)

"Of course, at my age," she continues, "I'd probably miss

and kill the Estate agent. Which wouldn't be an entirely bad thing, I guess..."

Mrs. M has been at a slow war with the Estate Agent (the King's land representative) for at least twenty-five of her years here. She is one of the last private owners of any of the properties that are encompassed by the 22,000-acre estate of Sandringham House, bought by the Windsors in 1856 and owned forever by Queen Elizabeth II (recently deceased, just a couple years older than Mrs. M). It was inherited by King Charles III, who in the next few days will fly over in his helicopter on his way home from the coronation. Sandringham Estate wants her property (three acres and the Old Rectory, a carstone structure first built in about 1646), and has the first rights to buy it upon her death. Unless, of course, someone in her family wants to inherit the place, in which case they would have to pay an enormous inheritance tax. Even though it needs a lot of work, The Old Rectory is worth millions of pounds. It's part of the price of being the Queen/King's neighbor.

L'Orvis, of course, loves the Old Rectory, and he is more than willing to do his part to chase the rabbits and muntjac deer out of Mrs. M's garden. The muntjacs are an invasive species brought to England from the Far East to be "ornamental." Now they've become hungry invaders with a fine taste for roses. I tell L'Orvis that wanting to do his part for Mrs. M is a nice sentiment and that he is welcome to do his best, but being a figment of my imagination, I'm not sure exactly how efficacious his efforts might be.

"Dude," he says, in his best French, "*tu viens certainement avec moi...*"

Which is how I find myself in the spring sunshine, wandering the back yard with a long-handled spade in my hands. I am following L'Orvis from one rabbit hole to the next. He sniffs out the burrows and I start by filling in each deep divot with a shovelful of loose soil and compacting it with my borrowed rain boots, of which there are several pairs near the back door. Green Wellingtons of various sizes. I wear the largest. The filling and compaction are almost certainly futile, but at least it looks like I'm doing something while Mrs. M watches from the garden room. She can't see L'Orvis as he snuffs at the ground in front of me and then freezes into a hunter stance as we both come face-to-face, not more than three meters away, with the resident male muntjac.

He appears to be eating the buds and flowers off a red-pink tea rose that is growing nicely along the side of a tipping, aging, trellis. He stops when he hears my spade and the stomping of my boots. He looks up at us, and I can see the felting brown moss of fur that covers the knobs of his two short antlers. I can see the two fang teeth that drop from the side of his jaw. And I can certainly see that he does not fear us.

L'Orvis lets out a low growl that is rendered somewhat ineffectual by his new French accent. It does not seem to register as a threat to the muntjac. He does not fear the French. But what will he think of an Angry American with a sharp spade?

Really? Thoughts of violence? I am a visitor here. Am I going to attack the local wildlife with a bloody outburst of Neanderthal rage? I'm an American—where is my pistol? With a silencer and exploding bullets. Where is Mrs. M's rifle? What sort of a man am I, standing there in borrowed Wellingtons, leaning on a shovel, with nothing but an imaginary dog at my side?

"Shoo!" I say. "Go eat some other rose bush, you rodent!"

My voice makes the muntjac's ear twitch. Like he almost understands. Then he looks me up and down and reaches his red tongue out and munches another rose blossom.

Who does he think he's dealing with here? A hippy Pacifist who hasn't killed anything bigger than a housefly in the last twenty-five years? Will I be forced into terrible spade-swinging violence?

This is when L'Orvis lets out a soft WOOF, and I see in the side of my vision a white-gray shadow swinging down out of the sky. In the next instant, something swoops a few feet over my shoulder, at least as fast as the speed of sound, and I'm actually watching the muntjac as this winged UFO dives directly toward the rosebush. I don't actually know what the muscle motor reaction time is of a male muntjac deer, but it has to be close to the electromagnetic speed of light, which, at least from my perspective, seems instantaneous. I don't even grok it as the muntjac suddenly lifts its head, jumps sideways two feet, and in one springing boing is about six feet in the air and flying over the back fence. The shadow that flew down over my shoulder makes a physics-impossible UFO turn in the air, banks hard to the left, and proceeds at full speed in the chase.

L'Orvis and I are left there staring at the empty air. It all happened so fast that we can't even believe that we imagined it.

"*C'était quoi, ce bordel*?" he says.

"I don't know what the hell it was. A giant owl? A flying hedgehog? A tiny alien spaceship hunting miniature deer?"

"*Incroyable*!"

"Well, the muntjac sure knew what it was, because he made himself scarce. I had no idea they could move that fast."

"*Je ne pense pas que ce soit un hibou. C'était un chien volant.*"

"A flying dog?"

"*J'en suis presque sûr. Une sorte de beagle.*"

"No way you could see that. It happened too fast. No way."

Silence descends on the backyard of Mrs. M. We have no agreement as to what just happened. At least I don't have to try to swat the muntjac with my spade. I can look down at L'Orvis and just shake my head. I hear the birds begin to sing again. The chirping of a Cetti's warbler. The short, skirring squawk of a brown thrasher. I turn and look across the lawn, and at the other side of the yard I see the soil moving where a rabbit is beginning to dig its way out of a burrow I just filled with dirt.

What mystery have we encountered here? More of the unknown. I'm happy to let it rest in the universe of unexplained enigmas. But one short glance at L'Orvis and I can see he is nowhere near resting.

"The work here is endless," I say. "We could certainly use the help of dive-bombing alien UFO's. Even if you think they are flying beagles..."

"*Certainement. Je vais commencer l'enquête...*"

"What, now you are some kind of French Hercule Poirot?"

L'Orvis shakes his head at my stupidity. "Poirot, as everyone knows, is from Belgium. I'm thinking more like Jules Maigret..."

Maigret? Commissaire of the Paris Brigade Criminelle? An obvious choice, I guess. Well, at least L'Orvis is speaking English again.

"Have at it," I say. "Begin your investigation. I certainly would like to know what the heck is going on back here. I'm sure Mrs. M will appreciate your report."

"Hmmmm," he says. "I've never actually prepared a full report…"

Turning and walking across the grass to see if I can hit the rabbit with my shovel before he digs himself out of the hole, I leave L'Orvis sitting there staring toward the fence where the muntjac and the UFO disappeared into the thicket of lilac trees. In passing, I say:

"No worries. Just use your imagination."

CHAPTER FORTY-NINE

Beneath the statue of Lord Horatio Nelson,
Trafalgar Square, City of Westminster,
Central London, England, UK

On Friday May 5, I wake very early in the big bed of the blue bedroom at the front side of the second floor of The Old Rectory, with a view from the tall windows out toward the circular drive and the tall stump where a majestic, centuries-old horse chestnut once stood. The Rectory is about 110 miles north of London (about the same north latitude, for American audiences, would be Great Sitkin Island in the Aleutian Chain of southwest Alaska). So in early May, the twilight comes very early, and by about 5 a.m. I have already decided, as I am lying there beneath the hand-sewn country quilt, that I have to go back down to London for the coronation of the king.

The issue has become slightly complex. Our British Friend has decided to stay at the Old Rectory and watch the coronation on the telly with her mum (Mrs. M). Orvis (he dropped the French name two days into his "investigation" for reasons that remain mysterious) has not been around for a few days. He has been deeply involved in the paranormal exploration of flying ghost beagles and frightened muntjacs, who may be conducting an intergalactic war in the back yard. He did not come home at all last night, and perhaps I should be worried, but then: really? My most recent estimation is that he can take care of himself. Far better, most probably, than I could ever do with my total lack of parenting skills.

So there I am, wide awake in the twilight before dawn, staring at the bookshelf of clothbound classics next to the hand-carved Ethiopian fertility goddess (the M family had many interesting guests over the years and they tended to leave interesting objects), which is highlighted by the background of bluebell wallpaper, possibly original to the latest rectory remodel (circa 1920). There isn't much that is more English-immersive than to wake up on the day before the coronation of the new king (Charles III) in an Edwardian-era bedroom, a scant 100 miles north of Westminster Abbey, bandoliers of Union Jacks hanging everywhere through the countryside, constant BBC coverage about the gold-gilded carriage that will transport the new King from the ceremony, the idea in the frontal lobe of your mind that you have traveled some 9,000-or-so miles to get here and you are a two-hour train ride away (roundtrip about $36) from the real thing and yet you are going to stay home and safe and watch it on the television? What kind of intrepid traveler/journalist are you, anyhow?

Even if your best friend and your dog don't want to come with.

Orvis doesn't want to come, even though he loves riding on the train. Initially I have trouble understanding this, but soon he explains that his new friend (possibly connected to the War of the Muntjacs) lives on the other side of the village, and he (named "Churchill") knows a secret way to sneak into the Sandringham House Estate grounds, where there is a huge fiesta taking place with big-screen televisions, picnic provisions, and a $75 ticket price. Oh yeah, and it's been sold out for six months.

"Churchill says that just the leftovers make amazing party pickings," Orvis says. "Not to be missed. A coronation party like this only comes around once in fifty years."

Which is actually an understatement. The last coronation of an English monarch happened on June 2, 1953. Just under 70 years ago, by my math. This is precisely why I want to make the trip back down to the city.

My only real support for this idea comes from Mrs. M. As it turns out, she was actually outside Westminster Abby in 1953 with her cousin, and she watched live and in person while the twenty-seven-year-old Lilibet Windsor became Queen Elizabeth II.

"I'll never forget it," she tells me. "We were front row, right there in St. James Park, and she came through on her way to the palace in the huge golden carriage. She wore white gloves. I remember her waving. She seemed to look right through us..."

My sudden plan is not without sacrifices from other family members. In her great indulgence, Our British Friend agrees that she will wake early on Saturday and tote my sorry ass to the train station so that I can catch the 5:15 a.m. London Express. It means getting out of bed by 4:30.

"Sure you don't want to come with?" I ask her brightly.

"Quite," she says with finality.

So I find myself reconciled to forced solitude, the lonely American tourist riding a mostly empty Saturday morning train toward a gathering of ten million people. With greater foresight and more planning, I could have at least wrapped myself in Union Jack-themed bunting. The only other passenger in my train carriage is a smiling woman with blue hair and bad teeth. She is wearing a knitted hat with two small flags on little sticks crossed and stuck into the back of her head: the Union Jack on one side, the Cross of St. George on the other. Below this, she appears to have a red jumper with blue-and-white piping down the side of her legs. In a canvas satchel on her lap (white sailcloth with the words "Sunday Times Coronation of Charles III" and the British flag stenciled on the side), I suspect she has cucumber sandwiches and at least two Cornish pasties. But this is pure speculation on my part.

Either way, it is highly probable that I will be both underdressed and underfed.

The train stops in Cambridge and a family of four step into the carriage. Only the children are in costume, the little girl with pigtails that end in little flags; the boy, even younger, in a sailor suit with a Union-Jack collar and a plastic display button on his chest with a photo of Charles III and the words "God Save Our King." The parents seem more conservative: blue jeans and practical shoes, rain jackets drooped over their arms, matching blue-nylon Tilley bucket hats. There are clues here about what is to come, but I somehow fail to notice. The woman is carrying a huge black golf umbrella. The man is lugging with him a six-foot stepladder.

Granted, it is before 8 a.m. on a Saturday morning, but King's Cross Station in central London is very sparsely populated. I expected to see hordes of Royalists streaming from the trains, bustling to get their place on the parade route to catch a fleeting glimpse of their beloved monarch. But the train station is actually very quiet. A few smiling dislocated tourists. A group of very old women, their walkers festooned with British flag bunting, being led by a caregiver/coronation guide to a waiting van. I find myself hoping they have a reserved space somewhere.

I am certainly aware that there are double-decker city buses that will take me to St. James Park, or at least somewhere in the vicinity. My plan, such as it is, calls for a brisk walk across town and a basecamp to be set in Trafalgar Square, somewhere beneath the statue of Lord Nelson. The buses scare me anyhow. Their routes impossibly confusing, their drivers speaking a subspecies of English that does not readily translate into American. I am more afraid to ask for directions in London than I was in Istanbul. Here, you see, I am expected to understand. At least in Turkey we could use hand gestures. All English was very slow and broken into easily understandable bits. London does not have this advantage.

As in most cities, the underground here is much easier to negotiate. But this day, in London, the subway has been shut down in key areas as a form of security. A seasoned rider would have no trouble finding proper rerouting. A confused American could just as easily end up in Upminster Bridge rather than Buckingham Palace. Too much risk for me. To come all this way and end up watching it on a television in the window of some appliance store in Lost Crossingly? All because I missed the proper stop on the tube? I'd rather walk and take my chances.

As it turns out, fate is closing in on me.

Feeling extra brilliant, I use my phone to give me directions. Or at least to point me in the proper direction. Mostly south. My poor dumb smartphone. Brilliant when fully charged. Totally useless with a dying battery.

But I'm foreshadowing here. Onward, I say, with the straightforward narrative.

The streets of London on this Saturday morning are mostly empty. It is a cool and overcast day. Are the sleeping citizens all more knowledgeable than I? Cozying in after a Friday night pisser? Or has everyone left town rather than deal with a million tossers trying to glimpse the king in a golden horse cart on his way from getting knackered with the Crown of St. Edward? If I actually lived in London, I would probably be spending the weekend at my country estate in Far Fastingham. Watching the coronation on the telly for two hours like the rest of the sane people. I would certainly NOT be striding steadily toward the chaos of St. James Park.

It is an epic walk downhill toward the river. I don't know the names of the streets, so I'm following my compass, but I do recognize the British Museum, then over to Drury Lane toward the Opera House, west toward Westminster and then the National Gallery. The Savoy Hotel is a couple of blocks from the river, and then I'm walking along the Strand toward Charing Cross. Slightly to my west is the tall tower at Trafalgar Square (Nelson's Column), with the famous one-armed admiral (Lord Horatio Nelson) looking south toward the Thames, his left hand steadying him as he leans on the pommel of his sword, a mere forty-six meters off the ground on the top of a solid granite column.

I'm starting to see more and more people on the streets, but it is certainly not crowded, and as the time spins toward 7:30 I start to think it won't be bad, not too crowded. I find myself a good place to stand at the foot of Admiral Nelson. The King's carriage will come down Cockspur Street and take a right to head west on The Mall toward St. James Park. I should be able to see him coming and going. I stand balanced on a concrete curb, a perfect perch slightly above the street. Sweet! What a smart and lucky guy I am…

I get to pat myself on the back over my good fortune for about one hour and then the place begins to fill with people. Standing next to me with their own short stepladder is a friendly couple from the Midlands (near Shropshire). It turns out he is the kit man for the English National Football Team. It's great that we have a lot to talk about. It is so engaging that over the next couple of hours I don't even notice that the place is becoming densely crowded. Still, I am good. Because I can see over everyone.

But then it starts to rain.

What is a little rain to an Oregonian? Maybe we turn up our collars or adjust the brim of our hats. Most likely we just ignore it.

This is not the case in London. The minute it begins to rain, everyone and their sister pulls out a "brolly" and inflates it over their heads. Now I am not looking at the parade route, my perfect clear view of the coming monarch. Now I am looking at the surface of a sea of umbrellas.

Really?

I turn to my new friends to ask if this is going to be our view and they motion to the stepladder they brought with them.

"What, mate? You didn't bring your step stool?"

Nor did I bring my umbrella. As the rain intensifies, I start getting wet, ducking between the brollies to the right and left of me while trying not to get poked in the eye. It's not much fun. And then the chanting starts.

By 9:30, I am totally stuck in the crowd. Nowhere to go if I wanted to. To the left of me, just out of sight around the corner, a few hundred people start chanting: "NOT MY KING! NOT MY KING!"

In reaction to this, on my right, an even bigger groups

starts singing at the top of their lungs: "HAPPY AND GLORIOUS, LONG TO REIN OVER US, GOD SAVE THE KING..."

The King's carriage is due at 10:15. Under their umbrellas, everyone seems to be watching the procession on their smartphones. The tension grows as they see the king on television getting into the carriage at Buckingham Palace. He's about twenty minutes away.

The chanting gets louder on both sides as the carriage approaches. But then it stops suddenly and is replaced by an even louder chant. Like everyone, Royalists and Non-Royalists all together.

"PUT DOWN YOUR UMBRELLAS!!!!!"

Wow! Amazing! Such Cooperation! All the people on the curbside actually respond by putting away their brollies.

There is an electric intensity in the air as the carriage approaches, coming down Cockspur. For two seconds I get a glimpse of the Royal Horse Guards and then...

The King is here. Right in front of me. But of course I can't actually SEE him because everyone in front of me has raised their smartphones over their heads to make ten thousand home videos that no one will ever watch.

Ah yes, the modern world. A little girl on her father's shoulders is next to me and she starts to cry.

"I couldn't see ANYTHING!" she sobs.

I feel her pain.

CHAPTER FIFTY

Sandringham House, Norfolk County, England, UK

Orvis and I come home at about the same time on the day of the coronation. He is very happy. He is spry and enthusiastic. Well-fed. Had a blast with his friend Churchill.

I am completely spent, cold and wet, having barely made it onto the train north to Kings Lynn. I had my return ticket in a quick response code on my phone. No paper ticket at all. Well of course my phone died as I was walking back across London to the train station. At the info booth, they told me there was no solution for this. Either buy a phone charger or buy a new ticket (one way, $65). In desperation, I had to jump the turnstiles in the middle of a crowd. Caught my knee on the edge of the kiosk and limped to the train carriage, hoping there was not a squad of security guards tracking me. It got my heartbeat up, I can tell you that.

By the time Our British Friend found me at the Kings Lynn station, I was numb with cold and non-verbal. All I could do was mumble.

"It was the worst," I told her.

By 8 p.m., I was snug in my room with a hot cup of Tiger Tea, the covers pulled up to my chest, when Orvis came bounding into the room and jumped onto the bed. He was beyond excited.

"It was the best!" he told me.

Honestly, I really didn't want to hear about it. But there was no stopping him.

"Churchill really knows his way around the estate. I guess he grew up like next door. Right on the other side of the Laurel Hedge. We snuck up to the big house on the hill and he took me through a tunnel under the wall that surrounds the kitchen garden. You should see that place. Amazing. A big country kitchen with a fireplace all along one wall. They were making all kinds of delicious stuff. We ate this thing called Blood Pudding. Like a big hotdog, only made out of old blood. A little bit rich for me, but Church says you have to acquire a taste for it."

"Church?"

"Yeah, Churchill. He's like my best friend now. Knows everything."

Maybe we need to stop here for a little clarification.

First there is Sandringham House, which is on the Sandringham Estate, which is about 22,000 acres and includes five villages. It's in the northwest of Norfolk County, which is northeast of London. The estate is famous in England because it was purchased in 1862 by Prince Albert Edward, Queen Victoria's eldest son. Since then, it has been one of the residences of the Royal Family, personally owned by Queen Elizabeth II and now the property of Charles III. The vast acreage now includes a large organic farm, a sawmill, thoroughbred horse stables, residences for the 200-plus employees, a 6,000-acre Royal Game Park, and seven very old stone churches, some of them dating to the fourteenth century. It is rumored that in all of the estate there are only two residences that are privately owned by someone other than the king. One of them is the Old Rectory, where Mrs.

M sits in her garden room watching the muntjacs eat up her backyard.

Secondly, there is this character named Churchill, Orvis' new friend. A little investigation and a short conversation with Mrs. M turns up the story of a family that rented the cottage next door and their famous beagle. Well, actually it was a series of beagles. One beagle after another, and they all seemed to have the habit of barking unnecessarily, befriending small birds, and sitting in slow observation on the roof of a doghouse built by Tom Slipsworth Sr., located just beyond the lilac hedge halfway along the back path to the Royal Park.

"We had a lot less problems with the muntjacs when those cross old beagles were around," Mrs. M tells me.

Well, the Slipsworths are long gone, and they took their barking beagles with them. So there is no actual Churchill-the-dog living next door. But perhaps, I am thinking, there is his ghost.

I put this proposition to Orvis. He looks at me quizzically. And then a little indignant.

"He is as real as anything else around here," Orvis says.

This makes me cringe.

"But he IS a little strange. First off, I noticed that he is able to fly. Most dogs can't do that. The other thing is that he sometimes walks through brick walls like they are not even there. Which is very cool, but also strange."

"He might be a beagle ghost," I say.

Orvis pauses to think about it. "I don't know about that, but he is certainly pissed off a lot."

"An angry beagle ghost?"

"Possibly, but do ghosts vote? Because he's always talking about 'the vote' and how he was bamboozled by lying politicians. Brexit was bullshit, that's what he says. They said it would cut off all the foreigners, those lousy immigrants eating the shrubbery. He says he voted for it because he was sure it would get rid of the muntjacs. Now he needs a passport to visit the Slipsworths, who have retired to the south of France. And the muntjacs are worse than ever. Churchill sure hates the Tories, whoever they are."

"Politics," I tell him. "It screws up everything."

So the question remains a question. But I am dying to meet Churchill.

And maybe I will get a chance, because Our British Friend has received an invitation to the Coronation Concert. Well, sort of. Not the actual concert, live Sunday evening at Windsor Castle. But a televised feed of the concert to be projected on a big screen in the parking lot behind Sandringham House. It's fine by me, because we can walk there from The Old Rectory. I've had quite enough of training it south to London.

Orvis says he will meet us up there. He's meeting Churchill Sunday night to have a little dogs-only banquet of banquet leftovers in a "secret" place that I suspect is next to the big dumpster behind the Royal Kitchen. Let him have his fun.

I sleep in on Sunday morning and have a big midmorning breakfast, a Full English, cooked on the big solid Aga stove in the rectory kitchen. A further nap in the afternoon and I am fully recovered. The gloomy rain on Coronation Day has passed and the day of the concert is bright and warm.

The Royal Park is glistening in the late-spring sunshine. There is a huge meadow that stretches all the way from the village of West Newton up a gentle slope to the grounds of

Sandringham House. A crew is working in the center of the field, where a food and crafts fair took place the weekend before. The Royal Park gets a lot of use these days. One festival or concert after another, all summer long. All of them are big productions, with rows of white festival tents and staging and a parking lot on the surrounding field for ten thousand cars. Coming in August, a four-day music festival with Van Morrison and The Who.

All of this in Mrs. M's back yard. The villagers will be offered free tickets, but Mrs. M will only have to open a window to hear the music.

But on this Sunday in May, the day after the coronation, there is almost no one in the Royal Park. Our British Friend has been wandering through these woods since she was a little girl in the 1950s. So it is safe to say she knows her way around. She leads me out the front gate of the rectory and down a peaceful lane, past the beautiful brick school where she went to first grade and through a hefty wooden gate that opens onto the park. We take a very circuitous route toward the King's house; she ushers me on a side trail through a meadow of milkwort and vetch and a long stand of Scotch Pine.

"We used to ride our ponies through here," she says. "Then on up to the pond in front of the house, where we would hobble the horses and steal the Queen's rowboat and have a good old time pirating bluebells that grew along the shore. That's all changed now."

It's getting dark by the time we make the top of the hill. A tall iron fence now separates the Royal Park from the close grounds of Sandringham Hall. Our British Friend is not exactly sure where we will have to go to get in the back way. We try a couple of locked gates and wave at a few security cameras. Eventually we find a muddy back lane that goes through a dark wood but ends on a main street that runs into the back car park. It takes us to the edge of the concert, and we step out of the forest into a sea of picnic tables and a crowd of revelers facing a giant TV screen.

The Coronation Concert was pretty spectacular, even though we missed the first part of it. I especially liked the humpback whale rising above Windsor Castle. Amazing what they can do with blue LED lights and a thousand computerized drones. Orvis was nowhere in sight, which I found only slightly concerning.

It was very dark when the concert ended, and I had to totally rely on Our British Friend to lead me home through the dark forest. We emerged on the field side of the pine forest just as the moon was rising. It was a Waning Gibbous, just two days past full, and it seemed caught in the branches of a giant oak tree that stood in front of the Estate Agent's house. A magical mist had condensed over the sloping field of the Royal Park. Mystery motions in the woods. Distant echoing of barn owls. The heavy dew on the lawn had made my feet wet, and I was disoriented from a loss of direction. I reached out to Our British Friend and she gracefully held my hand as we walked steadily toward the village.

Certainly the supernatural was at work. This was my first time in the nighttime mists of the English countryside, and if I could open myself to it, there were visions to be had. The moon became untangled from the magical oak trees and soon I was hearing voices. Two ghost dogs singing off key:

"Merrily, merrily merrily oh ho
Play it out stiffly we may not part so
Cast away care for he that loves sorrow

Lengthens not a day nor can buy tomorrow
Money is trash and he that will spend it
Let him drink merrily our fortunes will mend it
Merrily merrily merrily oh ho
Play it out stiffly we may not part so…"

We finally came to the gate into the village of West Newton. When we reached the other side and closed the gate behind us, I finally got the courage to ask Our British Friend…

"Did you hear all that?"

"What?" she said. "The owls?"

"The singing. Did you hear the dogs singing? It almost sounded like Shakespeare."

In the dim and confusing moonlight I saw her turn toward me and try to look into my eyes. She gave my hand a squeeze.

"I think you must be tired," she said. "We'll put on the kettle for a kind cup of chamomile. Maybe have a fire in the living room hearth."

"But the singing dogs?"

"I only heard the owls," she said.

"That's what I was afraid of," I replied.

There was no sign of Orvis.

CHAPTER FIFTY-ONE

Buxton, Derbyshire County, Peaks District, England, UK

It is somewhat embarrassing for me to admit, but I get quite teary-eyed when it is time to say goodbye to Mrs. M. I've enjoyed her hospitality for almost two weeks, and she has indulged all my questions with dignity and forbearance. It hasn't been possible to really explain to her why I am traveling with an imaginary dog; heck, I have trouble explaining it to myself. And when it comes to the ghost-dog Churchill, I have no explanation at all. So I do not mention him. There is no good reason to leave her believing that I am totally delusional, though I think she has strong suspicions. How did that old proverb go? "It is better to remain silent and be thought a fool than to open your mouth and remove all doubt…"

We are leaving early the next morning. Our British Friend will drive us on a tour of the Midlands, up through the Peak District and then on over to North Wales. From there, a ferry to Ireland and we will say our goodbyes in Dublin.

I am confused and a bit in doubt as to whether Orvis will be coming with us. I suppose it could go either way. Does he stay and become Shakespearean with the beagle ghost or remain faithful to his master? Do I even have a say in this? Sure, I suppose I could force my imagination on him. But it's awfully hard to impinge on someone's free will. Even if they are made up. And what does Orvis think about his future? Does he even think about it at all?

I don't really know, because he hasn't been home in two days.

You probably know what it is like to have a lost dog. There is no telling what they have been up to. You can go around and post their picture on all the neighborhood telephone poles, maybe offer a reward, but in the meantime, you just sit home and wonder. It's even more difficult when the dog is imaginary. Really, they could be up to *anything*...

So that's what I do until the night before we are planning to leave, when he drags himself through the kitchen door about ten in the evening.

Our British Friend and I are in the Sitting Room, snuggled side-by-side in front of the fireplace, a nice non-alcoholic noddy in our cups, digesting a fine dinner of roast beast and baby new potatoes. We have a map of England spread across our laps and are determining the best route to wherever it is we want to go. Mrs. M is lending us her Yugo, and Our British Friend has volunteered to drive. I will not drive in England. They have the steering wheel on the right and the lane on the left. No one knows why. But it is too much of a challenge for this left-hander, who already has trouble in a right-handed world. I'll be the chief tourist and navigator, thank you very much. Driving a car in this land of narrow lanes and whirling roundabouts? For me that spells disaster.

I hear something in the hall and then Orvis limps into the room. He looks very worn out, his hair matted and his eyes bloodshot.

"Well then," I say to him with a friendly lilt to my voice, "look what the cat dragged in."

He immediately snaps to attention and starts looking for the suspect cat.

"Relax. It's just an expression."

His shoulders slump and he looks at me pleadingly.

"We have to talk," he says.

I turn to Our British Friend as I get up from the loveseat.

"I'm going to have a word with Orvis," I tell her.

So I adjourn to the kitchen with Orvis following me down the hallway. There is a nice after-dinner heat glowing from the Aga. A prolonged twilight is still filtering grayness through the mullioned windows above the farm sink. Sweetbreads wrapped in waxed paper are stacked on the butcher-block table.

"What can I get you?" I ask him.

"Just some water." He croaks the words out with an exhausted sigh.

He drinks and I sit. There is a padded bench next to the kitchen door, and I relax back against the windowsill and give him my full attention.

The first thing he says is: "You've got to get me out of here."

This is certainly not what I was expecting. Of course there was a backstory.

It started with the night of the Coronation Concert and a bit of indulgence up at Sandringham House. A meal of headcheese and scrapple, a couple of Scotch eggs, snake and pygmy pie, washed down with darkened barley wine. Orvis was making me sick just describing it. The strength of the beer made his head spin, but Churchill was just getting started. What followed was a two-day pub crawl. They ended up behind the Gin Trap Pub in Dersingham. No sleep for thirty-six hours. And still Churchill was not even beginning to stop.

"What did you expect?" I interjected. "He's a ghost. They never sleep."

"I had to finally beg off. I told him I had to stop by the house, because you would be worried about me…"

He paused as we looked at each other. I believe I was smiling.

"You WERE worried about me, right?"

I just kept smiling.

"Anyway, he's expecting me to meet him tomorrow out by the back gate. He wants to hunt down a clutch of muntjacs. Then head over to the the Cock and a Bull at Castle Rising. It's the oldest pub in Norfolk County. Been abandoned for two centuries. He wants me to meet some friends of his. On Tuesdays they make Ghost Cheeze."

"Ghost Cheeze?"

Orvis shook himself like he was shedding his fur filled with pond water.

"It could be anything," he said. "Most likely made from pig parts. Or cow's tongue. Frog's feet. Pheasant beaks. Or turkey knuckles."

I couldn't help it; I was still smiling. "What doesn't kill you makes you stronger," I told him.

"But what if it DOES kill me?"

Am I an evil person because I was enjoying the pleading look on his face? I mean he had deserted me for his new friend, hadn't he? It wasn't my fault that it hadn't worked out.

We looked at each other. Honestly, I was just glad that he came home. I wasn't smiling because I enjoyed his pain. I was smiling because I was, at heart, very glad to see him.

"Anyway, you're in luck. We are leaving tomorrow morning. Our British Friend is driving. You are welcome to come with."

It doesn't happen often, but it seemed like there was real gratitude in the expression on his face. For a moment I thought he was going to jump in my lap and start licking my face.

But he's just not that kind of a dog.

We left the Old Rectory early the next day. A bit of morning fog glistening in the air, a strengthening sun rising over the tile roofs of West Newton Village. Orvis snuggled down among the luggage in the back seat. In case anyone was looking for him. I didn't tell him that I was pretty sure you couldn't hide from a ghost.

Thusly we began our trip across England.

It is quite a strange land in some respects. The major highways, four lanes wide, approximately equivalent to the Eisenhower Interstate System in the United States, only run from north to south. There isn't really a major route that runs east to west. I'm sure there is a quaint and illogical reason for this, and I'm open to an explanation, but anyhow, that's the way it is. To drive across England you are mostly on two-lane roads that cross each other in a myriad of roundabouts. Many of the two lanes are bordered by hedgerows. They can be quite tall. It is like driving through a green maze. You can't really see the countryside. The view is through a nice thick covering of vegetation. It looks soft and cozy. Only not so soft if you drive into it, because the vegetation is often covering a solid stone wall. Drive off the narrow lanes at speed and you are toast. Tourist mush. And it will take a bit of time before anyone comes out to scrape you off the ancient stones covered with blackthorn and hornbeam.

It is, admittedly, very beautiful. A compact geography, located on a temperate island, populated for ten centuries by warring peoples, green and fertile fields constantly fought over. Modern England is a patchwork of rolling countryside and villages condensed between large cities. Seventy million people, but most of them in and around compact, industrialized metropolitan centers, which leaves the space in between bucolic. But completely cultivated. Even the forests look trimmed and well-managed.

At my suggestion, because the distances are short and we have all day, I navigate us along the narrowest roads I can find on the map. My compass is set toward the northwest, roughly in the direction of Peak District National Park. We take the route of minimal traffic and maximum Englishness.

Some of the villages: East Heckington, Byards Leap, Brant Broughton, Stragglethorpe, Barnby in the Willows, Maplebeck, Eakring, Bilsthorpe, Tuxford, Edwinstowe, Chutney, Shirebrook, and on over to Clay Cross. We drive through some rolling hills, then on down the lane to the city of Chesterfield.

Mostly you will do a double take when you come into Chesterfield and first see the twisted spire of the Church of Saint Mary and All Saints. The church spire was built in 1362, when the European world was still recovering from the Black Death, and supposedly there was a lack of good builders and craftsmen. They constructed the spire (252 feet off the ground) from unseasoned oak timbers, and then a century or two later, when the roof was redone with lead sheets, the framing could not support the weight and the spire both twisted and leaned almost ten degrees to the northeast. It has stood that way for another 500 years or so, which remains a mystery but is certain to be explained by the parishioners as an act of God.

We take a break in Chesterfield. Our British Friend sits in the plaza next to the church to make a sketch and I wander the downtown, tipping into one charity shop after another in my continuous search for good used football jerseys.

When the journey resumes, we meander up through the south section of Peak National Park, very picturesque, and then end the day in the spa town of Buxton. We have reserved a cheap room at the Palace Hotel. It is a beautiful old hotel, cheap because we are mid-week, directly across from the Opera House, close by the River Wye.

We cruise into the front car park and as I am unloading the luggage, I notice that Orvis is still nestled down on the back seat, just the top of his head showing, as though he is still afraid to come out.

"We have arrived," I tell him, but he doesn't want to come out of the car.

CHAPTER FIFTY-TWO

Buxton on Wye, Derbyshire County, England, UK

A good wet springtime English rain is falling when we wake in our beds on the fourth floor of the Old Palace Hotel in Buxton. Floor-to-ceiling windows, narrow with a wooden sash, look out on the second-floor balcony, where once the fancy ladies and lords would sit at shaded tables to watch travelers disembark under the front portico. The Palace has seen better days, and maybe it is a slight bit seedy in its elder years, but it was once the home of choice for prosperous merchants and their wives, training down from Manchester or Liverpool to take in the mineral waters of the Roman Spa.

Buxton is a modest spa town that once had ambitions to become Bath.

It is an interesting mix of both Georgian and Victorian architecture. The mineral springs have been there from antiquity, gushing out of the woods at a constant 85 degrees F. The Roman invaders called the spot *Aquae Arnemetiae* (Baths of the Grove Goddess), developed it as a spa town, spent a couple of hundred years there, and then went home. In about 1780, William Cavendish, Fifth Duke of Devonshire, took his vast profits from copper mining and invested them in making modest Buxton into the next big thing. He built indoor arenas, an opera house, and a semicircular luxury hotel (The Crescent), which is located across the street from the thermal baths (also rebuilt with ornate tile work) and Saint Ann's Well, a fountain of miracle waters where to this very day you can fill your canteen with spring water that seems quite drinkable. There is also the imposing Devonshire Dome which, with a diameter of 144 feet, was the largest unsupported dome in the world, larger than Rome's Pantheon by three feet, but about a thousand years younger. The dome is now part of the University of Derby, which also occupies all the other Victorian buildings clustered along the River Wye.

The beautiful, bucolic River Wye, twenty-two miles long and flowing gently through the Peak District of Derbyshire, is a setting you would certainly picture as the place where young English gentlemen would slowly row wooden punts with their lovely ladyships (a long flowery summer dress, flowers in their hair, perhaps a parasol) sitting primly on the stern seat. There might be a wicker picnic basket placed between them, as they are heading to a private hidden bank for lunch, a soft blanket on the meadow grass. Imagine the opportunity; a possible innocent kiss or two (maybe three or four) and an afternoon of delight.

I would suggest such a thing to Our British Friend if it weren't raining and if there wasn't a thick springtime bloom of mayflies, caddisflies, sedge flies, and assorted shire midges layering over the waters. The bugs are keeping the rainbow trout and graylings happy and well-fed. It's charming, but not romantic for roaming tourists. Every paradise has its muddy backstory.

Our raingear wanderings take us past the Opera House, where I am keen to learn there is a performance the very next day of the English Touring Opera Company. As far as I know, I am the only enthusiastic opera fan in the immediate family, but Our British Friend, as always, is a good sport and I need to find some way to lure Orvis out of the back seat. He's never been to an opera, so he won't have any reason to believe he wouldn't enjoy it. He might hate me afterwards, but at least I will get him out of the car.

It also gives me another excuse to browse the charity shops. Our British Friend always travels with a smart black dress (she looks dazzling), but I have been on the road for several months and I have absolutely nothing in my small carry-on to wear to The Opera. I at least need a suit jacket. Maybe a nice classic tuxedo?

The charity shops in Buxton are a bit of a disappointment. I was hoping for a sophisticated blend of tweed and gaberdine, corduroy and linen. Mostly we found faded denim. Used fishing poles. Tattered copies of Stephen King. I was beginning to think I would have to wear my patched Patagonia down sweater (basic black) and wrinkled Ex-Officio travel pants (charcoal grey, campfire sparks having made little holes in the lower buttock.) But then we came to the proper mall.

Tucked into the former Buxton Baths, located over the spot where the Romans "discovered" a sparkling spring of hot mineral water, we found a cluster of small boutique shops. At one end was a square bathtub with a wooden chair suspended on a block-and-tackle, the purpose of which was to lower some pampered Lord slowly into the hot water. On the other end was a tiny men's shop where I found a beautiful black cashmere turtleneck sweater.

Perfect. Casual but elegant. I would have bought it in a minute until Our British Friend looked at the price tag. Three hundred and seventy-five quid.

Nice shopping mall though. The Cavendish Arcade. I highly recommend it. The stained-glass domed roof. The pink-and-green tile work on the former "Lady's Side." The proper old man in the men's shop who looked at me like I was working class and could never afford a thing from his racks. Until he heard my American accent. It perked him up. Americans can afford anything, even if they don't actually have the money for it.

I didn't buy the sweater. I ended up with a semi-wrinkled linen sport coat (slightly beige with tortoise shell buttons) from the Oxfam Charity Shop (93 Spring Gardens). It cost seven pounds, which Our British Friend thought extravagant, but she let me buy it.

The English rain had let up during our walk through downtown Buxton, and it almost became English sunshine except for the thick (though brightening) English overcast. By the evening, when it was time to walk over to the Opera House, it was raining again quite properly, and honestly, no one noticed what we were wearing under our umbrella. The inside of the Opera House was quite nice, not overly ornate, but a calming beige with gilt gold paint highlighting the various filigree. It matched my sport coat, though, again, no one noticed. We had good cheap seats in the balcony. The performance of Handel's *Giulio Cesare* was on the better side of adequate, though I did notice that the eyelids of Our British Friend had quite a droop midway through the second act. Orvis, who was sitting on my lap (he wanted to see over the heads of the folks in front of us), was attentive and excited for the first five minutes. Then he realized that the opera was NOT in Italian. He slept quietly through most of it. At least he doesn't snore or trot his legs when he sleeps.

It wasn't an entirely successful night in Buxton. Cold and wet as we wandered around after conquering the opera, we looked for a place to eat. We really didn't find anything. But as luck would have it, we finally noticed a tiny storefront where an enterprising local woman had set up a portable pizza oven. There was no place to sit in her little restaurant, but she told us if we wanted to eat we could go sit in the pub across the street and she'd have her teenage son deliver.

So we ended our night at the Blazing Rag, a proper English Pub. I drank two elderberry ciders and Our British Friend drank tap water. Orvis hid under the table and cautiously eyed a huge Saint Bernard that seemed to be the house dog. At least there were no pub cats around. Most likely they were out in the midnight gloom hunting endangered river voles.

Afterward, I could have used a good long soak in a hot Roman mineral bath, but unfortunately, all the public baths had closed in 1963.

We had soggy shoes by the time we made it back to the Palace Hotel. The television had nothing on but reruns of Downton Abby. We were forced to read guidebooks and try to plan our trip down to Shropshire County.

It can be rough out there in the wilds of England.

CHAPTER FIFTY-THREE

Shrewsbury, Shropshire County,
Midlands, England, UK

It is late afternoon by the time we reach Shrewsbury. We got a late start from Buxton and wandered our way down the A515, through the south side of the Peaks District and on over toward Uttoxeter, where we stopped at a roadside food truck that had pretty decent bangers and mash. The coffee was tolerable (so said Our British Friend), and I had a cuppa Earl Grey. The skies were clearing. Orvis was beginning to come out from beneath the suitcases.

The longest and largest river in England (220 miles, flow rate 3,800 cubic feet per second) is the River Severn. It begins in the Cambrian Mountains of mid-Wales and ends at the Severn Estuary of the Bristol Channel of the Celtic Sea. It curves through the counties of Shropshire, Worcestershire, and Gloucestershire. At a particularly beautiful meander near the western border of England and Wales is an ancient settlement now called Shrewsbury.

An interesting note here concerns architecture. One unique quality of an English countryside tour is that it is possible to drive a few dozen miles from one century to the next. Or in the case of Buxton and Shrewsbury, from the nineteenth century a few hundred years back to the sixteenth. Buxton is Victorian. Shrewsbury is a beautifully preserved blend of the Elizabethan times. Gothic Revival stone and brick in Buxton. Tudor timber frame and plaster in Shrewsbury. Dickens, Emerson, and Longfellow on one hand, Shakespeare and Marlow on the other.

The beauty of Shrewsbury is that it is a compact city centralized on a loop of the River Severn. The loop contains a steep hillside that prevents the tight meander from becoming an oxbow lake. The town was built on this easily defensible elevation, with a natural moat surrounding almost seven-eighths of the circumference of the original town. This allowed Shrewsbury to prosper. It controlled the river trade from the sheep farms of Wales to the woolen mills of Birmingham. It became a key stopping place on the stagecoach line from London to Holyhead and the ferry boats to Dublin. At a prosperous riverfront estate named "The Mount" (just across the Severn from the Old City), the naturalist Charles Darwin was born in February 1809.

All this would be merely history if the citizens of Shrewsbury hadn't had the foresight to preserve the original downtown. Any city, small or large, benefits from the elimination of most motorized vehicles in its center. Shrewsbury, which has mostly banned or limited automobiles from downtown, has thusly preserved much of its seventeenth-century style and layout. It is now a walking town, with very limited parking and many streets too narrow for motorized transit. You could argue that such an attitude for preservation has made it very touristy, and this would be true. But it has also kept the town a living museum of Tudor architecture and the effects of nascent mercantilism from the 1500s. It is a priceless collection of original Elizabethan design: timber-and-plaster townhouse facades with a commercial shop on the street level and residences on the floors above. Shrewsbury provides one of Shropshire County's best examples of this era of prosperity. And of course, the travelers and tourists (like me) love it.

We have a bit of a walk from the Frankwell public car park on the west side of the river down the lane to the English Bridge and across the Severn to Mardol Quay. Our hotel is still a bit of a hike north. A fine three-star named the Shrewsbury Hotel and owned by the J D Wetherspoon Corporation, something akin to Best Western in the United States. Strictly middle-class hotels built around historic buildings in picturesque villages. Our room is above a pub that appears to have no clever historic name, but which Orvis insists on calling "The Cat Had Puppies."

I don't know, it sounds like a pretty good name for a pub to me. After all, other pubs in our neighborhood are named: The Loopy Shrew, The Nag's Head, Alfred's Shed, The Book and Banter, The Abbot's Meade, Darwin's Doormat, King's Head, Hop and Friar, The Coach and Horses, The Three Fishes, The Hairy Walrus.

Our British Friend cringes when I tell her what Orvis names our pub. It has been a bit of a trial for her to be traveling for so many days with my sense of humor in the passenger seat. She begs off to spend some alone time with her sketch pad.

This leaves Orvis and I in our little room under the eaves, with a queen-sized bed, a water closet, and one small modern television anchored to the sloping ceiling and aimed in our general direction. I try to find a football game to watch, but it is of no use. It is international break, and the only thing on is a rerun of a friendly between England and Croatia. I already know that my team lost.

So after a short rest, we are back out onto the streets. The evening is pleasant and clear. A late sunset has watercolored the western sky in blues and burgundies, strands of pink and orange dispersed among the last gray rain clouds. We climb to the top of Claremont Hill to sit on the steps of St. Chads Church and look out over The Dingle.

A public park and botanical garden occupy the long meadow and woods next to the Severn. In British English, the word "dingle" means a narrow, mostly forested valley. This one is prone to floods, but is presently above water and lush with springtime fecundity. There are blossoming flowers in the gardens, a stretch of green grass surrounding the old quarry and stretching down to National Cycle Route 81, and then the footpath next to the water.

Orvis and I climb down a steep stone staircase and walk through The Dingle to the edge of the river. Darkness is lowering itself grayly toward the surface of the water. Lights have come on in the Pengwern Boat Club, close by the opposite riverbank. It's a beautiful brick-and-plaster building with a slate terrace that fronts on the Severn. We can see the tips of rowing sculls jutting out from the arched storage bins below the raised patio.

No one is rowing on the river tonight. It is very quiet along the footpath as we head south toward the Kingsland Bridge and then down and around the river loop, taking the long way home.

Hopefully, by the time we get to the Cat Had Puppies Pub, Our British Friend will have forgotten that we called it that and will be ready for a nice dinner.

I'm thinking Fish and Chips. With cocktail sauce rather than vinegar. Anything to get more horseradish in my diet. I am, after all, Ukrainian.

I mention my meal preference to Orvis, and he just shakes his head. He knows that when we sit across the table from Our British Friend and order something weird, it tends to lower our esteem in her eyes. It's bad enough that I have to drag this imaginary dog with us everywhere we go.

"Maybe," he says, "you ought to just try the vinegar with the fish. Try to be normal for once. Otherwise you just might be pushing your luck."

Ah yes, the wisdom of dogs. I think he may be right. This is our last night in England and I've already stretched the bounds of my welcome. It's an odd little country, and I might want to come back someday.

CHAPTER FIFTY-FOUR

Racecourse Ground, Wrexham,
County Clwyd, North Wales, UK

The fourth time I stop to ask for directions, I am standing outside the east gate of the Racecourse Ground, right in front of The Turf pub/hotel, and there are half a dozen football fans sitting at a picnic table drinking enormous pints of ale. This is a little odd, because it's about nine-thirty in the morning.

They hardly notice me until I open my mouth.

"Excuse me. I'm wondering if you know where the stadium store might be?"

Six men, none of them younger than late middle age, put their beers down and look up at me from where they are sitting. Two of them are wearing Wrexham football jerseys with a small shield on the upper left that contains two red Welsh dragons holding a soccer ball and the words "Ich dien" written above. "I serve." Across the front of the jersey, it says: "AVIATION American Gin."

It's just natural, they can't really help themselves, so they have to mess with me a little.

"*Rydych chi bron yno, ffrind. Mae o gwmpas y cefn,*" the man sitting closest to me says.

He doesn't say it in a bad way. Really it is more of an encouragement. The other men smile and even laugh a little bit. They expect that I don't speak Welsh. They would be entirely correct in expecting this.

As far as I can tell, there is no line in the sand or even any signage when you cross from England into Wales. I couldn't really tell where the border lies. We drive northwest on the A5. The border is somewhere between Gobowen and Chirk. In my experience, you know you are in Wales when the names of the towns get unpronounceable. When you see signs for Llanrhaeadr-ym-Mochnant, Cynwyd, and Cerrigydrudion, you know you have arrived. Welsh is an impossible endangered language, and you can't blame the people here for wanting to preserve it.

I smile at the men sitting outside The Turf. I'm pretending I understand.

"For sure," I say. "I'm wanting to buy a proper kit for my nephew in San Francisco. He's a big fan."

It is my American accent that disarms them. Now they are all smiling and telling me that the "kit" shop is on the other side of the stadium. They gesture and point north to a rim road that goes around the Racecourse Ground. The Wrexham store is beside a car park next to the university.

"You're an American, mate?" One of them asks.

"Or just another bloody idiot tourist," says the man sitting next to him.

"American, yes." I explain. "All the way from Oregon."

This leaves a quizzical expression on his face.

"Pacific Northwest," I tell him. "West Coast. The state just north of California."

I know what they are all thinking. Why the heck has he come to Wrexham? Then it occurs to them: The Red Dragons.

Honestly, they didn't see a lot of Americans in Wrexham until two years ago, when a couple of Hollywood actors (Ryan Reynolds and Rob McElhenny) paid two million dollars and bought the local football (soccer) team. The club, Wrexham AFC (The Red Dragons, founded in 1864), is something like the third-oldest professional football team in the world. Its stadium (The Racecourse Ground) claims to be the oldest international football pitch. Reynolds and McElhenny reportedly have a combined wealth only slightly south of 500 million dollars. This is actually a modest income for people who own British football teams. Mid-table, wealth-wise. In order to get the Wrexham Football Trust to agree to sell them the club, they had to promise to invest in the team. It seems they have kept most of their promises, because the first thing they did was to begin refurbishing the stadium and filming a documentary that they then sold to the streaming service FX. This documentary (*Welcome to Wrexham*) became a bit of a sensation. Two full seasons (thirty-two episodes) have come out so far. It has raised the profile of the club internationally, and especially in the United States. It has also injected the entire community with hope.

It's almost impossible to explain and describe how important football can be to a town. There is no logic to it. There is no rationality. Football, winning, losing, drawing, become life and death to football fans. It also has an effect on the local economy, which has not been good since the country (like the rest of the United Kingdom) left the European Union. The curse of Brexit.

Further, it is hard to believe, but the success or failure of the Wrexham football team, the fact that it has been purchased by Americans with deep pockets, the fact that it has a fair chance of being promoted up the ladder of British football...well, it is a VERY big deal to the people of Wrexham, even the ones who don't give a fuck about football. They might be struggling in everyday life, but their local football team is now FAMOUS. A few days before I come to town, they win three-to-one against Boreham Wood, which secures their promotion to the next league up (League Two). This made the people of Wrexham very happy. Like, ecstatically happy. This phenomenon was something I wanted to see.

In fact, it's the entire reason I worked hard to convince Our British Friend that we had to stop for a few hours in Wrexham.

Also, I wanted to buy a t-shirt.

As far as I can tell, the people in Wrexham are not used to having tourists come here to buy souvenirs. The people I talk to seem very surprised to see me. And also very happy. And somewhat amazed that I've come all the way from America to see their football stadium.

Wrexham is not a particularly picturesque city. It came through the 1800s as a rough, blue-collar mining town. Coal and tin mines, a hardscrabble working-class life. The fortunes of the people were tied to the price of steel. Up and down and never very far up. Currently, like much of England, it is stuck in economic stagnation. The downtown, a red brick mall lined with small stores and empty storefronts, is modest. We drive into town on Regent Street and the only landmark of note is the Gothic-style Catholic church (St. Mary's Our Lady of Sorrows). It is surrounded by a nineteenth-century churchyard and next to the Wrexham Borough Museum and Archives, which is closed (temporarily?).

We find a carpark to leave the Yugo. Our British Friend goes off to sketch. Orvis and I are left to wander the downtown.

Orvis is already a bit bored with Wrexham. We have only been here an hour or so. He became slightly excited when we found the Wrexham AFC gift shop.

He enjoys shopping sometimes. While I was trying to decide which authentic football jersey to buy (the old ones that said Aviation Gin, or the new ones that said Tic Toc?), he had found a whole rack in the store that sold sweaters for dogs.

"How much money do you have?" he asked.

"For what?"

"They've got these doggie sweaters that might fit. Very cool. They say: "Wrexham Dog Dragons."

"How much?" (Not that I was going to buy my imaginary dog a doggie sweater. I mean that seems a little obsessive, right?)

"Thirty-five pounds."

He could tell by the look on my face that it was a non-starter.

True confession: I spent almost $70 on Wrexham gear. Two championship t-shirts, a dated soccer jersey, and a metal plaque that said: "Racecourse Ground, Wrexham AFC." We left the store without a doggie sweater.

So I ended up wandering the streets of Wrexham with a very glum dog who didn't even want to speak to me. There were not a lot of things to see. I looked pretty hard for a charity shop that might have cheap doggie sweaters, but even the thrift stores were understocked. The Wrexham football phenomenon had maybe lifted the spirits of the locals, but it hadn't really lifted the economy very much. Not from what I could tell.

In an aging brick shopping mall near the center of town, I met a shopkeeper who was being quite friendly. It may have been because I was the only shopper in the mall. He had a good-sized three-table display of t-shirts he had printed up himself. They were red with white lettering, the words printed around a trophy cup that said Wrexham Champions 2023. They cost two for ten pounds.

As I was buying them, the man asked me where I was from and why I came to Wrexham.

"It's pretty famous in the United States," I said. "At least among soccer fans."

This seemed to brighten his day. Another little reason for hope. A thought occurred to me as he was wrapping up my shirts.

"You don't happen to have any Championship doggie sweaters, do you?"

It was fun to watch him as a little light seemed to go off in his head. He brightened up noticeably.

"Maybe," he said. "How long are you in town?"

CHAPTER FIFTY-FIVE

Llandudno, North Wales, UK

I have never been one to enjoy rollercoasters. The one time (only time) I visited Disney World (Orlando, Florida), my date took me on a ride called "Space Mountain" and I came very close to throwing up in her lap. That was in April 1979. My tolerance for whooping and swooping and defying gravity at speed has only become less since then. The best I can handle now is a slow elevator. And that is with my eyes closed.

So I am actually happy that the Ferris wheel on the beach at Llandudno (it's Welsh, pronounced "Clan-dun-dough") is still not open for the season. It's called the Llandudno Eye, and a sign says it will be opening soon. As soon as he sees it from our fourth-floor room at the Grand Hotel, Orvis gets all excited about going for a ride.

The Grand Hotel. I booked it online for two nights. It looked good, poised right there on the west side of the Strand, overlooking the Llandudno Pier, a short walk to the downtown, a big view of the Irish Sea. Possibly I missed the clue that it was only fifty pounds per night. I mean, it is the "shoulder" season, right? Things are a little bit cheaper. In the photos online, I did not notice that it is a little bit rundown.

The dreary, gray, and wet English weather has followed us to Wales, though there are breaks in the clouds, and a very cold and penetrating Irish wind is blowing from the northwest. We have plans to go mountain climbing in Snowdonia, but no plans at all to go riding on a giant Ferris wheel. In fact, I'm a little concerned about opening the door on our tiny fourth-floor balcony because the safety rail has spots of penetrating rust that they have not bothered to repair or paint over.

"Don't go out on the balcony," I tell Our British Friend. "It's the salt air. Everything gets rusted unless you paint it continuously. There's plenty of deferred maintenance around here."

"What?"

"Deferred maintenance. It means they don't have the money to keep things up. I wouldn't trust the rail. Or even the balcony, for that matter."

I know I am being overly dramatic. The Grand Hotel is really not THAT bad. It was once very posh, I am sure. But now it has joined that certain category of British hotels. The category of places that were fashionable, but are now economically challenged. In fact, you could say this about the whole town of Llandudno. The whole country of Wales.

That is the major problem with places of history. Places of historic significance. They're historic. They're old. It takes a lot of money and energy to preserve and restore them. Upkeep is a killer.

I won't go into a detailed description of the Grand Hotel. The stretched and wrinkled carpets. The clanking and jerking elevator. The sleepy staff, the empty dining room, the closed-off fireplaces. I actually like this kind of place. Not gentrified. Not stuffy. Not expensive. It's a little mildewy. A little haven for dust mites.

And I am very, very glad that the rusty Ferris wheel is not yet open for the season. The wheel stands tall at the foot of the Llandudno pier, a concrete and wood-plank walkway that juts 3,000 feet out into the Irish Sea. At the sea end, the pier spreads out into a large Y shape. There is an arcade in the center of the Y and a chippy stand and a sausage stand on either side. The arcade has a fancy metal dome, and the food stands are covered by mansard roofs. Along the pier, various square curio shops are spaced on either side, metal-clad hip roofs covering about fifty square feet of retail space. It is nicely thought out, but well-aged in the salt sea air.

At low tide, the water beneath the pier is not deep, but it is gray and cloudy and certainly not inviting.

There are big tides in parts of the Irish Sea. On the strand at Llandudno, the tide changes the water depth quite significantly. This means that waves are often lapping at the seawall on a high tide and then there is a half-mile of rocky beach when the tide goes out. Think of fishing boats sitting high and dry on their keels in the mudflats and then floating and ready to go out for the catch in ten feet of water at mid-tide. There is often less than six hours between tides, and within those hours, the water depth changes by twenty feet. It is a very fast suck and then an equally rapid regurgitation.

You would have to be a strong swimmer to enjoy the water at Llandudno. Crazy strong and with good timing.

Even with the sun shining, it is cold as we walk along the strand. There is a wide double-lane boulevard along the beach front (The Parade) and a solid concrete promenade (The Crescent). On the town side of the Parade, there are rows of Victorian townhouses and small hotels. They are all four- or five-stories-tall and painted in pastels that have turned mostly white with sun bleaching. The townhouses face north, toward the ocean. Walking back toward the hotel (west), we can see the south side of the town as it steps its way, one Victorian housefront after another, up into the limestone cliffs of the Great Orme. At one time (say about 1500 BC), it was the site of prosperous copper mining.

Because we are there off-season (it doesn't get warm enough to become a bustling resort town until about mid-June), there is not much to occupy us in Llandudno. We have a nice dinner at a good Bangladeshi restaurant (The Blue Elephant, highly recommended) and a stroll through town and are back to the Grand Hotel by about seven-thirty. We have a big day planned, climbing Mount Snowdon, for the following morning, so I have no problem hitting the hay early. There is no sign of my imaginary dog.

At eight o'clock, it is still quite light outside, and when I go to draw the curtains on our balcony doors, I take one more look out to the beach and the pier and the rusting amusement rides.

It is then that I notice Orvis. He is down at the foot of the Llandudno Pier, standing close by the pockmarked iron railing. He seems to be looking up at me, but then I realize this is not true. Even from the distance, I can see the wistful look on his face as he gazes up at the motionless Ferris Wheel.

As I go to sleep, I feel a little bad for him. But then I think: Well, he might as well learn sooner rather than later that not everything is going to go his way. Life is like that. Up and down like the tides. Like the Ferris wheel. A flow of good days and bad ones.

And sometimes filled with disappointments.

CHAPTER FIFTY-SIX

Snowdon Ranger Path, Yr Wyddfa,
Eryri National Park, Snowdonia, Central Wales

As you might expect as one travels deep into the heart of Wales, all the signage is written in Welsh. Underneath, there is usually an English translation. This means "Y Gar Yn Arfon" becomes "Caernarfun" and "Gwaun Mawr" becomes "Waunfawr." So really, the translation doesn't help all that much.

Hiking the back country is her idea, so I defer to Our British Friend to navigate and drive us through Snowdonia. It has been a lifelong dream of hers to climb Mount Snowdon (Yr Wyddfa), which, at 3,500 feet, is the tallest mountain in Wales. I like it when she becomes physically ambitious. Myself, I've mostly been in cities for the last few months, so a healthy airing out of my leg muscles and under-used lung capacity seems like it will be a good idea.

Of course, I could be wrong. But that doesn't become apparent until much later.

For his part, Orvis seems to have finally left his supernatural adventures behind him. He seems ready to run amok on the Ranger Path, up the mountain and through the countryside. Off leash. Isn't it great how some dogs do that? They sprint far ahead on the trail, following some delicious scent, and then come rushing back to make sure they haven't lost you. Orvis is sort of like that, only he knows he can never lose me, so sometimes he just sits next to a boulder on the side of the trek and waits for me to catch up. I wonder what he is thinking about when he is just sitting there waiting. I think he is tasting the air with his nose. A complex blend of sniffs and snorts and his tongue hanging out of the side of his mouth as he pants. There is so much to know of the unknown air. Two hundred million smell molecules to link into his 300 million scent receptors. Maybe he just sits and thinks, "How will I ever sort it all out?"

It's quite interesting to be a dog. Imaginary or not.

Our British Friend drives us down the A405, past the village of Betws Garmon, along the shore of Llyn Cwellyn, and to the car park at the Snowdon Ranger Path. She takes us, hiking, up through the gate of the Beddgelert Farm, through the sheep fields that wander toward the south, through another gate, and then we are on the main part of the Ranger Path. Or, as one guidebook describes it:

"At the top of the zig-zag section, the path levels considerably, and there is a gate. On your left are Foel Goch and Moel Cynghorion, with the pass of Bwlch Maesgwm in between. The footpath heading left from here goes to Bwlch Maesgwm and on to Llanberis; this is popular with cyclists and, of course, Hobbits."

Yes! And truly I feel like we have wandered into the realm of Middle Earth. Help me Frodo!!! It ALL starts to make sense…

I'd love to explain this to Our British Friend and my imaginary dog, but here, about half a mile into our nine-mile trek, I have already lost sight of them on the trail ahead.

Maybe this is because the trail is very circuitous and the boulders are numerous, but it is also (and perhaps mostly) because I am moving like a slug.

A slug is a snail-like creature without a shell. *Arion subfuscus* is the scientific name in my neighborhood of the Pacific Northwest. These forest mollusks are known for how slowly they crawl across the ground. Very, very slowly.

This should tell me something, because in the past I have been known as a very fast walker. I have motored through life on two strong legs, connected to two strong lungs and one strong heart. Certainly I am a bit older now. Certainly I am a bit slower. But never slug-slow.

Additionally, the guidebooks describe the Ranger Path as moderate to steep. Or as they say:

"The Snowdon Ranger Path (*Llwybr Cwellyn*) is located on the west side of the mountain, and is therefore much quieter. It is the oldest path up Snowdon, being in the eighteenth century close to Caernarfon on what was one of the best toll roads in the county. It is regarded as one of the easier paths, being just a long walk, albeit with steep sections; no hands are needed."

So, you ask, what is my problem?

I'm not quite ready to tell you my full medical history, but suffice it say, until very recently I have not been involved with doctors. I've been extremely healthy and always in pretty good shape. Hell, I just spent the last months hiking around the hills and staircases of several Eastern European cities. If I believe the guidebook, this hike should be a piece of cake.

My friend and my dog are kind enough to wait for me periodically as we make our way up the mountain. When the going gets very steep, I find myself mentally pointing to a boulder or an outcrop up ahead and then concentrating on putting one boot in front of the next until I reach my goal. Then a stop to catch my breath and then another goal upwards, 100 yards closer to the summit.

Eventually, we get to a flat spot up on the shoulder of the mountain, with the top of the trail visible in the short distance. Maybe one quarter-mile more to go. The weather is clear, with a cold wind blowing from the west. The landscape is a blend of stone outcrops and small sections of grassy meadow. There are green and gray rolling hills below us, and in the north, far away toward the horizon, a bank of white clouds just beginning to darken at the bottom.

I find a small shelf on the lee side of a cliff where we can sit out of the wind and eat our lunch. We have a great view down the north side of the mountain, and then up to our right there is a plateau and a wooden shed, and as we sit there eating egg sandwiches, we watch the train slowly make its way up the mountain toward the summit.

"You never told me there was a train."

Our British Friend smiles at me.

"It's for tourists," she says.

Orvis comes running down the path. He has already been to the summit, which he later tells me was just a flat spot with a flag on a pole and a plaque on the ground and a bunch of small Asian people making photos of themselves. Not very interesting. But then he saw the train. He loves trains and he is very excited that maybe we can go for a ride.

After climbing all this way, I tell him, there is no way that I'm taking a train to get back down. Besides, we have parked on the west side of the mountain and the train goes down the east side. We'd have to walk almost nine miles to get back to the Yugo. We have only four miles to get back to the carpark from our lunch spot. And it is all downhill.

Our British Friend is getting cold, so she gets up to reinvigorate her circulation and hike the last little bit to the top. I break out my heavy down jacket, pull my wool cap over my eyes, and settle down to a nice nap on the grassy flat spot. Orvis is already bounding back up the hill. He wants to see what the train looks like.

I'm not sure why I feel so tired. If I were less macho, I would probably admit to myself that something is wrong. Even though the latitude is pretty far north, we are not at much elevation (about 3,000 feet) and I should have no trouble breathing. But all of a sudden, my legs are heavy and my eyelids want to close, and very soon I am fast asleep.

I don't remember dreaming and I don't really know how long I was asleep, but Orvis tells me later that when he got back from the train, he looked at me lying there and for a second he thought I was dead.

He was breathing on my face when I came to. There was a look in his eye. A very worried look, and it seemed like he was going to ask me something, and then I realized what it was that worried him.

Dogs, as we all know, have a sixth sense about these sorts of things. Orvis was thinking:

"If he dies, does his imagination go with him?"

That was one I'm not sure I will ever be able to answer.

CHAPTER FIFTY-SEVEN

Dublin on Liffey, County Dublin,
Leinster Province, Ireland, E.U.

It is about a three-hour ferry ride from Holyhead, Wales, to Dublin, Ireland. Orvis and I spend most of that time sitting on a bench at the uppermost stern deck of the Stena Adventurer, a very large ferryboat. The sun is shining, but it's quite windy and cold up there and we shelter in on the lee side of the bridge-house. We're looking behind the ferry and I'm watching Great Britain fade and finally disappear in the wake of the ship. The ferry is creating a wide path behind us in the Irish Sea. The path eventually disappears into the choppy ocean waters and even more metaphorically, the land goes with it. Disappearing into my recent past. Goodbye, England. Goodbye, Wales. It's been nice to know ye.

Orvis hates it when I attempt to write in flowery or symbolic language. He especially hates foreshadowing. So I try not to do it.

You'll soon see how THAT goes.

The day before, when we came down off Mount Snowdon, I had no trouble hiking downhill. It felt like I was back to my old self, walking fast, taking long strides. I left Our British Friend far behind and had to stop periodically while she caught up. This was more like it.

Orvis took off and was already down at the gate to the farm. On the level ground and then on the descending path he could lope over the trail on his four imaginary paws, and it looked like he was almost flying. You know how dogs run, following their nose, close to the ground but seeming just slightly above it, their energy flowing like it is unlimited. My inexhaustible imaginary dog. That's what he looked like until he disappeared into a bend in the trail, and I did not see him again until I reached the car.

The next morning we drove to Holyhead, about one hour by car to the northwest, out on the thumb of Holy Island. We left the Yugo in the parking lot of the ferry terminal, dug our passports out, and prepared for the afternoon sailing to Dublin. The plan was to have a few days in Ireland. Our British Friend would then take the ferry back to Wales and I would board a plane to take me west. Orvis would be tucked neatly into my carry-on.

I had rented a flat near downtown on the Aston Quay along the river at the Ha'penny Bridge. It was across the Liffey from Temple Bar and a short walk to Trinity College. The flat was a bit spendy, but we were only going to be there for a few days. I wanted to try to do some writing at the Trinity library, as I had seen photos of the Long Room and I knew there was a long list of Irish Writers who had done work there. Everyone from Samuel Beckett to Bram Stoker. And not James Joyce.

It could be inspiring to sit and write a little story from the famous Long Room. I, of course, did not take into account the Book of Kells.

I have always been enthralled by libraries. From the one-room, wood-frame Public Library next to the Grange Hall, across the parking lot from Oxford Centralized School (my elementary school), to the new brick building, updated Federal style (Seymour Public Library) in my high school town, to my first college library (The Wilbur Cross) at my alma mater (University of Connecticut), to my tiny graduate student office in the old stacks at the University of Oregon (Knight Library). I finished writing a story one time while sitting in the reading room at the New York Public Library (Fifth Ave and 42nd street) and I started my first novel (unfinished, unpublished) at the Library of Congress in Washington, DC.

I find libraries inspiring. All those writers having written all those books was proof to me that it can be done.

But I also find libraries daunting and depressing: How can I ever add anything worthwhile to that historic lexicon of a hundred million other books? Seems like it would take courage and self-confidence that is far beyond my personal abilities.

Much like other aspects of life, it is a confusion to me.

Or maybe just an enviable mystery.

On our first morning in Dublin, I wake Orvis early and we head out the door before Our British Friend knows we are gone. With any luck, she will still be sleeping when we return with Starbucks coffee and some scones or soda bread.

It is only a short walk over the Ha'penny Bridge and through the Drinking District of Temple Bar, veering south past Parliament Square and the Irish Whiskey Museum and thusly onto the Trinity College Campus. The streets are fairly empty at 6 a.m., and there is a good heavy, hoppy smell of spilled beer, and then after a few wrong turns there is heavy dew on the grass as we walk across Fellows' Square to the front of the Old Library. To my amazement, there is a long line of people queued up to get in the front door. They do not look like students or writers or artists.

They look like tourists.

I guess I should have done a little more research. But planning is not my strong point. Spontaneous travel mistakes: That's what I'm good at.

Okay, so enter here into our narrative: The Book of Kells.

Of course you know the Book of Kells, correct? I mean, doesn't everyone? You are all much smarter than me then, because I had only vaguely heard of it. Or maybe I had just forgotten.

For people who are still in the dark here: A short explanation.

The Book of Kells is an illuminated manuscript created (or at least started) in the ninth century (AD 800) and hand-printed by Christian Monks. It contains basically unreadable calligraphy in Latin (the first four gospels of the New Testament) surrounded by amazing illustrations. It was bequeathed to Trinity College in 1661 after it had traveled through the centuries, ending up at Kells Abby (County Meath) and somehow surviving the pillaging of Vikings over the centuries. At one point (about 1659), after it was threatened by still another war, it was moved to Dublin and given to Trinity for safekeeping. It is currently (current to my arrival in Dublin, that is) housed under very thick glass in a climate-controlled box in The Long Room at the Old Trinity Library. More than 1.1 million people come to see it every year. The lines are long and it costs about twenty euros to stand in line and get a forty-five-second view of one page. They turn the page about eight times per year.

Okay, so anyone can get the above information from an online search engine in about two minutes. The information that is more difficult to obtain is that in May 2023 (about two weeks after my arrival), the Long Room was going to be closed for renovation. Carpenters work slowly in Ireland. They estimated the room would be closed for five years.

The Book of Kells, which had been at the library for 350 years, would be moved to a different, more secure, location.

Which, I suppose, was why all these folks were lined up at six in the morning.

So much for my desire to sit in the stacks of some old library and search the view for inspiration.

I had no desire to stand in line, no desire to be a tourist of that ilk, and no strong desire to see one page of The Book of Kells.

I would have liked to see the Long Room.

On our way back to the flat, Orvis found a good little independent cafe and we bought two lattes and a half-dozen sweet rolls. Our British Friend was awake and bright-eyed when we came in. She was sitting in the living room with a map of Dublin spread out on the coffee table with no coffee.

I'm not sure if she was glad to see us, or just glad to see the lattes.

As we sat drinking morning coffee, Orvis was studying the map. Perhaps it had been a mistake to teach him how to read, but how many dogs read these days? They all sit around doing video games.

In a moment his eyes were sparkling. He had found a place to visit. A place that excited him, and it was only three blocks away.

He pointed to the city map. The National Leprechaun Museum of Ireland.

Filled with imaginary beings. His people. Orvis can never get enough of that kind of stuff.

Inwardly, I groaned. I knew we'd be there all afternoon.

CHAPTER FIFTY-EIGHT

Dublin, Ireland

I once heard Dublin (and in implication, all of Ireland) described as a beat-up brutish boxer who keeps getting punched in the face, falls to the canvas, but time and time again refuses to stay down. The boxer is always ready to get back on his feet and take another swing at the world. Of course he needs a few drinks of whiskey in between rounds. Whiskey and Guinness. Then he's ready to jump up and do it all over again.

Our British Friend has been clean and sober for almost thirty years. This is one of the many things that I love about her. But it doesn't always make things easy. Anyone, like myself, who doesn't drink can have a pretty hard time socializing in pubs. Our British Friend, for instance, is a brilliant and accomplished songwriter (she would never agree with this estimation) and a good guitarist, and she often performs at folk festivals and in pub gatherings. She tends to drink tap water. I prefer mineral water from a well-shaped glass bottle. But it can be spendy.

I bring this up because one of the reasons we came to Dublin was to hear (live and in concert) some Irish music.

Earlier in my travels, I had been warned that the last place you want to go to hear Irish music was in the Temple Bar section of Dublin. But it was right across the river from our flat and we had a limited amount of time and...here could follow a litany of lame excuses.

The Temple Bar district is stretched along the south side of the Liffey River. It is about ten blocks long and three or four blocks thick, and it is an old section of Dublin with all the usual looks of Old Ireland: cobblestone streets, brick storefronts with cold-water apartments above, stone sidewalks hollowed out from hobnailed boots. Of course, it has been gentrified over the years and turned into a tourist mecca that pretty much obliterates the originality of the neighborhood. It covers most every variety of the tourist trade. The Hard Rock Cafe is on one side, the famous Temple Bar Pub is in the middle, and on the other end are Darky Kelley's and the Queen of Tarts. In between are various curio shops where you can buy an Irish Wool Sweater or a stuffed Leprechaun. A million permutations of the Irish Flag design (the "tricolor," green, white, and orange) or a dozen variations of dart boards with the Union Jack at the center (hostility toward Britain is pervasive). The lanes are closed to most traffic (who would want to try to drive through there) but clogged with pedestrians. The pubs (many, many pubs) are filled to overflowing. The Guinness Warehouse and Brewery is a few blocks west, just down the hill from St. Patrick's Cathedral.

From what we can tell on our first couple of nights wandering through, the Irish music in the Temple Bar pubs is most definitely third-rate. That is, if you can even hear it over the din of hard-drinking tourists. Sure, they try to turn the volume up. This only makes things worse.

I know, I know, I am sounding like a crotchety old teetotaler. Just drink my luxury mineral water and try to join the party, or shut the fuck up, right?

Well, stone sober, I get a little lucky. I mean, I'm in Ireland so it probably makes sense. One morning, while I am scribbling away at a cafe table in my favorite little funky coffee house (The Break in the Clouds, on Aston Place, across from the laundromat), I meet a man who recognizes my accent. He is a fellow American. He is young and polite, enthusiastic, and somewhat reserved, and we have a pleasant conversation. He is a student of literature at Trinity College. He has been in Dublin about one year. He also has dreadlocks wrapped with red and blue African beads and the most beautiful ebony skin. I take to him immediately.

We probably have a fifteen-minute conversation, maybe a little longer but not much. Somehow I comment about trying to find some good music. Some Irish music. His face lights up into a fantastic grin. His teeth are so white that they make mine look the color of banana skins in comparison.

"You should come hear our band," he says.

Absolutely. Wouldn't miss it.

Okay, so I'm very hesitant to mention any of this to Our British Friend. I have no idea what this band is going to sound like. For all I know, it could be some blend of Irish bluegrass and New York Hip Hop. Really, it could be anything. I already have a reputation with Our British Friend. Over the years, every film I've ever taken her to has been a bomb. Seriously, a bomb. Am I going to do any better with music?

Probably not.

But luckily, my luck holds. Our British Friend is hot to go see the Irish Museum of Modern Art. It is a trolley ride away (or a long walk) toward the west side of the city. I tell her I think I'll go to my coffeehouse to do some writing. Instead, I sneak off to Iveagh Gardens, across from Saint

Kevin's up the hill from Trinity College. This is where my American friend told me that his band plays on Thursday afternoons. I guess there is a tiny clamshell theater there with good acoustics.

I take Orvis with me, and of course he is complaining when I can't find the place and keep walking around and through Iveagh Gardens. We are about to give up, because for some reason his feet are hurting and he can't possibly walk another step, and "will I carry him?" (I will not), and then I hear music.

It is not coming from Iveagh Gardens. It's across the street. The music is coming from a spot next to the main entrance to the National Concert Hall auditorium. There is a little niche beside the stone staircase, tucked into the space between the auditorium and the John Field Room. A funny little space with grass growing between cobblestones and backed up by the gray granite wall of the concert hall.

He was right; the acoustics are great.

A small crowd of passersby are standing there listening to the music. The group consists of four musicians, all acoustic. A tall blond woman with ginger freckles playing the standup bass. A very beautiful East Asian woman holding something that looks like a cross between a guitar and a sitar. A banjo player right out of West Virginia in overalls and a flannel shirt, his hair wild and stringy, a wispy growth of unkept beard, a crazy-ass look in his eye. And then my new friend, dressed all in black, very classic, black vest, over black shirt, over black trousers, over black shoes. He is very sweetly playing the Irish fiddle. A slow Celtic reel.

We stood there at the back of the small crowd and listened to the music as it echoed off the granite wall. The tune, just the fiddle, went on for a short while, and then the sweetly sad melody was picked up by the bass, and then another moment or two and the guitar/sitar came in, and then the three of them played while the banjo player just looked on grinning, and then after quite a stretch they all stopped for a three-beat rest and the banjo started, and then in a measure or two the tempo picked up rapidly, same melody, and before we knew it things got wild. I mean, foot-stomping wild.

It was crazy good. Even Orvis's feet stopped hurting. The little crowd was hopping around. The music was bouncing everywhere, off the walls, off the cobblestones, off the gray Dublin sky.

Goddamn! I don't know if you could actually call this Irish music or not, and I still don't know if any of them were even Irish at all, but the sound? Nothing short of amazing.

To be honest, by the time we got there they were on their last song. They all seemed to have to be somewhere quickly, and I barely got to say hello to my American friend. I put twenty euros in their shoebox, and before I hardly knew it, Orvis and I were alone there on the sidewalk.

"Don't tell Our British Friend," I said.

"She wouldn't believe us anyway," Orvis replied.

That night, which was our penultimate night in Dublin, we went to a two-person play staged in a co-op restaurant just a couple blocks from where I heard the music. It was Our British Friend's choice. It wasn't very good. Not terrible, but not really worth the ticket price. Truthfully, it made me a little happy that it wasn't great. I felt like it made up slightly for the sucky films I had taken us to.

On our last night, we went to one more play. It was both our ideas. *The Best Exotic Marigold Hotel*, a full production at the Bord Gais Energy Theatre in East Dublin. We had to take a very long walk to get there, and it was cold when we came out, a stiff breeze coming down the river from the sea. The play was very good. Not five stars, but…well, Orvis liked it a lot.

So that was at least something. I felt like we were even. Well…not really.

In the morning we packed our bags, and mine was too full of junk, and we wheeled our stuff out the door and down the staircase and up the sidewalk to across the river, where we met separate busses. I left her to board the shuttle to the ferry terminal and then turned to cross the street and walk across the river, where I would find a bus to take me to the airport.

I have never been good at goodbyes. I'm always trying to be too stoic. As I was leaving, Our British Friend came back down the stairs off the bus where she had stashed her suitcase. We looked each other in the eye, and she gave me a big hug and a kiss and we said that we would see each other soon, though we both knew that was probably a lie.

Like I said, I'm pretty terrible at goodbyes.

And endings can be a son-of-a bitch.

CHAPTER FIFTY-NINE

Reykjavik, Iceland

Like so many of us, Orvis does not like to fly in airplanes. I give him the choice of either hiding out in my carry-on in the overhead bin or cuddling up under my seat, but neither option appeals to him, so he insists on sitting in my lap. Luckily, I have booked a window seat toward the back of the plane. We are flying Icelandic Airlines.

How long have we been traveling together? It is certainly over a year, maybe fifteen months. I can't exactly remember. I know he is getting tired of me. I'm a little tired of him too, but that doesn't stop me from telling him one more story.

"Did I ever tell you about the first time I visited Iceland?"

Imagine a dog rolling his eyes and then making a short circle, chasing his tail once completely around, and then settling down on your lap to immediately fall asleep.

It was 1973, and I was on my way home from Luxembourg. That summer it was the cheapest way to get to Europe: New York to Luxembourg on Icelandic Airlines, one stop in Keflavik at the one international airport in Iceland. Repeat to come home.

Because I thought it would be romantic, I decided to spend a week layover in Reykjavik. It was the end of my first European travels, and I was very nearly broke. Maybe $50 in

Traveler's Checks left. I probably spent $10 of it on the bus from the airport into town. I stayed one night in the youth hostel (I couldn't tell you which one—I remember a basement next to a church and a cute blond desk clerk who said "Bless, bless," when I left) and then I was out on the road with the intention of hitchhiking to some unknown place and camping out for free. I liked the sound of Thingvellir. It was the one placename I could pronounce.

Of course it's a big tourist attraction now, but then it was nothing more than a big split in the volcanic ground, a narrow canyon where the Vikings used to meet to make democratic laws. Very historic then, very historic now. But no people then. I got exhausted in two days. It was August and the sun never really set. There was no night. The stars were weird and every once in a while, the twilight at midnight would glow green in the north. Spooky. And the wind never stopped.

So soon I was back in the hostel, with enough money to spend one night and no place to go after that. This is when I saw the sign for Vestmannaeyjar Rescue Team. They were looking for volunteers.

Volunteers to dig a fishing village out from where it had been covered with volcanic ash.

EldFell Volcano had erupted earlier that year. It was located on Vestmannaeyjar Island. It had destroyed most of the town of Vestmannaeyjar, but some of it could still be salvaged. They were looking for teams of volunteers to go there and shovel ash. Great. Three days. Room and board provided to shovelers. Also, a plane ride to get there.

What an adventure! And at no cost!

I wish I could calculate how many years off my life it took to spend three twelve-hour days shoveling grit out of an old church on Westman Island. Sleeping in grit. Eating grit. Breathing grit. I had a red paisley bandanna wrapped around my mouth, but I doubt that helped much. It was very windy out there. I didn't even think the plane could land in that sort of wind. I didn't think it could take off. It made me wish I had more money. Or that I had never even come to Iceland.

But a great story, eh?

I look down to Orvis in my lap and I see that he has slept through.

Fortunately, on this return to Reykjavik I have reserved a room for the entire time that I will be here. It's good, because the weather is awful. Sideways rain. Gray on gray on gray (sea, sky, pavement) and all of it a cold, wet, springtime chill-to-the-bone experience.

In my latest estimation, Iceland is a large lava flow, slightly above sea level, covered with moss and lichen, glacial ice, steaming fissures, volcanoes ready to spew. There are five trees in the whole country if you don't count the ones growing in greenhouses. The rest is shrubs and grass. It is desolate in a way that is beautifully dramatic.

But you wouldn't want to live there.

Which is strange, because the people who DO live there are amazingly beautiful.

Norse gods and goddesses, every one of them. I distinctly remember falling in love with the girls at the youth hostel in 1973. They were all tall and sturdy and had the most brilliant blond hair, so blond that their eyebrows disappeared above their brown eyes set between silk-smooth cheeks of rose complexion. I was very blond then myself and I spoke not a word of Icelandic, but they loved my English and wanted to practice theirs. I was enthralled, until one morning when I had my cup of coffee and was going out onto the back patio (lee side of the church) and they were all there, six or seven young Icelandic women, every one of them charming and fit and filled with life...And they were all smoking pipes of tobacco.

Yikes!!! I never could handle smoking. No matter how cute the smoker.

But that is, of course, all in the past. Fifty years ago give or take a couple of months. Reykjavik is much different now. It is a beautiful small city, so neat and tidy, and everything in its place. It is also ranked among the top five most expensive places to live in the world.

I thought Paris and London were bad. Expensive for travelers. They are a bargain compared to Reykjavik.

Alright, I'm not to get into complaining. Orvis loved the city. He could wander everywhere because there was virtually no traffic. People rode bicycles. Buses were full.

Our section of the downtown ("Mioborg" or "101 Reykjavik") was mostly closed to traffic. A pedestrian street (Skolavordustigur) had little shops on every side, with stone-paved macadam that led up the hill to Hallgrimskirkja Cathedral (Lutheran Church of Iceland). It looked like a wild semicircle of grey plinths, like a giant's concrete organ creating a facade on the northwest side of the church. Opened in 1986, the cathedral is an ultramodern, 244-foot-tall stone and concrete structure, designed to resemble the trap rock, mountains, and glaciers of the Iceland countryside. Just like the rest of the island, it is constantly buffeted by wind that sings through the stone monoliths.

It was a great place to stay. We both enjoyed it, and right down the street you could get a burger and fries, or fish and chips, or an Icelandic burrito. Maybe a glass of pilsner, or white wine, or even mineral water. You could do all that and come home spending less than $100. And Orvis always ate for free.

The little room I rented was cojoined to three other rooms, and in the kitchen over morning tea I met a French family staying in the little room next to mine. They were enjoying a damp vacation and they turned me on to a short shuttle that I could take out to the nearest hot springs.

So this is what we did on our last day in Reykjavik.

Okay, I believe I did not find the hot springs they were talking about. There are lots of hot springs in Iceland. What I did find was a small van and a driver (Bjarki, or in English: Bear), and he was taking folks out to Reykjadalur Steam Valley, where, he said, there was a hot river that flowed down from the Mt. Hengill volcano.

Orvis was excited to hear this.

I will admit that it was a beautiful drive and a beautiful hike from the parking lot. Even though I was not feeling very good, the weather was pretty okay, and though I needed to stop six times on the three-mile hike up the mountain and down past Djupagil Canyon, I made it to the warm blue pool which was next to the steaming Reykjadalsa River.

I am an old man but not particularly shy, and I had enough energy left to dash out of my clothes and wallow down in the steaming water. Orvis was off somewhere in the grasslands that line the building, but I was not alone for long.

Through the steam coming off the water, I watched someone ride their pony (Icelandic, with a shaggy mane and shaggy withers, and a long forelock coming down its nose). It was a little funny, because the person was tall and their legs almost reached the ground on the sides of the small horse.

This person turned out to be an older woman. She had blond hair turning gray and a face wrinkled by the weather. She put the pony on a long tether that she anchored to a rock outcropping and came to the side of the pool. I am pretty sure she did not notice me.

This was going to be awkward. I was sitting with my chest above water, and I thought about making some noise, but then I didn't. She crouched by the side of the pool and tested the water with her hand. Then she stripped down and stood with excellent posture, fully naked, looked around her, and then looked me straight in the eye.

She knew I was there all the time. It sort of terrified me the way she looked over. But then she smiled and got into the pool on the opposite side.

Honestly? You know what my thought was?

This lovely local woman sitting in the hot springs across from me, her grey hair plastered to her forehead, the water up to her neck, a perfectly natural manifestation of some Norse goddess, met, perhaps on my way to Valhalla? My heart began to race a little.

I didn't know how long I could just sit in the hot water trying not to look too closely at her. I didn't know if there was anything I should say. Try to have a naked conversation? Try to say something that was not too stupid? I'm afraid my heart was not up to it.

My thoughts were: How am I going to gracefully get out of here before she starts smoking a pipe?

And where was Orvis when I needed him?

CHAPTER SIXTY

Keflavik, Iceland to Portland, Oregon, USA

Sometimes I think that I would be better off if I never made plans at all. Or at least if I always kept them to myself. But it doesn't seem to be in my nature to do that.

I have promised Orvis that we are going to New York City. I want to stop to see some friends who live on the Upper West Side (111th Street and Riverside Drive) and maybe sleep a few nights in their guest closet under the stairs. Then in a few days we can get on the train (Amtrak) and head out for a four- or five-day ride across the Great United States of America.

The United States. Yes, in my humble opinion, the States are all Great. They have always been Great. And they will, heaven help us, remain Great. Certainly with flaws, I grant you, but there is no reason to think that somehow they need to be made "Great Again." Especially not in a way that stresses authoritarianism, or the power of one individual. The States are "Great" precisely because they are not all "White" or "Christian" or "Straight heterosexual." America is a grand mix of colors and cultures, religions and genres and political opinions. Diversity and democracy and equal opportunity: this is what makes my country so "Great." I know this is still only a goal and it is far from being achieved… But as long as we continue to move forward in peace and gratitude…we can "Keep America Great." (Insert rainbow flag here.)

Back to our story.

I have said this time and again: dogs have a special way of noticing things that humans either don't (or don't want to) notice. Orvis knows that there is something wrong with my health. Maybe he can hear my heart murmur. Maybe he can smell stress on my breath.

In the shuttle van on the way back to Central Reykjavik he is sitting on the seat next to me. I'm not feeling bad, maybe a little out of shape, maybe my heart is racing a little and my lungs feel a bit weak…no big deal. Denial?

Out of seeming nowhere, Orvis turns to me and says:

"It is time to go home."

This was not something I was prepared to hear. So far as I know, he has enjoyed our trips together. It has been a great adventure for him after his humble origins in Eastern Oregon. I was very set on the idea of finishing it out with a train tour across America.

"Well," I said, "we are heading in that direction."

"No. We have to go back home. Home to your home. And as soon as possible."

I have to give myself some credit here. After all this traveling together, I knew better than to argue with Orvis. Or to ignore his advice, for that matter.

So I booked us a flight. Not to New York City, but to Portland, Oregon. There is about 1,000 miles difference. Portland is that much farther. But the one-way flight on Icelandic Air only cost about $60 more.

So off we were to Portland. I was quite disappointed. Orvis didn't seem to mind at all.

But there was some sunshine in this otherwise bleak and overcast change of plans.

I have an excellent long-ago friend that lives in Portland, Oregon. He is quite a brilliant writer, publisher, hip-hop DJ, and one of the most optimistic people that I know. Our friendship goes far back into the past. Back to the mid-1980s, when we worked for a publishing company in San Francisco and had many adventures in that fabled city. And I should mention (because it is virtually impossible to make a living off any of the things he is really good at) he also works at PDX. That is shorthand for the Portland International Airport.

A couple of messages later and my friend, whom I prefer to call "Reymundo" (King of the World), is set to meet our flight from Reykjavik.

Thinking that it will be his last flight for awhile, Orvis crowds himself close to the airplane window. There isn't all that much to see from 36,000 feet, just a layer of puffy white clouds below us. But soon there is a small break in the overcast, and we are suddenly looking down on Kalaallit Nunaat, which the English-speaking world calls Greenland.

Greenland is largely one immense sheet of ice, most of it over solid land, but some of it sea ice. It is called Sermersuaq. It covers about 660,000 square miles, and it about one mile thick. In mid-May, it should still be frozen solid. But nowadays the ice is melting fast. From above, you can see evidence of this by the reflection of deep blue from the melt ponds that now dot the ice flow. Pools of blue water, little lakes that make shallow depressions in the otherwise white glacial landscape. It has its own beauty, if you can somehow deny that it is a precursor of climate change. It's getting warmer on our planet, and nowhere more quickly than in the Arctic. No one knows exactly what will happen if the rapid seasonal melting of this ice sheet continues to accelerate, but all of the scenarios are pessimistic in relation to the human community at large.

Orvis is only a dog and so what does he know, but as our jet passes over the giant ice field, he says something strange to me.

"It doesn't look cold enough down there."

A couple of minutes later the aircraft is back up in the clouds, and we both try to sleep our way over Hudson Bay and then the rest of Western Canada. I have a weird dream about bright lights and white rooms and five doctors looking down at me and then I wake up just about when we are passing into US airspace.

Orvis does not have a passport, so I tuck him neatly into my shoulder bag as we are waiting in line at the immigration checkpoint. The customs officer looks closely at my passport and sees all the various stamps from various countries and then says:

"Where have you been?"

I'm a little tired to try to tell him everything, but I begin:

"Well we started out in Istanbul, and then there was the night train to Bulgaria, and then a bus ride to Serbia..."

He interrupts me by holding his hand up, palm pointing toward me.

"We?"

"Uh, yeah. I've been..." Honestly, my head is bleary from the flight and the time change and I'm not sure what to say exactly. "I've been traveling with my imaginary dog. But he's not here right now."

"So where is he?"

Wow. Should I lie or just tell the truth? “Mostly, he’s just in my head.”

This gives the agent pause. There is a long anxious line behind me of people with more reasonable situations. He looks down and stamps my papers and shakes his head in a tired way and hands me back my passport.

“Welcome home,” he says.

But I don’t think he really means it.

CHAPTER SIXTY-ONE

Northeast Portland, Oregon USA

In a more cautious and rational world, I might have arrived at the Portland International Airport and had my friend Reymundo take me straight to the emergency room of the nearest hospital. My choice would probably be OHSU (Oregon Health Sciences University), because it is a research hospital connected to the state university system. By virtue of graduate school, I am a full flying Duck (University of Oregon). In Oregon, you are pretty much a Duck or a Beaver (Oregon State), depending upon which football team you root for. Both varieties of mascot are welcome at OHSU. Well, I guess, so is everyone else. But when you put the word "university" next to something, it gives you the impression that people there are smart. So, you figure, they ought to be able to diagnose what is wrong with you.

Or, like me, you could just stay in denial.

Honestly, I didn't have a lot of symptoms. Shortness of breath, some tightness in my chest, a bit of sleep apnea. I was just feeling out of shape. Weary from so much traveling. Ready to return home and die quietly in my bed. At least temporarily.

But what would happen to Orvis?

Reymundo and his lovely partner (Claudia) hosted us for one night and then we would train down to Eugene for a triumphant return home. In our time there we would take a little tour of the city of Portland, which is a semi-tragic story unto itself.

(This all takes place in the late spring of 2023, so my estimation here might become quickly dated by the time anyone is reading this. Hopefully things have changed. Optimistically, they have changed for the better.)

It is necessary, I think, to attempt to describe my friend Reymundo, because in many aspects he is an exemplary example of a modern, urban-dwelling Oregonian. He is originally from Kansas (Junction City) and was raised by working-class parents (his dad was in the Army, his mom a schoolteacher), but his ancestry is set firmly in the slavery class of Jamaica and the Caribbean. He got his undergraduate degree from the University of Kansas, left there to make his way in publishing and advertising in Denver, was moderately successful, and then migrated to San Francisco, where we met one foggy afternoon on the 31st floor of the Chevron building at 550 Market Street (Financial District). This was sometime in the mid-1980s. Chevron Oil Company had a consumer products division that published how-to books: Ortho Books, named after the insecticide division. They printed *How to Grow Tomatoes, All About Evergreens, Deck and Fences, How to Remodel Your Bathroom*. The Editor in Chief was a Chinese American guy named Min Yee. He was the big boss. He had been bureau chief of *Newsweek Magazine* in Beijing. He would often forget my name and then say: "Whatever. All you white guys looks the same to me anyhow..."

At the point when we met, I was a blond white guy with a ponytail, a button-down shirt, and a striped, red-and-blue silk tie. Reymundo was the only black guy on the floor. He had horn-rimmed glasses, close-cropped tight-curl hair, a checkered blue-and-white Oxford shirt with a yellow tie, and the biggest grin on his face, because he had just been hired as an editor in the photo department. I'd been there about two weeks at most, a proofreader/associate editor in publishing. I wish someone had taken our photo, because we looked great together. Two straight guys in downtown San Francisco ready for whatever adventure might await. We became fast, tight friends.

I'm not exactly sure why that whole life in San Francisco fell apart. It sure was great for a good while. I think I realized that hanging out with writers and journalists and other ne'er-do-wells was quickly giving me an expensive and sickly cocaine habit. I got to be Min Yee's number one boy, the guy that picked up the lunch tab on the expense account, the guy that went out to get the takeout, the guy sitting in Min's living room in the Marina District, snorting coke and looking out on the city, convinced of his own genius without even lifting a finger or typing a word. It was all too much, and to my credit, I realized it was going to take me down.

In the meantime, Reymundo went out on his own in the book business. He eventually quit his job and started writing and publishing books. He had a very successful restaurant guide that supported him for a while. He had his picture in the SF *Chronicle*. He was among the rising stars in the under-forty best bets for publishing entrepreneurs.

Through it all, we were always close friends. Eventually I moved back to Eugene and Reymundo migrated with his family (a beautiful wife, two kids) to Portland.

In many ways, Raymundo's life paralleled the fortunes and misfortunes of the city. In the late 20th century, Portland became a mecca for creativity and possibility. It was an affordable city. If you were in your twenties or thirties, you could move there and find a small home in an interesting old neighborhood and start a storefront business or restaurant. It was a city filled with youth and weirdness. Very artistic and trendy. Good progressive energy. Inclusive and vibrant with multiculturalism.

Reymundo found that he was a good part of this trend. He published a newspaper. He wrote books. He did all of this while holding down a good job as a marketing executive for Hollywood Video. He had a big house. He had a nice car. He traveled. He did book tours. He took the new light-rail system to work. He would meet me downtown at a fancy cafe or bistro and he would buy me lunch.

But you have to be weary of boomtown economies. Capitalism can be unrelenting, and it does not care much for poverty. Progressivism is a very hollow philosophy when you have no place to live and not enough to eat. Like many big cities, Portland experienced a huge speculation bubble in the real-estate market. It took just a few years for the city to become unaffordable. Housing prices went up on the same curve as desirability. People, especially young people, got priced out of the economy, and wages did not follow the upward curve nearly fast enough.

Homelessness followed the real-estate boom like a poor hungry dog looking for scraps of food and getting more and more angry as it got more desperate. Soon the homeless bloomed like an outbreak of winter roof-moss, and tents and cardboard shelters grew to line the sidewalks. Where did all these impoverished people come from? The same neighborhood where the price of a fixer-upper was hundreds of thousands of dollars more than these folks made in a lifetime. You can easily see why this might discourage someone and turn them toward drugs and alcohol.

It all ended in conflict. Protest movements about other issues (national issues, international issues, climate issues) brought people out into the streets, and then the dogs of anarchy saw their opportunity. The anarchists hitched on to the protests, and it did not take long to loot and burn downtown Portland. Just one or two violent clashes with police and the war was on. And it only took the rumor of war to change the views of the outside world. In only a few years, Portland went from the weird and wonderful progressive city of the future to a prime example of the failures of liberalism. This was the view from outside the city. The worldview of Portland.

Reymundo survived all of this change, but it did not come without a price. He lost the big house. He lost the good job (Hollywood Video folded with the coming of streaming services). He went through a divorce and a healthy downsizing and none of it was easy or fun. But he lived through it, and in many ways he is stronger and more resilient now. Perhaps more realistic (though that might be a stretch for Reymundo, who is not normally subject to realism) and certainly not without unbounding optimism.

I can only hope that the City of Portland can do as well.

Reymundo is still in the publishing business, writing and self-publishing at least one book a year, planning his own performance art/book tour (Party Like a Writer) and hanging on to his creativity. To pay the bills? He drives a bus at Portland International Airport.

So it is a test of his generosity to come meet us after our flight comes in from Reykjavik. After all, it is his day off and probably the last thing he wants to see is the international arrivals curb at PDX. Orvis and I are standing there watching the traffic when he pulls up. Honestly, I have not seen him in a while, and I recognize him from his wide smile more than anything else. He is a bit thicker in the gut, not quite as bouncy on his feet, and his glasses have changed from horn-rimmed to jet black, framing his wide brown eyes in his dark face that is wreathed in a wash of curly dreadlocks with African beads woven into their texture. He is going slightly gray at the temples. His cheeks are slightly pockmarked with age. His hands are soft and big and when he hugs me there is still good stout strength in his arms and shoulders. He looks around and he smiles and he says welcome to Portland and then looks around some more, focusing on the empty space around my feet and my wheeled carry-on bag. He smiles broadly as though he is seeing a small vision. Then reaches down and moves his hand back and forth.

"This must be Orvis," he says, as he pretends to shake a paw.

We are smiling and laughing and we look each other in the eye as only old friends can; friends who have seen a lot and not enough of each other over the years, but who are bonded by a grace and humor that is too rare among humans.

I spend a couple of days with him and his partner and we talk about writing and publishing and how the whole thing has changed. I don't try to explain to him about Orvis or about my upcoming book, because we've heard all those stories before. We spend most of our time just laughing.

He hugs me again when he puts me on the train to Eugene. If there is anyone in the publishing world who deserves a big break and sincere acknowledgement of his skills, it is Reymundo. You can see it in the depths of his face that he knows this will probably not happen. But it does not cure his optimism.

“I love you man,” I say as I’m leaving.

“Write when you find work, mon.” He replies in a thick Jamaican accent.

It is an old joke between us.

CHAPTER SIXTY-TWO

Izee-Burns Road, Oregon Outback,
Harney County, Eastern Oregon, USA

Providing a perfect bookend to our story, my nonbinary friend Cait Z. meets our train at the Amtrak Station in Eugene. They are happy to see us, but I notice that they are looking closely at my face and the way that I am carrying my body and my whole attitude of fatigue.

"Have you thought about seeing a doctor?" they say.

In a former life, Cait was a nurse practitioner and then a licensed naturopath. They left those professions to become an attorney specializing in environmental law, and now they are deeply involved in their own plots to save the world. They are a very smart person, as you can expect. I'm very honored to be their friend.

As a public service, here I will include a note about their sexuality, because I know that you are probably wondering.

As far as I can tell from a casual reading of the science, human gender and sexuality has always existed on a spectrum. As much as we like to simplify things and classify our fellow human beings into two camps (male and female), that is a mistake. Most probably, the traditional bicameral nature of sex classification has been influenced more by cultural strictures than by biological reality. We needed humans to reproduce, so we bound them into hard categories: Males did this, Females did that.

In more modern times, as cultural mores have relaxed (slightly) and expanded, we have come closer to the reality of human gender. Every individual has both female and male characteristics embedded in their personalities. There are more male-like males and more female-like females, and then there is a whole variety of things in between. There are not just two genders. There is an almost infinite variety of ways to be a sexual human.

Is there any reason why an individual shouldn't be able to make a choice of where they fit on the spectrum?

You can answer that for yourself. My friend Cait has done extremely well in answering it for their-self.

They are the epitome of the modern human. Strong, intelligent, sensitive, brave, fearless, and with a sense of humor that does not take their-selves too seriously. They are perfectly capable of fucking around with their pronouns. They can be very "him" sometimes. Like with auto mechanics, for instance. He talks the man talk so he doesn't have to suffer any mansplaining. But they are also very "her" too. Like when she looks closely into my face and with her gentle female nurse voice tells me she wants to take me to the Emergency Room.

"I'm just fine," I tell them. "Some rest at home. A good home-cooked meal. I will easily be on the mend in the morning."

Luckily, we live only a few blocks from each other. Cait insists on checking in on me every day, bringing healthy food and good vibes. As a compromise, I agree to make an appointment with Dr. Tee, my primary care physician.

Like most things to do with medicine and the human body, it all becomes a long, complex, and expensive process. The thing that is so good about the American medical system is that it is filled with many very-talented and dedicated professionals, all doing an extremely good job of diagnosis and procedure. The difficult thing is that much of it is run by insurance companies and middlemen who make it all bizarrely complicated and outrageously expensive. A few years ago, Dr. Tee listened to my heart and refered me to Dr. Chappell (cardiologist), who also listens to my heart and orders an echocardiogram from Technician Ken, who sends the results to a radiologist who reads them and sends results back to Dr. Chappell, who tells me I have moderate-to-severe stenosis of my aortic valve. I will need surgery to correct this. In the meantime, he offers a few corrective medications that will help. Of course, I don't want surgery. At least not right now. So I decide to just go on with my life. A couple of years pass and a few more echocardiograms, this time under stress, and I'm doing well maintaining, but then I begin on this recent trip to feel something else. Something a bit worse. Shortness of breath, a tightness in my chest.

Keep in mind that all of these appointments and procedures are well spaced, time-wise. Like I said, the issue with my heart had been going on for a few years. It takes months to get to see a cardiologist.

Returning home, I get very lucky. Instead of an appointment in six months there is a cancellation and I get into see Dr. Chappell again just two weeks after my return. He orders up a catheter test of my heart. The results that come back are rather shocking. I have an aneurism next to my aortic valve that did not show up on the echocardiogram. He sends me immediately to see the cardiothoracic surgeon, Dr. Engstrom.

And so unfolds the scene in the surgeon's office where Cait and I are sitting in comfy chairs while a very young and articulate Dr. Engstrom is drawing us a picture on the erasure board of my aorta and the bulge of the aneurism and telling us how he wants to cut it all out (a full Bental procedure) and replace it with a synthetic valve and a sheath-like artery. What he doesn't say is that in order to get to my heart he has to saw open my sternum and pry apart my ribcage. He leaves that unsaid, but understood.

In response to Cait's question he says: "If the aneurism bursts? You probably die pretty quickly."

Reluctantly, I agree to the procedure. But the next question is timing. We are only midway through the summer, and I have many tasks and responsibilities I need to attend to. Post-operation, I will be laid low for at least three months. No work, no travel, nothing but rehab. There are many things I need to get done before I can afford that amount of layoff.

It takes some negotiation, but the three of us (me, Cait, Dr. Engstrom) decide the open-heart surgery can be postponed about a month. I schedule it to happen on Tuesday, August 22. The doc says he tends to do his best work on Tuesdays.

And so I have some time to think about my mortality. Nothing is certain with such a major surgery, and there is no telling if the aneurism will burst before I make it to the operating table. Then there is the question of how I explain this all to Orvis.

There is, of course, both a moral and ethical question underlying this part of the story. Part of the question is this: What happens to Orvis if something happens to me? If I die of a burst aneurism in my heart, then who is there to create and care for Orvis? Does he just disappear as my imagination evaporates into the darkness of non-existence?

The other part of the question: What is my responsibility for this situation? Sure, it's fine to just drive myself to the brink of death, but don't I bear some responsibility for those that I drag there with me?

And then, how do I explain this all to an imaginary dog?

I know that some people treat dogs like they are their children. They love and care for them in similar ways. I understand this completely and I think it makes sense. Dogs (and all pets, really) are so much easier to love than our fellow human beings. The love is so much simpler. They are either good dogs or bad dogs. They almost always return love with their own devotion, attachment, and unconditional joy. It is obvious and clear-cut. If only our relationships with other people, children, parents, friends, and strangers could be so easy.

Anyway, it is easy to see why people become so attached to their dogs.

I have certainly experienced this same attachment with Orvis. Over these last fourteen months he has become my indispensable travel companion. With his own personality. With his own point of view. With his own opinions. He has followed me with both skepticism and loyalty. Now my attachment is total, but I need to temper it with my own loyalty toward him.

He deserves his independence.

It is not so big of a problem explaining to him my health issues. He already knows more about it than I do. If he can see into my soul (which I am certain that he does), he can certainly see into my heart. He can see the steady decline of my aortic valve. He can see the thinning walls of my aortic artery. He probably knows better than I do when the walls will burst.

Does he know when I will die? Certainly. But I'm not at all interested in asking him about *that*…

Instead, I tell him that we have a limited time together, no one knows how long, and so:

"Let's just enjoy the rest of the summer," I say.

Faithful old Cait is also up for it, and so the three of us conspire to enjoy the great out of doors. Hardly any place is better to do this than during the summer months in Oregon. There is a perfect period—between when the heavy mosquito time ends in late July and the fire-and-smoke season begins in early September—that the Cascade Mountains are awesome. We decide to take full advantage.

It is, first off, a trip up to Crater Lake National Park, and we achieve it on a pristine clear day when there is hardly a whisper of breeze across the vastly deep and blue lake water of the caldera. The lake reflects the sky, the sky is an infinite vista stretching to the sides of the volcano, the pine and juniper trees smell of fresh pitch, and like us, there are about a thousand other tourists taking it all in. I just wanted Orvis to see this amazing natural wonder. He likes it so much he buys a souvenir coffee mug at the gift shop. He doesn't even drink coffee, but what am I going to say?

Our next excursion is even more dramatic.

Every year, about August 12 or so, the planet Earth on its path around the sun passes through the tail of the Swift-Tuttle comet and debris from the comet hits the atmosphere. This causes what we ground-dwellers have come to call the Perseid meteor shower (it appears to come from the direction of a star cluster known as the Perseids). In a clear sky with little or no light pollution, it is possible to see as many as sixty meteors (falling stars) per hour. It is a great time to get out and sleep under the stars.

So we pack up the taco truck and head into the mountains. At the top of the Aufderheide Road, up past the French Pete Wilderness and Cougar Hot Springs, we take a logging track further into the forest until we find an alpine meadow clearing among the Douglas fir trees. We are well away from any traffic, any noise, and most light pollution. It is a very dark night. We haul a double mattress out of the back of the pickup and set it out on a flat spot in the meadow. A couple of water jugs, a couple of firm pillows, a couple of sleeping bags, and we are all prepared to sleep under the Perseids.

We are not prepared for the night that awaits us. The intensity of the meteor shower after midnight is beyond all expectations. It is not that the falling stars are so numerous: we count about seventy or so during the entire night. But we have never seen anything in the sky so intense. The meteors seem to pass above us at a height that is just above the treetops. They are not just little streaks in the sky. They are quarter-inch-wide, white-hot stripes motoring across the sky. They look like glowing roadways burned through the atmosphere. It is almost frightening. It looks like they are coming to land next to our bed.

We don't get much sleep.

Orvis is suitably impressed. So are Cait and I.

And so it is with enthusiasm and anticipation that we set out on our last trip of the summer, just one weekend before I am scheduled for open-heart surgery. We are going to drive all the way out to Ontario, Oregon, just by the Idaho border, about 400 miles from my home in Eugene. We are going to visit some new friends who had restored the beautiful old house of the town surgeon and now had a music venue they were initiating. We were invited to the concert of Americana music. A band from Boise, Idaho, and the opening act of a young singer-songwriter from Nashville, Tennessee. The songwriter happened to be Mrs. M's grandson.

It was going to be a long drive, and I had every intention of making it even longer because I wanted to cut north up through Deschutes, Crook, and Grant Counties before we headed south to Harney County and spent a night in Burns. It would be a little tour of the Oregon Outback, as the tourist board had begun to call it.

There is some dramatic and desolate country out there in Eastern Oregon. Sunburnt hills and sagebrush canyons, juniper and pine trees above a certain altitude where a condensation zone occurs and there is snowfall to provide water. Rolling mountain ranges and long vistas on either side of the two-lane highways. Towns are far apart and are not much more than an intersection and a few abandoned buildings. Very large ranches and very few residents. The only traffic is from people passing through.

By late afternoon, we reach the unincorporated town of Izee, far out in Grant County. Named after the cattle brand of the local ranch (I-Z), it is nothing much other than an abandoned community hall (leaning wood beams eaten through by termites, ready to fall in the next big snow) and the old one-room former school. A warm wind is blowing when we get out of the truck. The air smells like dust.

We don't spend much time there. Orvis wanders a bit to check out the landscape. A rusted old tractor, a heap of coiled fencing, a collapsed corral. A rolling vista of grass hills crisped by the heat of the summer. Down in the wash there are a couple of cottonwood trees, their falling leaves yellowed in the sun where they stand next to a dry creek-bed. Crickets are cricketing in the brittle, late-afternoon heat.

We continue our drive. On impulse, I take a turn south on the Izee-Burns Road, and soon we run out of pavement and are riding on gravel. It slows us down and adds a bit of suspense. We drive toward an uncertain future as the sun drops toward the western horizon.

You have to understand that this kind of countryside is where Orvis first called home. His origins in Fossil had almost every aspect of this outback. Sparse open spaces. Sunsets setting across a wide horizon of mountains and hills. Cloudless skies and nights confused with countless stars. Both an intense heat in the day and a bone-chilling, numbing cold at night.

About twenty miles from the Izee turnoff the gravel road starts getting a little rough, and I begin wondering if it may become impassable. Cait is in the navigator's seat, and she estimates we are only about halfway to Burns. It is still light, the sun just hitting the western hills. I need to stop for a moment to stand and stretch and relieve myself. We all get out of the truck. I walk off for some privacy and when I return, I notice that Orvis is staring off into the distance. He has that structure to his stance that tells me he has found something.

"What is it? I ask.

Just as I say this, there is the howl of a coyote in the brush not more than a hundred yards from where we are standing. It is loud and it startles both Cait and I, but when Orvis turns to look at me, he is smiling. I have seen that grin before. It is both mischievous and happy. It is as though he has found an opening into or away from something that he doesn't want to deal with.

The coyote howls again, this time farther away, and then we hear the chipping little howls of a pack of coyotes who are answering from up on the nearest hill. Chipping and howling, chipping and howling, they are having a conversation. Before I know it, Orvis has moved farther away from the truck, out toward the sagebrush bramble by the side of the road. I begin to call to him, but the words kind of stick in my mouth, because somewhere inside of my own inabilities I know what he is doing.

Neither of us can ever really bring ourselves to say goodbye.

Orvis disappears into the brush. The coyotes are still talking, and by now the sun has set behind the hills and there is only the summer twilight to see by. It's not that far away and I watch as he comes out of the brush and climbs the hill toward where the coyotes are calling.

I expect him to stop and turn and look back at me, but he doesn't. At the top of the hill I see his silhouette against the empty skyline. I think I see him raise his head at an angle and I think I hear him howl, but I can never be sure, and then in a moment he is gone.

EPILOGUE

Intensive Care Unit, McKenzie Heart Associates,
McKenzie-Willamette Hospital,
Springfield, Oregon, USA

Early in the afternoon on August 22, I came back into consciousness after a six-hour surgical procedure that replaced a valve, repaired an aneurism, and bypassed a blockage in my heart. My first impression was that I was about to drown. There was a ventilator in my throat and drain tubes in my chest and the anesthesiologist telling me that I was doing fine. But I was not doing fine at all. I felt like I had been hit by a freight train and dragged along the tracks. I could not breathe and I was certainly going to die. To be truthful, I did not feel very much like coming back. The blackness was far more comfortable.

If that was death, I would choose it. Compared to what I was then feeling.

There is really no one to blame as to why my pain medications were not working. It is impossible to tell how any given individual will react to certain drugs. In my case, it was very difficult to communicate, and I could not tell my attending nurses that the drugs were making me crazy. I could not tell them about the grand hallucinations and the confusing semi-consciousness that I was experiencing. The first hours of it were very bad, extremely disorientating. I was completely convinced that I was losing my mind.

When this state of pain and suffering lasted a couple of days, I was ready to give up entirely. Just put me to sleep, I asked the nurses. I don't care if I ever wake up.

But the thing about sleeping is that it tends to create dreams. And my dreams during these first days of recovery were as bad as my hallucinations. Confused images of corkscrews worming their way through my brain. Multicolored dragons breathing fire into my chest. Lime-green plastic unicorns gathered at a watering hole being blasted to bits by a great white hunter that looked like Donald J. Trump. A true nightmare this. I squished the hunter with the hard knuckles of my right hand and the scene was covered with crimson blood. But even after saving the unicorns, my mind twisted back on itself, and soon I was being chased by a deadly herd of Republican Rinos, running for my life, my legs moving in slow motion, my breath coming in short gasps, my vision narrowing into a spiraling scotoma of blind fear.

Was there no relief?

On the third day, my surgeon came to see me. He was upset that I had been in such a state and ordered a strong painkiller. Finally I had a space away from the pain to relax. I slept without dreaming and in the morning I awoke very early, feeling better, perhaps ready to live again, and when I opened my eyes, there was Orvis standing next to my bed.

"Hey" he said. "You are alive."

"Just barely," I replied, and the miracle was that my voice came out normal. Ordinary. Like a dream recovery.

"I just stopped by to give you a couple of messages."

"Messages?"

He seemed a lot bigger, not a little dog anymore, not something you could fit into a suitcase or a carry-on. He was right there by the side of my bed, but he stood eight feet tall. He was actually looking down on me.

"Messages from me, from the other coyotes, from the world at large."

"I like messages," I said.

"Well, I guess it is really only one message, when you come down to it. I mean, there is no reason to complicate things, is there?"

"Not at all."

"The message is that you are going to be okay. You'll get through all this. Slow recovery, but everyone thinks you will make it."

"Good to know," I said, "because for a while there it didn't seem like it."

"You'll be fine," Orvis said.

"I hate it when people say that," I replied.

We spent a moment just smiling at each other. It had been a very long journey and it seemed like we had shared some unique moments. I knew that I missed him even if I didn't want to admit how much. There was very dim light in the room, just the hall lights filtering in through glass doors and the sunlight reaching around the edges of the blinds. His eyes glowed a little, and I could see him smiling in that doggy grin he liked to give when something was either comically fucked-up or exceptionally cool.

"How is it out there?" I finally asked.

His eyes glowed a little brighter and he pricked up his ears.

"Amazing," he said. "The world is big and round and at night it stretches up into the stars and the landscape is always changing and everywhere you look there is another story. There are so many cool stories. No wonder people like to tell them."

"Yeah," I said. "Lots of cool stories."

Orvis turned and looked over his shoulder. I could tell he was about to leave.

"You take care of yourself," he said. "Sometime I'll be back and we can sit around the fire. We'll talk some more and I'll tell you a great story and you can write it all down. Okay?"

"Okay," I said. "I'll keep my pencil sharp."

That made him smile. Just before he disappeared.

The End

Acknowledgments

The writing of this book is the culmination of sixty years of practice and untold help and teachings from so many people that the list would certainly fill another entire book, if not two. It is my belief that no author reaches into the universal pool of creativity and climbs out alone or without the help of those that have reached in before him. That's a very, very long list of reachers and helpers.

So let's compress my thank-yous into a manageable group. First, there is my sister Rosemary (Sunny) Schneider, who supported me and encouraged me throughout. This would not be a book without her. Second, there is my close friend Mary Catherine Martini—traveling companion, reader of first drafts, companion by the Baja campfires... again, there would be no book without her. I am deeply indebted to both of these amazing women.

During my travels, I had untold help from many sources. I'd like to thank those who guided me, including, but not limited to: Kate Martin, Blue Lake, CA, Pier and Norma Azcona in King City, California; Debra Hawkins and Dan Harrington, Temecula, California; Joy and Jon Sperry in Palm Desert; Erica Hawley and Kenny Paasch in Bolinas, California; Rhonda Sable and Ambhoda Hanson in Seattle, Washington; Ron W. Bailey of the Moisture Festival; Betal in Istanbul; Daniel Ayodele and Genille Asmatova in Sofia, Bulgaria; Damir Koboevic in Zagreb; Kersten Costantini

Sigurdsson in Paris; Barbara and Atul Arora in London; Phylis Martini in Norfolk County, UK; Thomas Kerrtak in Wrexham, Wales; Patrick Lincoln in Dublin; Sig Sigfinnur in Reykjavik; Raymond Quinton and Claudia Schroeder in Portland, Oregon; and Scott Landfield of Tsunami Books in Eugene, Oregon.

A special thank you to Jose Esteban Martinez in Mexico City whose paintings inspired me (website: Joseestebanmartinez.com) and who graciously allowed me to use a detail of *Los perros se van al Cielo* on the front cover.

I'd like to also thank the designers, editors, and professional encouragers at Luminare Press. Their guidance and help was invaluable.

And lastly, to all the far-flung friends and friends of friends, and everyone else who said, at one time or another: "Why don't you get a real dog?"

I promise I never told Orvis you said that.

About the Author

Mose Tuzik Mosley has been a travel writer for more than twenty-five years and has traveled extensively, throughout the world, on a wing and a prayer and a budget that few could match for its paucity. He has earned degrees from the University of Connecticut (BA Political Science/Journalism) and the University of Oregon (MS Journalism). Still, he has not let higher education stop him from becoming a writer. He currently resides in rural Lane County, Oregon, USA, and Cabo del Este, Los Cabos, BCS, Mexico. This is his first book.

Author photo: Ken Anderson

www.ingramcontent.com/pod-product-compliance
Lightning Source LLC
Chambersburg PA
CBHW032049020426
42335CB00011B/250

* 9 7 9 8 9 9 0 6 5 2 6 1 3 *